FREE EXPRESSION

Free Expression

ESSAYS IN LAW
AND PHILOSOPHY

W. J. WALUCHOW

McMaster University
Hamilton, Ontario, Canada

CLARENDON PRESS · OXFORD
1994

Oxford University Press, Walton Street, Oxford OX2 6DP
Oxford New York
Athens Auckland Bangkok Bombay
Calcutta Cape Town Dar es Salaam Delhi
Florence Hong Kong Istanbul Karachi
Kuala Lumpur Madras Madrid Melbourne
Mexico City Nairobi Paris Singapore
Taipei Tokyo Toronto
and associated companies in
Berlin Ibadan

Oxford is a trade mark of Oxford University Press

Published in the United States
by Oxford University Press Inc., New York

British Library Cataloguing in Publication Data
Data available

Library of Congress Cataloging in Publication Data
Free expression: essays in law and philosophy /[edited by] W. J. Waluchow.
p. cm.
Includes index.
1. Freedom of speech—Canada—Congresses. 2. Freedom of the
press—Canada—Congresses. 3. Freedom of speech—Congresses.
4. Freedom of the press—Congresses. I. Waluchow, Wilfrid J.
KE4418.A66 1990
342.71'0853—dc20
[347.102353]   93–42518

ISBN 0–19–825800–3

1 3 5 7 9 10 8 6 4 2

Typeset by Create Publishing Services Ltd., Bath, Avon
Printed in Great Britain
on acid-free paper by
Bookcraft Ltd., Midsomer Norton, Avon

For Carrie and Rob

Preface and Acknowledgements

Freedom of expression is an issue of obvious and perennial interest to both philosophers and non-philosophers alike. Its relevance is evident throughout history, from Plato's advocacy of censorship of the poets on through to modern calls for restricting the free expression of such notables as Philip Rushton, Salmon Rushdie and Madonna.

Freedom of expression encompasses a wide variety of questions, only some of which are discussed by the contributors to this volume. One question is why freedom of expression enjoys the importance it has within liberal societies. According to Joseph Raz, the right to free expression is generally given far greater legal protection than a person's interest in having employment, or in not running the risk of accident when driving on public roads. This is true despite the fact that most people value the latter interests more than they value the right to free expression. Raz attempts to solve this liberal puzzle by developing a theory which explains the special importance attached to the right to free expression within pluralistic societies. David Richards links the importance of free expression to the value of toleration, while Jan Narveson attempts to forge a connection between a duly limited right to free expression and the principle of liberty.

In addition to general questions concerning its bases in political and legal theory, the right to free expression gives rise to a variety of more narrowly focused questions involving the many forms which human expression can take. Some of these are addressed by the contributors. Roger Shiner is concerned with freedom of commercial expression and the question whether it deserves special legal protection. Leslie Green examines whether freedom of expression includes the right to express oneself in one's native language. Green's question is of obvious theoretical and practical importance in multi- and bilingual countries like Switzerland and Canada, and uncovers a dimension of free expression which has hitherto received little attention. An issue which has received considerably more attention is the existence and enforcement of laws proscribing 'hate literature'. Three of our authors address this vital issue. James Weinstein and Joseph

Magnet provide highly critical, comparative treatments of hate propaganda laws, practices, and policies in Canada and the United States of America, concluding that the case in favour of such laws, practices, and policies has yet to be made. Wayne Sumner, on the other hand, is guardedly in favour of the laws which Weinstein and Magnet so vigorously oppose. Sumner wishes to provide reasons for thinking that minority groups in Canada today are vulnerable to racist propaganda, that criminal sanction can provide some of the protection they need, and that effective legislation need not trench too deeply on freedom of expression.

The essays included in this collection were first presented at a conference entitled 'Freedom of Expression' held at McMaster University in May of 1990. The conference was sponsored by the Guelph-McMaster Ph.D. programme and funded by the Social Sciences and Humanities Research Council of Canada. I wish to express my gratitude to each for these bodies for the support they provided. In organizing the conference I profited immensely from the invaluable assistance of Joe Murray. For his patience, expertise, and remarkable attention to detail, I express my undying gratitude. Unless otherwise indicated, all the essays in this volume reflect the state of the law at the time of the conference, May 1990.

Two of the essays included in this volume have appeared in other places. Joseph Raz's 'Free Expression and Personal Identification' was reproduced in the *Oxford Journal of Legal Studies*, 11/3 (1991) and Les Green's 'Freedom of Expression and Choice of Language' was published in *Law and Policy*, 13/3 (1991). Thanks are due to the publishers of these journals for permission to include these papers.

W.J.W.

Table of Contents

Notes on Contributors

LESLIE GREEN is an Associate Professor in the Department of Philosophy and Osgoode Hall Law School at York University. He is the author of several articles on legal and political philosophy and of *The Authority of the State* (Clarendon Press, Oxford, 1988). He is also the co-editor (with A. Hutchinson) of *Law and Community: The End of Individualism* (Carswell, Toronto, 1989).

JOSEPH MAGNET is a Professor of Law at the University of Ottawa and was a Law Clerk to the former Right Honourable Chief Justice of the Supreme Court of Canada, R. G. B. Dickson. Professor Magnet is the author of numerous papers on constitutional law and is the author of a widely used text, *Constitutional Law of Canada*, 4th edn. (Blais, Montreal, 1989) and the co-author (with E. H. Kluge) of *Withholding Treatment from Defective Newborn Children* (Les Editions Yvon Blais, Montreal, 1985).

JAN NARVESON is a Professor in the Department of Philosophy at the University of Waterloo. He is the author of countless articles in moral and political philosophy and of *Morality and Utility* (Johns Hopkins, Baltimore, 1967) and *Libertarian Idea* (Temple University Press, Philadelphia, 1989). He is also the editor of *Moral Issues* (Oxford University Press, Oxford, 1983).

JOSEPH RAZ is Professor of the Philosophy of Law, Oxford University and Fellow of Balliol College, Oxford. He has published numerous articles in the areas of moral, legal and political philosophy and is the author of *Practical Reason and Norms* (Hutchinson, London, 1975), *The Authority of Law: Essays on Law and Morality* (Clarendon Press, Oxford, 1979); *The Concept of a Legal System,* 2nd edn. (Clarendon Press, Oxford, 1980); and *The Morality of Freedom* (Clarendon Press, Oxford, 1986). He is also the editor of *Practical Reasoning* (Oxford University Press, Oxford, 1979) and (with P. M. S. Hacker) *Law, Morality, and Society: Essays in Honour of H. L. A. Hart* (Oxford University Press, Oxford, 1977).

David A. J. Richards is a Professor Law at New York University Law School. He is the author of many articles in the areas of constitutional law, and legal, moral, and political philosophy. His books include *A Theory of Reasons for Action* (Oxford University Press, Oxford, 1971); *The Moral Criticism of Law* (Dickenson-Wadsworth, Belmont, Calif., 1977); *Sex, Drugs, Death and the Law: An Essay on Human Rights and Overcriminalization* (Rowman and Littlefield, Lanham, Md., 1982) and *Toleration and the Constitution* (Oxford University Press, Oxford, 1986).

ROGER SHINER is a Professor of Philosophy at the University of Alberta. He has published widely in the areas of Greek Philosophy, aesthetics, and moral, political, and legal philosophy. He is the author of *Norm and Nature* (Clarendon Press, Oxford, 1992).

L. W. SUMNER is a Professor of Philosophy at the University of Toronto. His main research interests are in the areas of moral and legal philosophy. Among Professor Sumner's many publications are *Abortion and Legal Theory* (Princeton University Press, Princeton, NJ, 1981) and *The Moral Foundations of Rights* (Clarendon Press, Oxford, 1987).

JAMES WEINSTEIN is a Professor of Law at Arizona State University. He has published several articles in the area of constitutional law, including 'The Language of Impeachment', *Arizona Law Journal* (1988) and 'The Dutch Influence on the Conception of Judicial Jurisdiction in 19th Century America', *American Journal of Comparative Law* (January 1990).

W. J. WALUCHOW, the editor of this volume, is an Associate Professor of Philosophy at McMaster University. He has published several articles in the areas of moral and legal philosophy and is the author (with J. E. Thomas) of *Well and Good: Case Studies in Biomedical Ethics*, rev. edn. (Broadview Press, Peterborough, 1990) and *Inclusive Legal Positivism* (Clarendon Press, Oxford, 1993). He is also the co-editor (with D. Poff) of *Business Ethics in Canada*, 2nd edn. (Prentice-Hall Canada, Scarborough, 1990).

Table of Cases

Table of Statutes

Table of Constitutions and International Conventions

1. Free Expression and Personal Identification

JOSEPH RAZ

1 THE PUZZLE

Freedom of expression is a liberal puzzle.[1] Liberals are all convinced of its vital importance, yet why it deserves this importance is a mystery. The source of the problem is simple. While a person's right to freedom of expression is given high priority, and is protected (or, in political morality, is held to deserve protection) to a far greater degree than a person's interest in having employment, or in not running a risk of an accident when driving along public roads, it is evident that most people value these interests, and many others which do not enjoy special legal protection, much more than they value their right to free expression. Worse still, there can be little doubt that most people are right not to value their right to free expression highly. With few exceptions people's interest in their right to free expression is rather small.

The right of freedom of expression protects people's freedom to communicate in public. 'Communication' is to be understood broadly to include much more than the communication of propositional information. It includes any act of symbolic expression undertaken with the intention that it be understood to be that by the public or part of the public. Thus communication here covers not only all the forms of language-dependent communication but also pictorial and musical communication, and a whole range of symbolic acts such as picketing, displaying banners, wearing uniform. It does not cover acts of expression which are not convention-based

This article benefited from comments on earlier drafts by John Finnis, John Gardner, Avishai Margalit, Sandra Marshall, Hans Oberdiek, Quentin Skinner, Andrew Williams, and participants in the political thought seminar conducted by Professors Skinner and Dunn in the spring of 1990, and especially from the detailed comments of Ron Garet and Carl Wellman.

[1] In this paper 'Liberalism' refers to a political culture which dominates in some societies, or sub-cultures, and not to any particular philosophical doctrine.

symbolic expression such as blushing, or expressing anger at one's competitor's success by setting fire to his shop.[2] Furthermore, to be protected communication has to be public, i.e. addressed to or made available to the public or any section of the public. It is essentially a right actively to participate in and contribute to the public culture.[3]

Given this understanding of the scope of the right the liberal puzzle is apparent. Rights protect interests and it is natural to expect the importance or stringency of the rights to reflect the importance to the right-holder of the interest that they protect.[4] But most people participate in public expression rarely, if at all. For most of them their participation is confined to addressing local communities about local matters (e.g. concern with the maintenance of street lights in one's neighbourhood expressed in a local paper or a local meeting). While that interest is important to a large number of people it can be protected by a much weaker right than the one the liberal doctrine of free expression upholds. It is true that we have an interest in the freedom to engage in activities we are unlikely to engage in, but other things being equal that interest is proportionate to the likelihood, and for most people it is very small indeed.

I should be careful not to underestimate the interest people may have in the freedom to engage in public speech. It is not part of my case that most people have no interest in the freedom of public expression. All I am arguing is that many other interests most people have are much more valuable to them than their interest in this freedom. Yet it is the freedom to express oneself publicly, rather than the more valuable interests, which enjoys special protection.

The responses to the puzzle are numerous. Most of them fall into five categories. First is the contention that appearances are misleading and that people have a great interest in their own freedom of expression. It lies at the heart of their humanity, is a requirement of personhood or rationality, etc.

---

[2] Many acts which carry a symbolic meaning also have some other standard consequences, e.g. pickets impede traffic. This may affect 'balancing tests' but does not exclude them from protection.

[3] Freedom of expression includes the passive freedom to listen and the corresponding negative freedoms, that is the freedom not to communicate and not to listen.

[4] For a discussion of rights in general see my *The Morality of Freedom* (Oxford, OUP 1986), ch. 5. Constitutional rights are discussed in ch. 8. The discussion in this paper relies, and further develops, the framework discussed there.

Second comes the contention that while people's interest in their own freedom of expression may be small there is absolutely no reason, or only minuscule ones, for curtailing it. At least there can be no legitimate reason for curtailing it since its possession and its exercise do no one any harm. Words do not kill. To the counter-argument that they do the reply can be to redefine the right so that where words infringe other people's interests (as in libel, or invasion of privacy) there one's freedom does not stretch, or at least there it has to be balanced against other interests. A sophisticated version of this argument regards the right to free expression as a right against its curtailment for certain reasons, e.g. that what is expressed is false, or an abomination, or repugnant, etc. This allows one to restrict the freedom, provided this is done for other reasons.

Third comes the contention that while people's interest may be small the risk that curtailment will be unjustified is particularly great in this area. This could be because governments are worse judges of the justification of public expression than they are of welfare and other matters, or because they have an institutional interest in restricting expression unjustifiably (it threatens their power), etc.

Fourth are the arguments which suggest that, while the likely harm to the right-holders in cases of curtailed freedom of public expression is not particularly great, the wrong done to them is great. The wrong done to them, according to this argument, is not to be measured in consequentialist terms. The very act of censorship insults the censored, denies their rationality, treats them as means rather than ends in themselves, etc.

Fifth come the arguments that a person's right to free expression is protected not in order to protect him, but in order to protect a public good, a benefit which respect for the right of free expression brings to all those who live in the society in which it is respected, even those who have no personal interest in their own freedom.

Of course these different avenues are not mutually exclusive, and quite a number of writers have buttressed their defence of the right to freedom of expression by combining arguments from different categories. In this article I will examine just one idea which leads to two arguments which belong respectively to the fourth and fifth types; both arguments regard free expression as a public good.

It is not my purpose to propose a comprehensive account of freedom of expression. The considerations I will put forward are insufficient in several respects to justify the right of free expression as it is practised in some Western democracies and advocated by some political theorists. One possible conclusion is that the liberal emphasis on free expression is overdone. Another is that there are other important considerations in support of the right which I will not consider. The second conclusion is certainly warranted, and possibly there is something in the first conclusion as well. All this will remain unexplored here.

Furthermore, I will not be concerned with questions of the outer boundaries of the right, not even in as much as these are affected by the considerations here examined. It seems to be a common philosophical mistake to think that the core justification of a right or any other normative institution is sufficient for fixing its boundaries. The boundaries of a right are greatly affected by existing local conventions and practices, and by institutional considerations. Rights are compatible with a variety of institutional arrangements. Contrary to some views constitutional judicial review is but one possible institutional expression of the right of free expression. A strong common law tradition is another, equally viable institutional framework for the right.[5] The traditions and prospects of different countries may well make one or another institutional framework the preferable one for that country at that time. But often there is no reason to prefer one institutional arrangement over another. This does not mean that different institutions will, should or are capable of protecting the right within identical boundaries. It means that, so far as the core justification of the right goes, there is a flexible range of permissible or acceptable boundaries; the choice between them turns on their suitability for the institutional arrangements in the different societies.

2   FREEDOM OF EXPRESSION AS A PUBLIC GOOD

So much by way of general caution regarding the ambitions of my arguments and the hedges around them. As I said they hold that, whatever else it may be, freedom of expression is a public good. Therefore the right to it is also a public good.[6] I believe that it is

---

[5] I say that it is equally viable, meaning in principle. It is not my contention that the British courts do justice to freedom of expression.

[6] As will be emphasized below it is important to distinguish between freedom of expression, as an actual social situation, and the right to it. The distinction does not avoid the present difficulty for if freedom of expression is a public good so is the right to it if it does protect and promote it.

regarded as such in the common law, but would not argue for that conclusion.[7] Instead I will try to justify that view of freedom of expression first by removing a conceptual objection to the view that a fundamental civil and political individual right can be justified as a public good, and second by pointing to one uncontroversial public good served by free expression.

The conceptual objection is encapsulated in the view which I have already expressed. The considerations which justify rights, I said, are that they protect an interest of the right-holder.[8] Furthermore, their importance depends entirely on the importance of the right-holder's interest which they protect.[9] Both propositions are true and wrong— wrong in excluding the relevance of other considerations. That the first proposition is true is hard to deny.[10] On the one hand stands the fact that rights are necessary to what is in the interests of the right-holders.[11] One cannot have a right to a disadvantage, or to a penalty, etc. unless it is, at least in part, to one's advantage to have the disadvantage or the penalty. This cannot be just a coincidence. The

---

[7] As Mark Kelman remarked to me, the frequent invocation of the slippery slope or the thin end of the wedge argument in cases dealing with free expression itself lends some support to the view that the right is regarded as resting on the need to protect a public good rather than as a matter of protecting the right-holder from a violation of a very important interest of his in the case under consideration. This matter also has bearing on the availability of the right to corporations and other legal persons.

[8] A right protects an interest if and only if respecting it leads to the interest being better protected than it would be if the right did not exist. The argument for a right also shows that whatever disadvantages it brings to others are justified given the interests it protects.

[9] More accurately, their importance is often thought to be a function of the net gain from respecting their existence, i.e. the benefit to the protected interest which such respect brings (compared with a situation in which the right does not exist) discounted by the loss to others, if any, resulting from restrictions it imposes on them.

[10] The so-called 'choice theory' of rights, most notably defended by Hart (see his *Essays on Bentham*) does not deny it. One way of reinterpreting the choice theory, not one favoured by its supporters, is that it identifies the interest in choice as the only, or at any rate the primary, interest for the protection of which one may have a right. Nor does the view that rights are side-constraints (held, regarding some rights, by Nozick in *Anarchy, State and Utopia*) necessarily conflict with the first proposition. It is compatible with holding that only acts detrimental to the right-holders' interests can give rise to rights. The side-constraint view is, of course, incompatible with the second proposition. It regards all rights as absolute, regardless of the importance of the right-holders' interest they protect. This understanding of rights, therefore, supports, but for other reasons, my rejection of the second proposition.

[11] Or, in the case of legal rights, only what the law considers to be in the interest of the right-holders can be so protected. See my 'Legal Rights', (1984) 4 *OLJS* 1.

natural explanation is that the reason for the right is (at least in part) that it serves the interest of the right-holder. Pointing to the interests of right-holders is the standard argument for rights. This would suggest that the importance of the right-holders' interest is a factor in assessing the importance of the right. But it does not establish it as the only factor.

There can be no denying that other people's interests are often served by behaviour which respects rights, and harmed by behaviour which violates them. Assault, or burglary, apart from harming the victims, also instils fear in others, with, sometimes, considerable consequences for their lives. Do the benefits of the right to people other than the right-holder count in assessing the importance of the right? I have argued elsewhere[12] that, when the benefits to others are the result of the benefit the right brings to the right-holder (rather than merely a coincidental independent effect), they do. Given that the right has these consequences any consequentialist morality is committed to taking them into account. Indeed, any morality with a consequentialist component (i.e. one which allows that consequences matter even if they are not all that matters) is bound to take them into account. The most natural way to take them into account is to allow them to be reflected in our judgment of the importance of the right, respect for which secures these consequences.

Once we have gone that far it is but one further step to suggest that the further benefits to third parties which respect for a right brings count, alongside the interest of the right-holder, towards establishing the claim that that person has a right. The problem is this. Rights exist only if the interest they protect is sufficient to hold another person to be under a duty to respect it. That is so only if the interests in question are greater than the disadvantages, if there are such, of being subject to the duty to respect them. Judgment of the existence of a right does, therefore, involve a comparison of interests protected and sacrificed. The question I gave an affirmative answer to is the question whether the interests of those who benefit from the fact that the would-be right-holder's interest is respected count in the case for the existence of a right. Again the reason is that that seems to be the most natural response by every morality with a consequentialist component to the fact that respect for the interest of one person sometimes essentially serves the interests of others as well. To deny the relevance

---

[12] *The Morality of Freedom*, ch. 10.

to the existence of a right of third party interests which it so serves would be odd since it amounts to asserting that considerations which affect the importance of a right are irrelevant to its existence.

Given that the interests of third parties count towards the justification of a right we can begin to see how rights can be justified by their service to public goods. But the case for justifying rights by their service to public goods is not based merely on the abstract argument preceding. It relies in part on the fact that such justifications are deeply embedded in our practices. After all, the argument we are engaged in at the moment, the argument about the nature of rights, is an attempt to understand the basic structure of some of our practices. If it can be shown that those practices are not intelligible except on the assumption that rights are advocated and upheld by reference to their service to public goods then that is strong evidence that such considerations are relevant.[13]

The paradigmatic public-good argument for freedom of expression is also the least problematic argument for the importance of the right. Freedom of expression is an integral part of a democratic regime, i.e. one based on some form of institutional arrangements designed to ensure significant responsiveness of government to the wishes of the governed. Whatever justification democratic government may have, and whatever form it may take, two implications are bound to emerge: (1) Governmental responsiveness to the wishes of the governed is to be desired only if those wishes themselves are not entirely the product of manipulation by the government.[14] (2) Other things being equal, the better informed the governed are and the better able they are to evaluate the information at their disposal the stronger the case for heeding their wishes.

These two considerations serve as a foundation for the democratic defence of freedom of expression. In contemporary multi-candidate electoral systems these considerations lead to a right to the free

---

[13] I have delineated the outline of such an argument in *The Morality of Freedom*, ch. 10. My argument is not 'intuitionist'. It is not based on accepting current moral views, and regarding their vindication as the aim of moral or political theory. I am merely saying that structural features of concepts should be recognized. It is the fact that what is, if a good at all, a public good counts towards the justification of rights that I am relying on, not the actual beliefs in the value of particular alleged public goods.

[14] It is perhaps arguable that there is nothing wrong in governments manipulating the interests of the people so that the perpetuation of those governments in power should be in the people's interests. My concern here is merely with manipulating information and the ability to judge it, and not with the manipulation of interests.

dissemination of information and opinion which may affect judgment on matters of public policy, i.e. on issues which are, or may be, objects of a political decision. It has often been pointed out that democratic justification is insufficient to account for the full scope and importance of the constitutional protection of freedom of expression called for in liberal political theory. This is partly because that freedom extends to matters which are not subject to political decisions, nor likely to affect opinion on issues which are (e.g., publication of research on the burial customs of the ancient Egyptians), but also because the importance of the right in such theories does not reflect the importance of the information for political decisions (e.g. the right is supposed to protect views about the authorship of the Gospels as much, if not more, than views about the causes of inflation, even though the latter are more relevant for political decisions). This is not a refutation of the democratic argument. There is no reason to think that just one consideration can provide a complete account of the right. My purpose in adverting to the democratic case for free expression is both to highlight this fact and to point out that it is a public good justification.

From the point of view of the democratic argument, whatever value the right to free expression has for an individual right-holder derives from his interest in being able to participate in the democratic process. It is, however, notoriously difficult to show that people have a rational reason to cast a vote in any election with a sufficiently large electorate. Arguably, therefore, the value of the right to vote largely depends on the symbolic recognition of full membership in the community which it expresses, rather than arising out of the value of actually being able to vote. How does this reflect on the right of free speech? It carries, though to a lesser degree, the same symbolic value as the right to vote, i.e. its denial implies less than complete membership. Its actual exercise can be of greater value than the right to vote, since it may enable a person, like Springer, Murdoch, or a Kennedy, to affect the votes of many. But for most people the exercise of the right to free public political speech (by which I mean the right of free expression as justified by the democratic argument) has little value, and most people refrain from exercising the right in more than a minimal way.

This argument notwithstanding, the right is essential for the survival of democracy, and everyone has a great interest in the survival of democracy. The point is that this interest is not limited to those who have the vote or the right of free expression. Members of the public in general, be they infants or convicts without the vote, or without a right to free expression, have an interest in the prosperity of democracy, since we assume that democracy is a better form of government than its alternatives, and therefore more likely to ensure that people get what they deserve and are entitled to, and what would be good for them to have. This good, i.e. living in a democratic country, that most people have a personal interest in having is clearly a public good. Its existence is, in part, the existence of the right to free public political expression. Hence that right is a public good, a good not merely to its holders but to the public at large. Furthermore, it follows from the above that the right's service to this public good is a major reason for its importance, a reason of greater weight than the value of the right to each individual who has it.

3   THE CORE CASE: VALIDATING FORMS OF LIFE

With this clarification behind us it is time to turn to the core case behind the two arguments to be presented here.[15] They are primarily arguments for freedom of expression, and only secondarily for a right to it, on the ground that that is a good way of protecting and promoting it.[16]

Much public expression, in books, newspapers, TV, cinema etc., portrays and expresses aspects of styles or forms of life. Views and opinions, activities, emotions, etc., expressed or portrayed, are an aspect of a wider net of opinions, sensibilities, habits of action or dressing, attitudes etc. which, taken together, form a distinctive style or form of life.[17] An important case for the importance of

[15] The view I wish to explore is closely related to the general position expressed by J. Nickel in 'Freedom of Expression in a Pluralistic Society', (1988/9) 7 *Law & Philosophy*, 281.

[16] I will talk both of rights and of duties as protecting interests. Duties protect interest inasmuch as their observance promotes the interests or their violation damages them. Rights protect interests inasmuch as they are the justifying reasons for duties which protect the interests.

[17] Though naturally any single act of expression can be an element of, or fit in with, various forms of life. The only point is that it does not fit with all. Note that nowhere do I define 'forms of life'. For the purpose of this argument the precise understanding of the term is immaterial. The only material points are that different aspects of activities, tastes, styles and attitudes are seen to belong together, in the ordinary way in which we can distinguish the yuppy, or the middle class, or the 'Sloane Ranger', etc. Whatever other aspects of styles or forms of life are material to the argument will emerge as the argument of the article develops.

freedom of expression[18] arises out of the fact that public portrayal and expression of forms of life validate the styles of life portrayed, and that censoring expression normally expresses authoritative condemnation not merely of the views or opinions censored but of the whole style of life of which they are a part.

The fact that much public expression expresses or portrays aspects of ways of life is often either overlooked or taken for granted as a trivial and irrelevant point. It is overlooked because often writers on freedom of expression focus attention on types of speech of which this is not true, or at least not true in any straightforward way. For example, claims about the relative merit of high interest rates versus high taxation as a means of dampening consumer spending do not express any way of life. The same goes for publication of an academic article about the origin of galaxies, etc. When discussing such cases attention is normally focused on the importance of the information conveyed and of being free to convey it. But these cases have an additional aspect. Engaging in such speech is part of the normal activities of economists, politicians, journalists, or scientists. Prohibiting or censoring such speech distorts and impedes these activities, and if it is far reaching it renders them impossible and can constitute their public condemnation. This is true of interference with much free expression. It points to the fact that public expression is itself an element of several styles of life.

Of course this fact in itself is no argument for the *special* protection of free expression. Many non-speech activities are integral to many different styles of life. One should be aware of this factor whenever the State criminalizes or otherwise impedes various activities. It would be wrong, however, to dismiss this consideration just on the ground that it is not unique to acts of expression. Even though it applies to other cases too it may justify greater protection of free expression than of freedom to engage in other activities, if only for the reason that the justification of each freedom involves comparing good and ill, merits and demerits; and the demerits, the disadvantages of engaging in various activities, are not the same. Prayer may be part of a religion which involves ritual bodily mutilation of young children. Respect for this religious style of life may weigh equally in favour of tolerating both prayer and mutilation. But the arguments

---

[18] i.e. a situation in which freedom of expression occurs, not of a right to free expression.

against tolerating the two practices are far from equal, and the result need not be the same.

The argument that I wish to explore covers cases in which the very act of expression is an element of a way of life as a special case. It covers also speech by people who do not share the style of life about aspects of which they express themselves. That is why I refer to portrayals or descriptions of ways of life as the paradigmatic, though not the only, case my argument applies to. These include cases in which the concern is not with the interest of the speaker and the way his speech is an aspect of his life, but the way it reflects, expresses or describes the life of others.

A typical example of this is a portrayal of a family in a TV sitcom. Let's say, husband and wife have two children, an adolescent girl, romantic and full of dreams about poetry, her boy-friend, her studies, her tennis, and a younger boy, continuously quarrelling with the neighbours' children, making his first steps as a computer hack, teasing his older sister to tears. While such portrayals are typical of the kind of expression I am concerned with, they are not the only ones. The argument extends to discussion and comments on activities, beliefs, attitudes, and of responses to them. It also, and most importantly, extends to pornography, and to prayer books and much else which, while only sometimes portraying ways of life, are always meant to be used as part of certain ways of life.

The reason to focus on acts of expression of this type is that they fulfil important functions in contemporary societies.[19] Three are of prime concern to my argument:

— They serve to familiarize the public at large with ways of life common in certain segments of the public.

— They serve to reassure those whose ways of life are being portrayed that they are not alone, that their problems are common problems, their experiences known to others.

— Finally, they serve as validation of the relevant ways of life. They give them the stamp of public acceptability.

I shall talk of portrayal in the public media as validating the experience or way of life portrayed or expressed, as a shorthand to refer to

---

[19] By 'contemporary societies' I mean societies like ours. Many past societies shared these features, and some contemporary ones lack them. But it seems to me important to start from the here and now, and not from an abstract enumeration of relevant features.

all three functions of such expression. The use of the term 'validation' suggests the direction of the argument.

That public portrayal has an important validating function is a contingent fact of human nature. But although contingent it is deeply rooted and of great importance to the preservation of any culture. Even traditional homogeneous societies in which individuals find themselves enmeshed in closely knit social networks depend for the legitimation of their culture and its transmission and renewal on its expression and portrayal in the public arena. The difference is that contemporary pluralistic societies place a high value on recognizing the existence of a plurality of valuable ways of life, and of the possibility of change and the generation of novel valuable forms of life. Furthermore we depend more than ever before on a culture which saturates us with images and messages through the public media, which have acquired a great power both to encourage and to stifle and marginalize activities, attitudes, and the like.

To a large extent the validating functions of public expression acquire their contemporary importance from two much discussed aspects of contemporary societies, their urban anonymity and their cultural and ethical pluralism. These mean that people depend more than ever on public communication to establish a common understanding of the ways of life, range of experiences, attitudes, and thinking which are common and acceptable in their society. They also depend on finding themselves reflected in the public media for a sense of their own legitimacy, for a feeling that their problems and experiences are not freak deviations.[20]

4 THE FIRST ARGUMENT: TOLERATING AND ENCOURAGING VALIDATION

Freedom of expression touches on the validation of ways of life in two ways, yielding two distinct arguments for it. First, while it exists and in as much as it is exercised, ways of life which are portrayed and expressed are validated through their portrayal and expression. People get the reassurance that others know of their problems, experiences, attitudes etc., and that they are acceptable in the society. Second, because of this significance of expression, censorship and

---

[20] For the existence of the problem, viz. the proliferation of support groups for people who are drug abusers, smokers, teenage mothers, fat, thin, etc.

criminalization acquire a wider negative significance. They express not merely disapproval of the particular act of expression which is censored. They express disapproval of the whole way of life (of all the ways of life) of which it is a part. In contemporary societies public portrayal validates ways of life, whereas censorship is authoritative public condemnation of the way of life. The first argument for freedom of expression arising out of these considerations asserts that freedom of expression renders a great service to people's well-being. This service takes three forms.

First, validation of a way of life through its public expression is of crucial importance for the well-being of individuals whose way of life it is. It helps their identification with their way of life, their sense of its worth, and their sense that their way of life facilitates rather than hinders their integration into their society.

Second, such validation is important for making ways of life a real option for people. Absence of validation makes them suspect, and unattractive, and jeopardizes the chances that people will choose them.

Thirdly, public validation is an essential element in the process of cultural transmission, preservation, and renewal. It is one of the central arenas for the assertion of traditions, and for challenging traditions and experimenting with new forms of relationships, new attitudes and styles of life.

This argument shows freedom of expression to be a public good, a constitutive element of a public culture. It points to a strong, positive case for free expression. It points to the importance not only of the absence of censorship but of providing access to the means of public expression to those who portray various ways of life, and express different points of view.[21] At the same time the argument supports only a weak, overridable right. Like all public good arguments it is weak on setting boundaries. No major difficulty arises if one allows, say, private TV stations to deny access to certain views, so long as those views can find other avenues of expression. No major problem arises from restricting the areas in towns in which demonstrations can

---

[21] At its most abstract level, the argument does not distinguish between privately owned and publicly owned means of expression (such as land, newspapers, public halls, or TV stations). It establishes a reason for all those who control means of public expression to allow access to them. But in establishing the ways such abstract reasons are to receive institutional support and become enforceable by law it may be reasonable to distinguish between privately owned and publicly owned means of expression and to impose lesser duties on the former. Such matters cannot be determined in the abstract.

be held, so long as the areas available provide for a reasonably effective way of expressing views and displaying the intensity with which they are felt.

5 THE SECOND ARGUMENT: CENSORSHIP AS INSULT

To a certain extent the issue of boundaries is helped by a second argument. It derives from the evil of censorship and criminalization, which extends a good deal beyond denying people the benefits of a culture in which expression is free. Because of the validating function of public expression pure content-based censorship[22] has acquired a symbolic meaning. It expresses official, authoritative disapproval and condemnation of the style of life of which the censored communication is a part.[23]

People's relations to the society in which they live is a major component in their personal well-being. It is normally vital for personal prosperity that one will be able to identify with one's society, will not be alienated from it, will feel a full member of it. The importance of this factor derives from two concerns. First, a significant part of the activities and pursuits through which people prosper (or fail to prosper) involves engagement with larger groups (their workplace or trade association, their city, sports or other leisure association, a variety of civic activities in support of the homeless, single mothers, war veterans, etc.). Full membership in the society is essential for free participation in the activities of such groups (except in those which are dedicated to achieving full membership for certain subgroups—membership of such subgroups sometimes presupposes

---

[22] 'Pure' content-based censorship is marked by the reasons for the censorship. Censorship is pure content-based if the reason for it is the disapproval of the content of the act of expression, rather than merely an attempt to avoid undesirable consequences of its publication. So that prohibition of the publication of military secrets is content-based but not 'purely' content-based. 'Content' is meant to include style. E.g. expressing a view by the use of violent language or gesture has, for the purposes of this discussion, a different content than its expression in polite academic language. This follows from the fact that attitudes, emotions, etc. and not merely a cognitive content are covered by 'expression'.

Pure content-based censorship can take the form of prior restraint, criminalization, or regulation. But the last is characteristically based on desire to minimize the consequences of the act of expression, and is only very rarely purely content-based. Criminalization and prior restraint can be either purely content-based or based on a perceived reason to avoid or mitigate the consequences of the speech.

[23] I use this expression to indicate both acts of expression which are themselves a part of a form of life, and those which portray, describe, discuss, etc. aspects of forms of life. Both are covered by the arguments advanced in this article.

absence of full membership in one's country's society). Second, the very ability to identify with one's society is an independent background good, and feeling alienated from it is a significant handicap. They have a considerable, often imperceptible impact on people's ability to engage in activities involving relations with other people, or contributions to their well-being or to the common good. Official denunciation or condemnation of one's way of life is a major obstacle to identification with one's society, and this is a powerful argument against it.

Just like the first argument the second rests on a public good case for free expression. The evil to be avoided is not a specific special harm to the interests of the right-holder caused by denying him free expression. It is a harm to the common interest of all, and especially of those whose interests are served by the condemned way of life and its prosperity. Because this is the meaning of *every* act of content-based censorship, and of *every* content-based criminalization of acts of symbolic public expression, the second argument solves many of the boundary problems which the first argument generates.

In some ways this second argument is the more powerful of the two. Content-based censorship and criminalization are a public and authoritative condemnation. Their repudiation of ways of life which they reject is insulting and hurtful and their negative meaning is a stronger reason against censorship and criminalization than the reason for free expression deriving from the value of the validation of styles of life through their public portrayal. In a culture in which expression is free, validation is provided by people exercising their freedom. They provide validation and not the state, not society using its authoritative voice. Society's official attitude welcomes and facilitates such validation, but it is given only where members of that society wish to give it through their exercise of freedom of expression. Content-based censorship and criminalization not only deny individuals the opportunity to provide validation but constitute official condemnation of the way of life aspects of which are censored or criminalized.

The symbolic meaning of content-based censorship and criminalization gives the second argument considerable weight where it applies. But its range is limited compared with the first argument. The symbolic meaning of condemnation of the style of life to which the expression belongs is a feature of pure content-based prohibitions. It is not typical of other restrictions on free expression, e.g. banning demonstrations from the vicinity of churches during the high holidays, out of respect for the feelings of worshippers, or banning them on certain highways during the rush hour, in order to facilitate commuters' journeys home. Similarly the interest of would-be speakers to have access to the public has to be reconciled with the interest of the public not to be made a captive audience, a reconciliation which requires many pragmatic compromises between speakers who wish to address people where they are likely to be, and members of the public who wish to be able to use public arenas without being subjected to acts of expression which they regard as odious.[24] The second argument does not extend to such cases, and while the first argument does it establishes only a weak right, which is subject to compromises when it clashes with such legitimate concerns.

The weight and scope differences between the two arguments should not be exaggerated. Limited acts of prior restraint by a minor official, even though content-based, do not carry the message of official condemnation to the same degree as major legislation extensively criminalizing the portrayal of a group's way of life. Even pure content-based censorship is a matter of degree, though this is normally relevant to the degree of wrongness of the act, rather than to its justification. Justification is however at stake in mixed cases. Often criminalization or prior restraint[25] is based both on pure content-based reasons and on a perceived reason to avoid the consequences of acts of expression. Furthermore, given that the underlying reasons for such criminalization and prior restraint are so commonly mixed, almost every content-based criminalization or prior restraint is perceived as expressing in part official condemnation of the content of expression.[26] Since the evil is in the public perception, almost every content-based criminalization and prior restraint is subject to the considerations of my second argument.

These observations presuppose that the public meanings of permitting and prohibiting are not contraries. Whereas prohibition

---

[24] Of course, members of the public also have an interest in easy access to information which they wish to receive. The conflict I am alluding to is not between speakers and the public. It is between speakers and the sections of the public who wish to have easy access to them, and other sections of the public who wish to be free of their intrusion.

[25] I have in mind all content-based criminalization and prior restraint, pure or impure, that is excluding only those which are designed merely to enforce regulatory measures rather than to stop all expression of a certain content.

[26] The exceptions are instances where the importance of the noncontent-based reasons is clear, as with vital military secrets.

(i.e. censorship and criminalization) condemns the prohibited conduct, permission does not endorse what is permitted, it merely toler-
ates it. How should facilitating actions be judged? How should one
judge state subsidies to science? Does their denial to astrology
amount to its condemnation? How should access to the media be
judged? Does the provision of TV time to Muslims and its non-
provision to Buddhists constitute condemnation of the latter and
endorsement of the former? The main point to bear in mind is that the
issue is factual, not logical. It is not to be resolved by arguing, say, that
subsidies are a positive interference, like censorship, and not merely a
non-interference, like permissions, and that therefore they are an
endorsement, whereas a refusal to facilitate is no condemnation. Nor
would it do to argue that since no effective access is likely to be
possible to some ideas or ways of life (since they have no rich
supporters) it follows that refusal to facilitate is condemnation. The
only issue is what is the public meaning of certain acts, and the same
act can have different meanings in different societies.[27] The meaning
may depend on considerations of the kind mentioned, and on many
others (the reasons for lack of facilitation being obvious ones,[28] as are
the normal expectations in that society). I am assuming that generally
providing access to the public media in our society does not speak of
approval, but of toleration. And that its denial does not amount to
condemnation by the society. Therefore, the second argument does
not support a positive right of access to the means of public expression. The State's failure to give philosophers an assured access to
the means of expression does not amount to an authoritative condemnation of philosophy by the State, whereas censorship and criminalization of philosophical publications are such a condemnation.

Broadly speaking the position is this: regulatory restrictions are
subject to the first argument only. In general content-based criminalization and prior restraint are subject to the second argument, for
in most cases they express condemnation of the way of life portrayed
or expressed. Where the restriction is pure content-based the argument is normally decisive. Where the restriction is based also on good
reasons to avoid certain consequences of the act of expression, the

---

[27] More awkwardly for setting the boundaries of the right it may have different
meanings to different groups in the same society.
[28] Compare denying subsidies to Buddhists on the ground that there are none in the
country with their denial on the ground that Buddhism is repugnant, or morally
corruptive.

need for such restriction has to be assessed against the reasons against it adumbrated above.

Finally, neither of the two arguments protects most acts of expression about particular individuals. Similarly, the democratic argument for free expression does not concern, with some obvious exceptions, speech regarding identifiable ordinary persons. Naturally it does protect many comments regarding individuals who are holders of or candidates for public office, or who are otherwise involved in politics. Similarly, the arguments I am considering here do protect speech about individuals who become symbols of certain cultures, or ideologies, or who have acquired a status of paradigmatic representatives of styles of life, or cultures, etc. But with these exceptions the right to freedom of expression does not conflict with the law of libel and right of privacy.

6   PROTECTING BAD SPEECH

Any doctrine of freedom of expression must face the question: why should society respect people's freedom to express false, worthless, degrading, depraved, etc. views and opinions? It is an essential aspect of any doctrine of free expression that it purports to justify the freedom to what we can generically call bad speech (by which I do not mean that it must justify the freedom to express anything however bad). Does my argument do that? Does it not depend on the value of the protected speech? This objection misunderstands the nature of my argument. It does indeed depend on the value to be found in the ways of life of which protected speech is a part. But bad speech is often a part[29] of a good way of life, or at any rate one which should not be condemned by society through its official organs. This point is important not only for the justification of freedom of expression but for any doctrine of toleration.

Take two examples. First, an atheist may say that since there is no God it is permissible to censor public expression avowing belief in the existence of God, or propagating arguments purporting to prove his existence since they only spread error. Second, a person of cultivated taste may say that the high volume of rock music detracts from its value, and the law may, perhaps even should, restrict the volume at

[29] Either in being strictly speaking a part of, or in portraying something which is part of, a bad style of life.

which it is played, for to do so can only improve people's taste and the quality of their lives. Let us assume that we agree with the atheist about the non-existence of God, and with the finely cultivated person about the worthlessness of loud music. Does it follow that censorship is justified?

Of course not. There are many other questions which have to be faced. Is such speech protected by other principled arguments for free speech? Can we trust the legislature with the power to take such decisions? Even if right in these cases is it not likely to reach wrong conclusions more often than not? Would the consequences of restriction of speech have the desired results? Or will it lead to enhancing the appeal of the forbidden speech by lending it the aura of anti-establishment heroism? Will restrictions have undesired side-effects (undermining confidence in the government, providing the police with excessive powers which invite abuse, etc.)? There is always also the consideration which elsewhere[30] I made much of that any prohibition of victimless crimes brings with it punishments which infringe people's life, and deny their autonomy in ways which exceed the authority of the State, since they cannot be justified on the ground that they are necessary to protect the autonomy of others. For the purpose of the present argument I want, however, to leave all these considerations on one side and concentrate on a question of first principle. Do the considerations I canvassed above establish any reason of principle against the State curtailing free expression in the two examples we are discussing?

They do, for by curtailing these acts of bad speech the State condemns, and impedes the existence of, good ways of life of which the acts of bad speech are parts. I am assuming here that we will all agree that the religious life, and the life of rock fans, are valuable despite the presence in them of these objectionable features.[31] The real question is one of separability. Can it not be said that in condemning these aspects of these ways of life one does not condemn the whole way of life? It is to be welcomed, and even encouraged, but it should be purged of its objectionable features.

---

[30] In *The Morality of Freedom*.

[31] Two caveats: first, I am not assuming that all religions embody valuable ways of life, only that at least one does. The same goes for the life of the rock fans. Second, while the notion of a religious life is familiar, there is no equivalent term to describe the disjunctive set of features which make one or the other styles of life in which rock music features importantly. But the absence of a handy phrase does not mean that rock music is not an important part of the life styles of many people.

It cannot be said that it is impossible for people to go to church, perform church music, continue with the complex social, charitable and educational activities of their churches, but abandon their belief in the existence of God. There is good reason to think that this is indeed the way that quite a few people conduct themselves. Similarly it cannot be said that rock music is not improved if played at lower volumes. Yet such claims are beside the point. For the believer belief in God is an essential part of the religious life. For the rock fan volume is essential to his favourite music, and its significance for his life. We can say to them that there is an alternative way of life which is better, but we cannot deny them sovereignty over defining what their way of life is, and what is integral to it. This question is answerable entirely from the point of view of those whose way of life it is. *Their* way of life is the activities, practices and attitudes which are meaningful and rewarding in their life.[32]

The censoring government can say that it does not intend to condemn the style of life as a whole, that it rejects only the censored aspect of it. But such response even when truthful is inadequate. What is condemned is an objective matter, which does not altogether depend on the government's intentions. The perceived significance of the act is more sweeping. For reasons which are not hard to seek it is reasonably seen as a condemnation of that way of life as it is. Given that that is the social significance of such acts of censorship, that is that they are perceived as condemning the way of life as a whole, such censorship constitutes condemnation. The defence 'we did not intend to condemn' is of no avail. What counts is what the government did, not what it intended to do.

These observations relate to the second of my two arguments. Similar considerations apply to the first argument. In denying public expression to aspects of a way of life the government restricts and impedes the ability of that way of life as a whole, and not just the offending aspect, to gain public recognition and acceptability.

Does all this matter? It is conceded that the ways of life my

---

[32] And it is not determinable in the abstract. It depends on the actual practices of real people. This is consistent with allowing that individuals may make mistakes about what is meaningful in their lives. They do not enjoy an epistemically privileged position. But I mean styles of life to be understood flexibly, to include more or fewer aspects of a person's life. All that matters for this argument to apply to any act of expression is that it reflects or portrays an aspect which is either pervasive in itself or is an integral element in a pervasive aspect of that person's life.

argument intends to protect are deficient, and that they can be improved by changing them in appropriate ways, or by substituting alternative ways of life which preserve much of the good but avoid the shortcomings of the ones portrayed in the offending speech. Does not that provide sufficient grounds for restricting free expression? Assuming that the bad speech expresses or portrays elements of a valuable way of life, does not the fact that there are better alternative ways of life justify restrictions of free expression if they are likely to encourage a change to the better alternatives? There is nothing wrong in principle in governments trying to promote valuable ways of life, and to improve them. But here the proposed measures to that end include impeding or denying public recognition to a good (though imperfect) way of life, or its public, authoritative condemnation. Such measures cannot be justified. They are wrong in themselves.[33]

So the arguments I am advancing provide reasons to protect much bad speech. But they do not protect all bad speech. To be protected by these arguments it has to be an expression or portrayal of something which is a part of a valuable way of life. Some ways of life are without redeeming features. Some of their aspects have no place in any worthwhile way of life and their expression or portrayal is not protected by the arguments advanced here.

This is not the place to discuss in detail what makes a way of life totally unacceptable. This is one of the central questions of ethics. But it is worth noting that the task is not straightforward. Moral philosophy tends to concentrate on single items: which acts are wrong, or right, which character traits are admirable, and which are not. The character of a way of life depends on evaluating a much broader canvas—of practices, character traits, attitudes, beliefs, and so on. It raises questions rarely discussed by theorists. Some tests seek perfection and would disallow any but forms of life without any blemish. They are based on a misunderstanding of the task. It is not to imagine perfect or saintly lives, but good and worthwhile ones. Other tests while sensible in their motivation may be deemed too lenient. For example, it may be suggested that any form of life which may enhance the quality of life of a person, while not involving him in any major

[33] Remember that so far as the first of my two arguments is concerned it is subject to adjudication between conflicting goods. The second argument is different and it seems that only extraordinary circumstances will justify overriding it.

sin, is acceptable. By this test, which is admittedly too vague to be accepted without much further development, even Nazism is acceptable. Many youngsters were rescued from a life of drifting and petty criminality, into organized, spirited activities in Nazi youth clubs, enjoyed camaraderie, and a sense of proud membership of their nation, partaking of its culture and traditions, as well as a sense of purpose in their life, while being lucky enough never to have become involved in Nazi crimes. Such cases raise difficult issues which I will leave on one side.[34] One sufficient condition for the unacceptability of a style of life is that the activities essential and distinctive to its pursuit are rightly forbidden by law. But this test is incomplete, and in any case merely defers the question. For it all depends on what is rightly forbidden by law.

7 ATTACKING SPEECH

For more than two years now Britain's liberal conscience has been shaken by the Rushdie case. The thought that a novelist may find himself pursued by murder gangs, that he should go into hiding, lose contact with people and places, that his creative life no less than his personal life will be for ever indelibly marked by a campaign of mass hysteria and hatred, shocked and horrified the public. Personally I was touched by another aspect of the affair. I suddenly found myself living among neighbours some of whom believe that they have a duty to kill Rushdie if the opportunity comes their way. Liberal-minded people everywhere found themselves torn between their belief in free expression and their abhorrence of racism and acceptance of pluralism. How were they to react to the claims of many Muslims that Rushdie, under the protection of an alien and hostile culture, has blasphemed, and has also grossly defamed their religion?

The Muslim response to Rushdie, where even moderates called for the banning of the book, on the one hand, and the campaigns by gays and lesbians for gay culture to find expression in the public arena, were the main triggers for the thoughts I have been outlining in this article. Both highlight the considerations on which I based my arguments, i.e. the validation of ways of life through their public

---

[34] One response, suggested to me by Antony Duff, is to distinguish between morally mistaken and morally evil beliefs. The latter can perhaps be said to diminish the quality of one's life, as well as one's character, even if one does not act wrongly as a result of such beliefs.

expression. The Muslim campaign to suppress speech which attacks and vilifies their religion raised the question of the limits of the protection. Do not the very considerations I pointed to suggest that, while positive portrayal of ways of life, or aspects of them, should be tolerated, a critical or hostile discussion or portrayal of them is to be banned?

There are two tempting mistakes in understanding these arguments. One is to invoke a presumption of freedom. After all, we are told, no one is compelled to read novels, or newspaper articles, or to watch films or TV. I have remarked at the outset that acts of expression have consequences, even as acts of expression, for the life of others. One important interest which all people share is an interest in the character of their environment, cultural and social as well as natural and physical. It is short-sighted to condemn the reaction of the Muslim community to a culture which is critical of their religion as meddling in things which are of no concern to them since they can avoid reading the offensive literature. It is a legitimate concern of gays that our culture is swamped with displays of heterosexual relations, whereas homoerotic ones are *de facto* denied public expression. These facts do undermine the public acceptability of gay relations, or of Muslim culture.

But it is wrong to react by embracing the other mistake and censor critical or hostile portrayals of Muslims or gays. Two considerations establish the need to tolerate hostile speech. First, while content-based censorship or criminalization is an expression of authoritative condemnation of the views censored and the way of life they are a part of, criticism, hostility or neglect by individuals or sections of the public express only their hostility or condemnation. They do not carry the authoritative voice of society. This again is a matter of fact, a matter of the social significance of our acts of toleration in the public culture of free societies. It is otherwise in illiberal societies. Since in them only those who express approved views are allowed to express them, the fact that an opinion is tolerated shows that it has authoritative endorsement. By their very nature this is not true of free societies.[35] Hence the second argument for protecting free expression does not extend to censorship of private hostility and condemnation. Second, criticism of rival ways of life is a part of any way of life in the sense that it is implied by it, and is felt by its adherents. Hence the

[35] Though it is worth remembering that freedom is a matter of degree, and so is the social significance of toleration.

arguments I advanced for protecting free expression also protect expressions of critical and hostile views and attitudes.[36]

One needs to distinguish here between incompatible and rival ways of life. Two ways of life are incompatible if they cannot both be adopted by the same person.[37] Many incompatible styles of life are displayed in any society. For example, the way of life of town dwellers is incompatible with the way of life of the inhabitants of the prairies or of remote mountains. There is no inconsistency in approving of different ways of life just because they are incompatible. Rival ways of life are ones which it is inconsistent to approve of without reservation. Islam and Christianity offer rival ways of life. A Christian can approve of the way of life of the Muslim, and vice versa, in that they can and should find each other's way of life valuable and worthwhile. But not without reservations. There are aspects of the other's practices, attitudes, and beliefs that each of them must take exception to, must disagree with. Disagreement, condemnation, and even hostility to certain aspects of rival ways of life is an essential element of each way of life. That is why the argument of this article protects its expression.

The argument for a right of free expression I am defending is 'perfectionist' in the sense that it is based on the need to fashion legal institutions to promote people's ability and prospects of having worthwhile, good lives. But it is not perfectionist in the more ordinary sense of the term. It recognizes that imperfect ways of life may be valuable. Moreover, imperfect ways of life may be the best which is possible for people, given the society to which they belong, and the course of their life to date. This view is strongly pluralistic. It recognizes the value of many incompatible ways of life, but also the value of many rival ways of life. Strong pluralism of this kind finds itself, as the Rushdie case illustrates, approving as valuable, though imperfect, ways of life which themselves deny the truth of pluralism. Of course the anti-pluralistic views which underlie such ways of life are regarded as wrong, and the ways of life that they inform are correspondingly

[36] As mentioned in the section above there is always a need for a compromise between the interest in addressing the public and the interest of individuals not to be made a captive audience. This applies to offensive and hostile speech as well. The rules which apply to, say, books will therefore differ from those which apply to TV in a country where there are only a few TV stations and thus less choice for members of the public.

[37] Throughout a whole lifetime. Within limits people can change from one to another.

imperfect. They are rival ways of life, but none the less recognized as valuable, that is as enabling those who follow them to have good and rewarding lives, and as being for some people, due to their circumstances, the best kind of life possible to them.

Where a dominant pluralistic outlook leads to the recognition of the value of rival ways of life conflict is inevitable. The pluralist while finding value in the ways of life informed by some wrong beliefs must inevitably differ from the people who have those wrong beliefs about what precisely is valuable in their lives and why. The Christian will regard his life as good because he is following the word of God. The atheist will approve of that person's life because it is informed by respect for human beings or because it values religious art, and therefore manifests aesthetic sensibility.

The respect that the pluralist shows for the anti-pluralist may disguise the difference of values, even from the eyes of the pluralist. The seeming harmony is fractured when cases such as Rushdie's make it plain. At such moments the anti-pluralists challenge the sincerity of the pluralists. You never really respected us, they say. You only approved of us when it suited your outlook. But you never respected our views out of respect for them, for the truth they express. All along you were merely enforcing your views on us, allowing us to go our own way only when it suited you. Your claim of pluralism is therefore a sham. You enforce your toleration of Rushdie on us in an intolerant spirit (since you do not tolerate our rejection of him), and at the same time you object to us, the anti-pluralists, enforcing our beliefs in the name of a toleration of other people's views.[38] Pluralists often feel uncomfortable when faced with such accusations. They feel that their pluralism is indeed inadequate for they do not allow (when they have the political power to decide such matters) the anti-pluralist cultures which they claim to respect, to have their way of life (including its anti-pluralist aspects) fully enacted. They pick and choose what to allow and what to disallow.

But the accusation is groundless. The accusers seize on aspects of the pluralist position while misunderstanding their significance. Pluralists have the virtue of recognizing the value of rival ways of life. But such recognition does not stem from abandonment of judgment, or

---

[38] There are of course other claims made in this context. One of them, that if one is to tolerate other cultures then one should censor attacks on them, has been dealt with above.

from general scepticism. Such positions are incoherent.[39] Consistent pluralists have their own firm views about the qualities which make for a good life. They are distinctive in recognizing the plurality of incompatible and even rival but nonetheless valuable ways of life. Pluralism is misunderstood when it is assumed that it is committed to approval and support of every aspect of ways of life it recognizes as valuable, or that it is committed to taking these ways of life at their own estimation. Because it recognizes the value of ways of life which it (partly) disagrees with, pluralism is committed to a society in which conflicting ideologies and beliefs are accepted, and tolerated. But it is an illusion to think that accepting conflict is a way of avoiding conflict. This is the substance of the accusation of hypocrisy against the pluralist, that in the end he has his own position which he is willing to back against those he 'pretended' to tolerate. So he does; so does anyone who has a coherent position. Pluralist toleration is real enough, but it is no recipe for the avoidance of social conflict. Conflict is avoided not by pluralist toleration but by repressive perfectionist uniformity.

There is of course the question of how conflict should be conducted. Should the supporters of rival views be allowed to use the law to promote their views? This question finds its answer in each of the rival views out of its own internal logic. The attempt by some thinkers[40] to find an extra, or meta-position from which to reconcile the conflicting views does not seem to hold much promise. The views explored here are the implications of a pluralist position to the question of using the law to suppress free expression. It shows that freedom of expression can be supported as part of a pluralist argument for using the law to promote pluralism in the society.

8   THE CASE FOR SPECIAL PROTECTION

So far the article has advanced a case for respecting freedom of expression. I said nothing about the justification of a right to freedom of expression, let alone of a constitutional right. This concluding section will briefly address this last issue. The point I wish to highlight is that the stringency and the constitutional standing of the right need

---

[39] See my 'Facing Diversity: The Case for Epistemic Abstinence', *Philosophy & Public Affairs*, 19 (1990), 3 and 'Liberalism, Skepticism, and Democracy' (1989) 74 *Iowa Law Review* 761.
[40] Most notably Rawls.

not be justified by showing that freedom of expression is more important than relative economic prosperity, or full employment. The right can be justified on the ground that the institutional arrangements best suited for the protection of freedom of expression are best operated through the institution of a constitutional right.

As indicated at the outset the institutional arrangements proper for the protection of freedom of expression depend to a considerable extent on the tradition and practices of different countries. But some general observations about contemporary societies can be made. First let it be noted what the argument of this article does *not* establish. It does not establish that freedom of expression should never be compromised. As noted above, the second of the two arguments I presented comes close to doing so, but it applies only to pure content-based censorship and criminalization, which is but a small part of the protected acts of expression. Second, the arguments do not even establish that free expression should be protected as a matter of individual right of the speaker. The arguments are public good arguments. The case for a right is institutional. Vesting speakers with a right to free expression is an efficient way of protecting freedom of expression in the community, for it enables people whose freedom to express themselves is restricted to invoke the law, rather than relying exclusively on governmental institutions whose motivation to protect freedom of expression is often suspect. Furthermore, giving individuals a legal right to free expression is one way of making the courts guardians of this freedom, and as we shall see there are institutional reasons for doing so. With all that it still seems to me that the protection of freedom of expression should not in most States rest entirely on the individual right to free expression. It requires additional recognition in public culture and legal institutions.

Needless to say, my arguments do not establish a universal moral right to freedom of expression. Nor do they establish that the value of freedom of expression is universal to all human societies. The core considerations on which the arguments rest apply to most familiar societies. But even they are not universal, and certainly the ramifications of the arguments depend on cultural features which vary from country to country. Finally, while the arguments of this article do not cover all aspects of the conventional liberal doctrine of free expression their implications are not confined to freedom of expression. They may have special force in cases of expression, but they can be applied to condemn some forms of moral paternalism, such as forcing people to refrain from sexual activities which are, let us assume, immoral.

Having said all that, the arguments do point to the great importance of free expression. They turn on the fundamental need for public validation of one's way of life, and on the need for public recognition as a way of transmitting, preserving and developing ways of life. In the circumstances of contemporary life these considerations touch the very foundations of pluralistic societies. In this respect the argument I adumbrated here joins three other arguments to form the foundation of a liberal doctrine of free expression. The other three are: (1) freedom of expression as a prerequisite of a democratic government; (2) freedom of expression as vital for the prosperity of a pluralistic culture; (3) freedom of expression as a crucial element in controlling possible abuses and corruption of power. All four arguments point to the need to make freedom of expression a foundational part of the political and civic culture of pluralistic democracies.

There is reason to favour legal arrangements which provide institutional recognition for the distinction between everyday short term politics, and those aspects of our political life which protect the basic features of our culture. Freedom of expression belongs to the latter, and should receive the kind of institutional protection given to the fundamentals of our culture. One way of doing so, suited for countries with a strong tradition of the rule of law, and a politically sophisticated and enlightened judiciary, is by assigning primary responsibility for its protection to the courts. This is the main justification for its inclusion in entrenched bills of rights. The significance of such entrenchment is that it removes the matter from the short-term pressures of ordinary political decision-making. It places decisions in the hands of courts which enjoy, under the doctrine of the rule of law, independence from everyday political pressures. This does not mean that decisions about freedom of expression are apolitical or undemocratic. They are political through and through, both in their implications and in the reasons underlying them, which all too often have to do with striking compromises between conflicting interests. They are also democratic in that the courts are properly responsive to public opinion. But they are responsive to public opinion not as expressed in public opinion polls, but as expressed in the public culture of their country. It may have implications which do not curry favour with the public, implications which remain unpopular for a long time. In respecting those implications the courts avoid degeneration of the public culture, which does, by definition, enjoy public support.

The entrenchment and special protection of legal rights, we thus learn, can be a reflection of the institutionalized arrangements for settling disputes concerning them, and not only a reflection of the importance of their subject matter.

2. Free Speech as Toleration

DAVID A. J. RICHARDS

The theory of free speech is a natural subject of interdisciplinary and comparative study for both political philosophers and lawyers. First, it has a highly abstract component, in which issues of general normative philosophy (for example, utilitarian or perfectionist teleological consequentialism versus deontological natural rights) are at stake; and second, it has a historical and contextual component, in which free speech is embedded in a historically evolving tradition of constitutional thought, including both political and legal arguments made over time about its proper meaning. The proper balance between these two components (political theory and interpretive history) differs in various legal systems all of which are committed in some form to free speech. Nations with written constitutions and judicial review (the United States, Canada, Germany, and the nations governed by the European Convention of Human Rights) give greater play to abstract normative argument than a nation like Britain, in which free speech is a principle of common law in light of which supreme parliamentary law is interpreted;[1] and those nations with long traditions of judicial review under written constitutions with highly

Work on this essay much profited from a seminar on comparative German/American civil liberties given at the NYU School of Law during the spring term of 1992 jointly with my colleague, Professor Thomas M. Franck, and with a Visiting Professor at the School of Law, Dr Georg Nolte of the Max-Planck-Institut für ausländisches öffentliches Recht und Völkerrecht, Heidelberg, Germany. Both Tom Franck and Georg Nolte graciously read and wisely criticized this essay, and saved me from many errors; those remaining are my own. Nolte suggested to me that the argument offered here has a family resemblance to that offered in Lee C. Bollinger, *The Tolerant Society: Freedom of Speech and Extremist Speech in America* (Oxford University Press, New York, 1986). For an argument exploring critical differences, see David A. J. Richards, 'Toleration and Free Speech', *Phil. & Pub. Aff.* 17 (1988) 323.

[1] For a good treatment of this question, with specific focus on the British law of free speech, see Eric Barendt, *Freedom of Speech* (Clarendon Press, Oxford, 1985). In addition to its own common law of free speech, Great Britain is a signatory to the European Convention for Human Rights and, to the extent required by the Convention, is governed by its written guarantees and interpretive institutions. See, in general, Mark W. Janis and Richard S. Kay, *European Human Rights Law* (University of Connecticut Law School Foundation Press, Hartford, 1990).

abstract language (like the United States) refer more often to both abstract arguments of political theory and the long history of their interpretive experience than nations (such as Germany) with relatively recent post-World War II written constitutions (with US-style judicial review) in which guarantees have been drafted in more specific terms.[2] The two components of the study of free speech will accordingly interact in different ways depending on such distinctions. For example, the normative theory of utilitarianism may naturally fit the British constitutional landscape of free speech, while a deontological theory of rights may be the better account of both US and German constitutionalism. Even systems (like Germany and USA) that appeal to a comparable rights-based deontological theory and judicial review may, as we shall see, quite differently interpret such theory in ways that bear directly on central issues of free speech (for example, the constitutionality of group libel laws).

This essay addresses both components of the theory of free speech from a US constitutional perspective on these issues. I begin by sketching and criticizing two general normative theories of free speech (namely, utilitarianism and the argument from democracy), and then present a third view (free speech as toleration) and discuss its substantial merits both as political theory and an account of America's historically continuous interpretive experience. I bring the force of my argument into sharper focus in the form of a concluding defence of US constitutionalism's quite distinctive view that the principle of free speech renders group libel laws constitutionally problematic.

1 UTILITARIAN MODELS OF FREE SPEECH

Utilitarian arguments for free speech take a wide variety of forms, such as J. S. Mill's classically complex and nuanced arguments in *On*

---

[2] For example Article 5 of the German Basic Law textually distinguishes freedom of speech and of the press (in Art. 5(1)) from freedom of art, research, and teaching (in Art. 5(2)), imposing specific textual limitations on the former (in Art. 5(2)) but no such limitations on the latter. See *Basic Law of the Federal Republic of Germany* (Press and Information Office of the Federal Government, Bonn, 1987). In contrast, Article 10 of the European Convention on Human Rights provides a general guarantee of the right to freedom of expression (in Art. 10(1), subject to general restrictions applicable to this right in general (in Art. 10(2)). See Janis and Kay, *European Human Rights Law*, p. xx.

Liberty[3] and Oliver Wendell Holmes's crude appeal to the amoral deliverances of Social Darwinian competition in his dissent in *Abrams v. United States*.[4] The abstract structure of these arguments is that protection of free speech is justified because over all (its tendency to advance truth, and the like) it promotes the greatest net balance of pleasure over pain among all sentient creatures. But such arguments will not justify principles of free speech of the sort that US constitutional law now requires. The net aggregate of pleasure over pain is often advanced, not frustrated, by the restriction of speech. Large populist majorities often relish (hedonically speaking) the repression of outcast dissenters; the numbers and pains of dissenters are by comparison small; and there is often no offsetting future net aggregate of pain over pleasure to make up the difference. Holmes's more sceptical and less humane utilitarian vision may therefore reflect a sounder balancing of the competing utilitarian consequences than Mill's. For Holmes, free speech values should protect only those 'puny anonymities'[5] unlikely to harm anyone and from whom something might be learned; it would not protect a more politically effective speaker (like the challenge of a Eugene Debs to US involvement in World War I, or comparable dissenters to the Vietnam War later) whose threat to existing institutions and policies was clear and whose benefit to those institutions and policies was unclear.[6] But that approach is decidedly not the current approach to free speech protection in US constitutional law, and rightly so. The credible critical challenge to US war policies in both cases was precisely the dissenting speech most worthy of protection. Otherwise, free speech protection would be extended only to the incredible fatuities of the lunatic fringe.

---

[3] See John Stuart Mill, *On Liberty*, ed. Alburey Castell (Appleton-Century-Crofts, New York, 1947), chs. 2–3.

[4] 250 US 616 (1919).

[5] *Abrams* v. *United States*, 250 US 624 (1919), at 629.

[6] This interpretation of Holmes's views on free speech is not inconsistent with the rather more expansive language of his dissent in *Gitlow* v. *New York*, 268 US 652 (1925) ('[i]f in the long run the beliefs expressed in proletarian dictatorship are destined to be accepted by the dominant forces of the community, the only meaning of free speech is that they should be given their chance and have their way') if that language is to be contextually understood in terms of the protection of a political group of fringe left-wing socialists whom Holmes regarded as, in contrast to Debs, politically impotent.

2 POLITICAL PROCESS MODELS OF FREE SPEECH

The political process model of free speech conceives the core function of such speech to be the protection of the democratic political process from the abusive censorship of political debate by the transient majority who has democratically achieved political power. In the form of this view offered by John Hart Ely, the appeal of the theory is its forthright response to the democratic objection to judicial review.[7] On this model, judicial review on free speech grounds does not fall foul of the democratic objection to judicial review; judicial review here protects the integrity of democracy itself from the illegitimate attempt of a transient majority to entrench its own power by manipulating the agenda of political debate in its own favour. The judiciary does not, on Ely's view, illegitimately impose on democratic majorities a substantive value, but legitimately insists upon and monitors a view of democratic procedural fairness.

The very coherence of this approach to free speech protection requires a background conception of democratic legitimacy, i.e., forms of political power that democratic majorities may and may not legitimately exercise. But the idea of democracy is essentially contestable; views differ as to what is and what is not essential to a well-functioning democracy, or, conversely, what counts as democratic 'pathology' for purposes of determining the legitimate scope of free speech.[8] For example, the legitimate scope of democratic debate may be interpreted either narrowly or broadly. The narrow interpretation limits such debate to the issues directly in controversy in political campaigns among the main contenders for majoritarian political power;[9] the broader interpretation construes such debate as extending to any possible issue, including the very legitimacy of political power in general and democracy in particular.[10] Neither of these

[7] See John Hart Ely, *Democracy and Distrust: A Theory of Judicial Review* (Harvard University Press, Cambridge, Mass., 1980), esp. ch. 4.

[8] For a range of perspectives on the democratic pathologies that free speech should remedy, see e.g. Vincent Blasi, 'The Pathological Perspective and the First Amendment', *Colum. L. Rev.* 85 (1985), 449; and Owen M. Fiss, 'Free Speech and Social Structure', *Iowa L. Rev.* 7 (1986) 1405; Owen M. Fiss, 'Why the State?', *Harv. L. Rev.* 100 (1987), 781.

[9] See Robert Bork, 'Neutral Principles and Some First Amendment Problems', *Indiana L. J.* 47 (1971), 1. As a federal judge, Bork later offered a more expansive interpretation of this requirement, see *Ollman* v. *Evans*, 750 F.2d 970, 995 ff. (DC Cir. 1984).

[10] See Alexander Meiklejohn, 'The First Amendment Is an Absolute', *Supreme Court Review* (1961), 245.

interpretations provides a secure and convincing basis for the protection of speech. The narrow interpretation trivializes free speech by
restricting its scope to consensus politics; it thus excludes from protection precisely the dissenting discourse outside the political mainstream often most crucial to critical examination of central issues of
justice and the common good. The broader interpretation seems itself
to compromise democratic legitimacy by protecting attacks on the
very foundations of such legitimacy, including attacks on free speech
itself. If such attacks should be protected, as current US law indeed
requires,[11] it seems rather strained to justify such protection on the
ground that it invariably advances democracy when the speech it
allows may sometimes self-consciously aim to subvert it. We value
such speech intrinsically, certainly not because it always advances
democratically determined policies and aims.

This latter point suggests that we value democracy or, to be more
precise, democratic constitutionalism to the extent it respects independent substantive values of free speech; and those values cannot
themselves be plausibly understood in terms of perfecting the majoritarian political process. C. Edwin Baker has recently put this point in
terms of a substantive value of equal respect for the moral self-
determination of all persons, and assesses the legitimacy of democracy, to the extent it is legitimate, as a political process that realizes
that independent value;[12] and Kent Greenawalt has advanced a
similar argument in terms of the remarkable US constitutional
commitment to principles of religious liberty and the important place
of free speech in giving proper expression to these principles.[13] To the
extent free speech must give expression to the communicative
interests of liberty of conscience, the limitation of protection of free
speech to politics is clearly inadequate. As Greenawalt puts the point:
'Once freedom of religious ideas is acknowledged, distinguishing
protected speech from unprotected speech, say about science or
personal morality, becomes almost absurd.'[14] From the perspective
of Baker and Greenawalt, constitutionally legitimate political power
must respect substantive spheres of moral independence like liberty of

[11] For pertinent discussion, see David A. J. Richards, *Toleration and the Constitution* (Oxford University Press, New York, 1986), 178–87.
[12] See, in general, C. Edwin Baker, *Human Liberty and Freedom of Speech* (Oxford
University Press, New York, 1989), esp. ch. 3.
[13] Kent Greenawalt, *Speech, Crime, and the Uses of Language* (Oxford University
Press, New York, 1989), 177–9.
[14] Ibid. 178.

conscience (including all matters of fact and value fundamental to the exercise of conscience); the right of free speech, through which persons exercise their constructive powers of moral independence, must correlatively extend to all such matters. The limitation of free speech protection to politics is, on this view, illegitimate because it allows forms of censorship that deprive persons of the inalienable liberties essential to the moral self-government of a free people. Many of these liberties are not, in their nature, political. The limitation of free speech protection to the political is therefore illegitimate because it fails the ultimate test of rights-based constitutional legitimacy, the equal protection of the basic rights of free persons.

Baker and Greenawalt suggest (in my view quite rightly) a larger research project about the principles of democratic constitutionalism. Those principles cannot, as a matter either of sound interpretation of US constitutional tradition or of defensible democratic political theory, be understood on the political process model of perfecting the majoritarian political process, i.e., rendering the political process more truly majoritarian (and therefore democratic). As an interpretive matter, the constitutional tradition regards all forms of political power (including the power of democratic majorities) as corruptible; it subjects such power to a system of institutional constraints (including judicial review) designed to harness such power to the legitimate ends of government, namely, respect for human rights and the use of power to advance the public good.[15] A perfected political majoritarianism, often hostile to respect for both human rights and the public good when involving minorities, cannot be the measure of constitutional legitimacy. As a matter of democratic political theory, political process models familiarly rest on a form of preference utilitarianism. Such utilitarianism not only has already mentioned defects as an account of current US law; it has independently been subjected to searching contemporary criticism as an inadequate normative theory of equality. Part of this criticism has been that its theory of equality fails to give adequate expression to the place of respect for human rights in the normative idea of treating persons as equals.[16] We need an alternative view of democratic constitutionalism that

---

[15] See, for extensive development and exploration of this theme in US constitutionalism, David A. J. Richards, *Foundations of American Constitutionalism* (Oxford University Press, New York, 1989).

[16] The now classic contemporary treatment of this point is John Rawls, *A Theory of Justice* (Harvard University Press, Cambridge, Mass., 1971).

better captures, both as a matter of sound interpretation and of defensible political theory, the ways in which constitutional principles subject the exercise of political power to scrutiny and constraint.

3   THE TOLERATION MODEL OF FREE SPEECH

The theories of religious liberty and free speech are natural starting points for this alternative research project because the US doctrines of religious liberty and free speech are pivotal constructive components of the kind of reasonable public argument in terms of which exercises of political power must be justified if they are to be constitutionally legitimate. Constitutional argument has in the USA a dignity and weight distinctive from ordinary political argument because it addresses the fundamental question of what lends legitimacy to any exercise of political power. It was fundamental to this constitutional project from its inception not only that all forms of political power were corruptible, but that they had been and were corruptible in a distinctive way. Corruptible political power had deprived persons of the capacity to know, understand, and make effective claim to their basic human rights. As a consequence, political power had been distorted from its proper role in the pursuit of the justice of equal rights and advancing the interests of all alike in pursuit of the public good.[17] The argument for religious toleration was, for leading US constitutionalists like Thomas Jefferson and James Madison,[18] a model for both the corruptibility of political power (subverting the right to conscience) and its constitutional remedy (namely, depriving the State of any power to enforce or endorse sectarian religious belief). In effect, the exercise of political power for religious ends had entrenched a sectarian conception of religious truth as the measure of all reasonable inquiry about religious matters; it thus had deprived persons of their inalienable human rights reasonably to exercise their own moral powers about such matters. Such exercises of political power entrenched a kind of self-perpetuating political irrationalism that deprived people of reasonable government; political power was exercised in ways that neither respected people's right to reasonable self-government in their own moral and religious life, nor subjected its own power to reasonable criticism in terms of equal justice and the

---

[17] See, for a general development of this theme, Richards, *Foundations of American Constitutionalism*.

[18] For further discussion, see Richards, *Toleration*, 111–16.

public good. Arguments of constitutional principle have the weight that they do precisely because they subject such corruptions of political power to appropriate constraint in service of the reasonable justification of political power in terms of respect for rights and the use of political power to advance justice and the public good.

The principle of free speech plays the central role it does among constitutional principles and structures because it deprives the State of power over speech based on self-entrenching judgments of the worth or value of the range of speech that expresses sincere convictions about matters of fact and value in which a free people reasonably has a higher-order interest. That interest is nothing less than the free exercise of the moral powers of their reason through which persons give enduring value to their lives and communities.[19] Speech in the relevant sense must be free from certain forms of State control both to insure that censorious state judgments are not the measure of reasonable discussion in society at large and to allow the broadest possible exercise of the reasonable powers of a free people consistent with both respect for their human rights and their rights as citizens to hold political power accountable in terms of its respect for such rights and the public good. If constitutional argument depends for its dignity and weight on subjecting political power to such independent tests of reasonable justification, free speech is the foundation for the practicability of such justification; it insures a constitutional space for the kind of reasonable public argument against which, on grounds of constitutional legitimacy, all forms of political power must be subject to open debate and criticism. It would, of course, doom the entire project to emptiness and triviality if the State's majoritarian judgments of the worth or value of speech were the procrustean measure to which all such discourse must be fitted.

The nerve of this argument is implicit in the way James Madison argued that the principle of free speech is an elaboration of the argument for liberty of conscience as an inalienable human right.[20] The argument for religious toleration was, as I earlier suggested, that the State may have no power over religion because enforceable State judgments about the worth or value of particular religious beliefs fail to respect the right of persons reasonably to make such judgments for themselves. The idea is not that the state is always mistaken in judging

[19] See, in general, David A. J. Richards, *A Theory of Reasons for Action* (Clarendon Press, Oxford, 1971).

[20] See Richards, *Foundations*, 173–82.

certain religious views to be false or noxious; rather, judgments of that sort cannot, in principle, be made by a State committed to respect for the right of people reasonably to exercise their own judgment in these matters. In his seminal formulation of the Virginia Bill for Religious Freedom, Jefferson put the point thus:

to restrain the profession or propagation of principles on supposition of their ill tendency is a dangerous falacy [*sic*], which at once destroys all religious liberty, because he [the civil magistrate] being of course judge of that tendency will make his opinions the rule of judgment, and approve or condemn the sentiments of others only as they shall square with or differ from his own.[21]

In effect, abridgement of religious liberty could not be justified on sectarian grounds but could only be justified on independent grounds of preventing harms to secular general goods like life, liberty, and property. As Jefferson put the point, 'it is time enough for the rightful purposes of civil government for its officers to interfere when principles break out into overt acts against peace and good order'; the normal means for rebuttal of noxious belief, consistent with respect for the right of conscience, is 'free argument and debate'.[22] As he wrote elsewhere: 'it does me no injury for my neighbor to say there are twenty gods, or no god. It neither picks my pocket nor breaks my leg.'[23] The limitation of the exercise of State power to the protection of general goods expresses respect for the diverse ways that people may interpret and weight life, liberty, and property consistent with the independent exercise of their moral powers.

Madison saw that the same argument justified a special protection for speech because the State was inclined to make and enforce the same kinds of illegitimate judgments about the worth of the speech through which we express, develop, and revise conscientiously held beliefs. Accordingly, the principle of free speech took the form of a prohibition against the enforcement of State judgments about the truth or worth of what is said (thus anticipating the contemporary free speech doctrine forbidding content-based restrictions on speech[24]). The criterion for the abridgement of speech was the same as Jefferson's criterion for the abridgment of religious liberty; speech

---

[21] Julian P. Boyd, ed., *The Papers of Thomas Jefferson, 1777–1779*, ii (Princeton University Press, Princeton, NJ, 1950), 546.

[22] Ibid., 546.

[23] Thomas Jefferson, *Notes on the State of Virginia*, ed. William Peden (University of North Carolina Press, Chapel Hill, 1955).

[24] See Richards, *Toleration*, chs. 6–7.

may be abridged only 'when principles break out into overt acts' inflicting secular harms (a criterion anticipating the highly demanding contemporary US requirements for satisfaction of the 'clear and present danger' test, namely, the danger of some imminent, non-rebuttable, and very grave secular harm[25]).

Madison's expansive view of protection derives from a contractualist conception of political legitimacy; State power is only acceptable when it acts in ways that no person, understood to have basic higher-order interests in rational and reasonable self-government, could reasonably reject.[26] From this perspective, conscience is an inalienable human right constitutionally immune from political power because, consistent with this contractualist conception, it is the right that enables persons, on terms of equal respect, to be the sovereign moral critics of values, including political values like the legitimacy of government. Constitutionally guaranteed respect for this right insures that free and equal persons are the ultimate judges of whether the government respects their rights and pursues the public good in a way that justifies obedience and, if so, on what terms and to what extent. The scope of free speech protection, thus understood, must in its nature be much more expansive than the actual cases when political power is illegitimate, or, more extremely, when revolution might be justified. The point of free speech is not that revolution, on grounds of rights-based political illegitimacy, is often justified, but that the deliberative question of ultimate political legitimacy must, consistent with respect for the inalienable right to conscience, be always vividly addressed to the public mind of a free people if they are to be the ultimate free and equal sovereigns in terms of whose just claims political power must be searchingly tested and held accountable. Persons could not reasonably reject this constitutional principle because it insures the only reasonable basis for holding political power accountable to the basic requirements of its own legitimacy. But the protections of speech—which are also protections of conscience—cannot be limited to religious speech narrowly understood (as Jefferson, for example, supposed).[27] Madison's objection to the

[25] Ibid. 178–87.

[26] See T. M. Scanlon, 'Contractualism and Utilitarianism', *Utilitarianism and Beyond*, ed. Amartya Sen and Bernard Williams, (Cambridge University Press, Cambridge, 1982), 103–28.

[27] For Jefferson's quite restrictive conception of the scope of free speech (in contrast to his expansive protection of religious liberty), see Leonard W. Levy, *Jefferson and Civil Liberties: The Darker Side* (Quadrangle, New York, 1973), 42–69.

prosecutions brought by the federal government under the Alien and Sedition Act of 1798[28] was that they sought to enforce a suspect judgment of the worth of speech (notably, speech critical of the government) that improperly allowed the government's own beliefs about the legitimate scope of political criticism to settle the issue of what people might and should find reasonable. This was, of course, the same abuse of State power Jefferson noted in religious persecution. If anything, the temptations to such abuse would be greater in the case of speech expressly critical of the State. Accordingly, speech should enjoy at least a comparable kind of protection.[29]

The scope of such protection is clearly responsive to an evolving public understanding of the extent of reasonable conscientious debate about values; as the scope of reasonable application of the idea of protected conscience widens, so must the scope of free speech. Such background shifts explain the expanding class of expressions to which the US judiciary now applies the guarantees of free speech and free press. For example, subversive advocacy[30] and group libel[31] are now fully protected; and much that was traditionally excluded from free speech protection—fighting words,[32] defamation of individuals,[33] obscene materials,[34] advertising[35]—is now more fully protected. Madison himself expanded the scope of the argument from free conscience to protect public criticism both of religion and of the State; and the modern judiciary has further expanded the argument to protect expressions of dissent from suppression by majorities essentially motivated by hostility to such dissent, rather than by the desire to combat clear and present dangers of secular harms. As Madison clearly saw, the pattern of intolerance familiar in unjust religious persecution occurs as well in the censorship of speech; and the

[28] See James Madison, 'Report on the Virginia Resolutions', in *Debates on the Federal Constitution*, iv, ed. Jonathan Elliot, (Washington, DC 1836), 546–80.

[29] For a recent important historical study of the background of early American journalism that was the context of Madison's argument, see Jeffery A. Smith, *Printers and Press Freedom: The Ideology of Early American Journalism* (Oxford University Press, New York, 1988).

[30] See *Brandenburg* v. *Ohio*, 395 US 444 (1969).

[31] See *Collin* v. *Smith*, 578 F.2d 1197 (1978), *cert. den.*, 439 US 916 (1978).

[32] See *Gooding* v. *Wilson*, 405 US 518 (1972).

[33] See *Gertz* v. *Robert Welch, Inc.*, 418 US 323 (1974). For an illuminating recent commentary on this development in American constitutional law, see Anthony Lewis, *Make No Law: The Sullivan Case and the First Amendment* (Random House, New York, 1991).

[34] See *Miller* v. *California*, 413 US 15 (1973).

[35] See *Virginia Pharmacy Board* v. *Virginia Consumer Council*, 425 US 748 (1976).

modern United States Supreme Court has correctly understood that the same protections fundamental to our Jeffersonian conception of religious liberty apply, as a matter of principle, to free speech.

The theory quite cogently explains, for example, something that both the utilitarian and political process models have difficulty in explaining, namely, the inclusion of subversive advocacy in free speech protection. From a utilitarian perspective, as Holmes himself clearly saw, speech advocating the subversion of constitutional institutions, at least when made by a socialist political leader of the eloquence and effectiveness of Eugene Debs,[36] is sufficiently dangerous to warrant suppression on utilitarian grounds ('puny anonymities' are quite another matter[37]). And from the political process perspective, as earlier suggested, why should speech itself subversive of democracy be protected at all? But from the perspective of the toleration model here proposed, subversive advocacy, precisely because it makes substantive claims that go to the very legitimacy of constitutional government, is at the very core of free speech protection. Such advocacy conscientiously addresses the public conscience of the community in terms of putative failures to so respect rights and the public good that disobedience, indeed revolution, is justified. From the perspective of a conception of free speech rooted in respect for freedom of conscience about ultimate issues of value like justice and the right to rebel, that is the speech most worthy of protection. It raises the questions of public conscience central to a free society; the constitutional guarantee of the moral independence of such speech and speakers from State majoritarian censorship ensures that the legitimacy of State power is subject to searching and impartial testing in terms of its respect for universal human rights and the public interest. It is very much the point of such robust protection of free speech that, precisely because of such protection, the claims of subversive advocates thus protected will be tested by the deliberative judgment of a people empowered by their freedom responsibly to assess such claims. Often they will reject such claims as false and unjustified; sometimes, they will accept them. The meaning of free speech is the impartial moral independence of the testing.

The theory of free speech proposed here straightforwardly explains both the special priority of free speech and our grounds for scepticism about certain State abridgements of speech. The speech protected is

[36] See *Debs* v. *United States*, 249 US 211 (1919).
[37] See Holmes J., dissenting, *Abrams* v. *United States*, 250 US 624 (1919), at 629.

coextensive not with all speech, or with speech as such, but with the independent communication of willing speakers and audiences sincerely engaged in the critical discussion and rebuttal central to the conscientious formation, revision, and evaluation of values in living. Some communications do not serve such independent conscientious expression and rebuttal about critical values. Some may bypass reflective capacities (subliminal advertising); others do not express sincere evaluative convictions but make knowingly false statements of fact (fraud and knowing or reckless defamation of individuals[38]); and still others state true facts in which there is no ground for a reasonable interest from the perspective of the critical expression and discussion of general values. Because of the fundamental structural importance of the protection of the right to conscience to political legitimacy, the line between protected and unprotected speech should be drawn in the way that gives the broadest reasonable protection to moral independence in the expression and discussion of values; speech should be regarded as unprotected only on a strong showing of no reasonable ground for protection on this basis. In such cases of unprotected speech, the State may, consistent with the principle of free speech, pursue legitimate secular interests such as protection from consumer fraud and protection of individual reputation and privacy, harms to individuals not subject to rebuttal in public debate in the way in which disagreements over values are. It is therefore not an objection to a theory of free speech grounded in the communicative independence of our rational powers that the theory fails to accommodate such legitimate regulatory interests; the theory, properly understood, gives them proper weight.[39] In general, free speech has the priority we accord it against a background of reasonable State regulations (including fair time, place, and manner regulations)[40] that afford a supportive framework of communicative dialogue among

[38] By reckless defamation, I mean not mere negligence in stating a false fact, but subjective awareness that a fact stated is likely to be false. On my view, both knowledge of the falsity of one's statements of fact or awareness of likely falsity thereof remove such statements from the core of free speech protection, since in both cases the statements are not the sincere expression of conviction. In contrast to *New York Times Co.* v. *Sullivan*, 376 US 254 (1964) and subsequent cases, my view does not turn on the speech being about public officials or figures, and would tend wholly to immunize conscientious public speech from abridgement by libel actions of any kind.

[39] For somewhat fuller development of this theme, see Richards, *Toleration*, ch. 7; Richards, *Foundations*, 195–201.

[40] For somewhat fuller development of this point, see Richards, *Toleration*, 173, 194, 217, 220, 225.

free, rational, and equal persons and a constitutionally reasonable pursuit of legitimate State interests without prejudice to free speech.

Correspondingly, our scepticism about State power over speech is rooted not in a general suspicion of the State as such, but in a desire to avoid specific evils that our constitutional tradition identifies in historically familiar patterns of persecutory State intolerance of moral and political criticism. This explains the background principle of toleration that prohibits the State's enforcement of its own judgments about the critical worth of public speech. Laws condemned by this principle include not only seditious-libel laws that prohibit either express or implied criticism of the government. This principle condemns as well State prohibitions of speech motivated by the offence taken by groups of citizens at the critical advocacy of values of other groups; such prohibitions improperly substitute State enforcement of general views believed to be true for the play of the critical moral powers of free and equal people engaged in responsible discourse. It is this reason of principle, I believe, that explains why group libel laws (laws making it a criminal and/or civil wrong to engage in defamation of racial, ethnic, or religious groups) are currently constitutionally suspect in the United States.[41]

The reason is this. The principle of free speech, properly understood, discriminates among kinds of interests that may enjoy weight in the balance of political argument about free speech (for example, consumer protection or reputational integrity or privacy), and disentitles certain other interests to any weight whatsoever. These latter interests include offence taken at the exercise of the right of conscience itself, i.e., arguments for the repression of conscientious speech based on offence taken at the general evaluative merits of what is said, in effect, a kind of general 'ideological fighting words'.[42] A free speech balancing consequentialism predicated on giving weight to such interests (triggered by offence of this sort) is radically misconceived. Whatever a clear and present danger may reasonably mean, it cannot, consistent with respect for the right to conscience,

[41] The constitutionality of such laws (directed at general normative claims) must be distinguished from the question of laws directed against *ad hominem* insulting epithets of a sort contextually highly likely to lead to violence, so-called 'fighting words'. See *Chaplinsky* v. *New Hampshire*, 315 US 568 (1942). However, constitutional protection of offensive public speech, making general claims, may require that the latter laws be narrowly construed. See e.g. *Gooding* v. *Wilson*, 405 US 518 (1972).

[42] See Harry Kalven, Jun., *A Worthy Tradition: Freedom of Speech in America* (Harper & Row, New York, 1988), 95.

mean this. This conception of 'harms' (sufficient to justify State action) in this case is defined by the objection that offended people take to the conscientious advocacy of certain general views, and the enforceable State judgments are based on this sense of offence. At bottom, the offence taken at a form of conscience (viewed as corrupt) is taken to be sufficient to abridge the exercise of conscience. Such a ground for repressive State action is, in principle, unacceptable, for the same reason that the equal moral independence of conscience is, in principle, immune from State power. The State can, consistent with respect for conscience, no more proscribe conscientious moral convictions on such a basis than it can religious or political convictions. Disagreements about issues of conscience (including the corruption of conscience) must, in a free society, be resolved through the free exercise of conscience in debate that appeals to free public reason. Conscience can only be free in this way if a putative error in conscience is not sufficient for State censorship in the domain of conscientious conviction and expression.

If this argument is based on a proper understanding of the right to conscience as an inalienable human right, it will clarify its force and weight to contrast its American interpretation of these matters with the ostensibly rights-based forms of constitutionalism that take a different view of the constitutionality of group libel, indeed that accept group libel as itself a protection of rights. German constitutionalism is usefully illustrative. This constitutional system, like many others,[43] justifies the prohibition of group libel in rights-based terms of another right defined either as 'the right to inviolability of personal honour'[44] or a general guarantee that '[t]he dignity of man shall be inviolable'.[45] This general framework of free speech analysis in Germany is older than the current German constitutional order. Its current sense is, however, framed by a distinctive feature of current German constitutionalism, its commitment to militant democracy; on this view, democracy must be protected against groups and

[43] See e.g. Art. 10, European Convention for the Protection of Human Rights, in Janis and Kay, *European Human Rights Law*, p. xx.

[44] See Art. 5(2), *Basic Law of the Federal Republic of Germany*, which sets limits on the scope of protection of the rights of free speech and press under Art. 5(1).

[45] See Art. 1(1), ibid., which sets general limits on otherwise absolute rights like the right of art and science, research, and teaching under Art. 5(3). For an example of judicial balancing of this sort, see *Mephisto Case* (1971), 30 BVerfGE 173, translated into English in Donald P. Kommers, *The Constitutional Jurisprudence of the Federal Republic of Germany* (Duke University Press, Durham, 1989), 309–12, 426–30.

persons that would subvert its general constitutional principles.[46] As I earlier suggested, some rights (like that of individual reputation, and of privacy) may reasonably be legally protected to the extent they do not conflict with the right of free speech. But these rights in their nature fall in spheres (wilfully false statement of facts about individuals or statement of private facts in which there is no reasonable public interest) that do not trench upon the core interests of free speech, the conscientious discussion and criticism of public matters of fact and value by people free of improperly censorious State judgments about the worth or value of such discussion. But the German rights of honour or dignity are not similarly so limited.[47] Rather, the State may prohibit conscientious expression of general evaluative views essentially on the ground that persons experience such expression as disrespectful.[48] In effect, the scope of public debate is to be circumscribed to the measure of ideological inoffensiveness to important persons and groups in society (as those persons and groups are defined by the State).

---

[46] See Art. 5(3) (obligation of loyalty of university teachers to the constitution); Art. 9(2) (prohibition of associations directed against the constitutional order); Art. 18 (abuse of rights like free speech can lead to forfeiture of such rights); Art. 20(4) (in the absence of any available alternative, all Germans given right of resistance against anyone attempting to overthrow the constitutional order); Art. 21(2) (on the basis of a finding of the Constitutional Court, unconstitutionality of political parties directed against the basic democratic order), *Basic Law of the Federal Republic of Germany*. For associated legal developments, see Eric Stein, 'History Against Free Speech: The New German Law Against the "Auschwitz"—and Other—"Lies"', *Mich. L. Rev.* 85 (1986), 277.

[47] The problem is not limited to group libel alone; German constitutional law, like that of other European countries, permits its individual libel laws to encompass disparaging value statements about public figures. See, for a case illustrative of this approach, *Street Theatre Case* (1984), 67 BVerfGE 213, reprinted in Donald P. Kommers, *The Constitutional Jurisprudence of the Federal Republic of Germany*, 431–6. For the contrasting US approach, see *Hustler Magazine* v. *Falwell*, 485 US 46 (1988).

[48] It would be a closer case if group libel laws were limited to knowingly false statement of facts about groups, statements that therefore do not express conviction and are not therefore sincere expressions of conscience. In my judgment, the constitutionally relevant difference between such a more circumscribed form of group libel action and an individual libel action would be that the former is embedded in general debate about values that can be rebutted in the usual way; in contrast, individual libel is targeted at an individual as such, and can only be adequately rebutted by the forms of legal actions through which persons uphold their reputation. For this reason, even a more circumscribed form of group libel action would violate the principle of free speech. I am indebted for this clarification of my thinking to Thomas Franck.

People do often identify themselves with some larger group with whom they associate their self-respect; and they take a lively interest in how they take such groups—and thus themselves—to be represented and discussed in the public culture of their societies, and sometimes experience reasonable indignation at such discussions as forms of heresy or blasphemy or group libel challenging their essential values in living, indeed the very core of their identities. Such indignation cannot, however, count as a harm sufficient to limit free speech protection, as it would be if such indignation gave rise to a right of sufficient force (as it does under German law) to limit the scope of application of the right of free speech. The German constitutional theory wrongly counts the occasion of such indignation as a secular evil from which free people may, like threats to physical integrity, be protected. In fact, a proper understanding of free speech as toleration regards such occasions as precisely the kinds of spiritual challenge to public discussion and debate that the tradition of free speech should protect and encourage. Otherwise, the essential public rights and responsibilities of a free and democratic people (indeed, the core of their inalienable rights) are illegitimately transferred to others, who protect citizens from even hearing speech they might find offensive. A people, thus protected, may privately gain in peace of mind, but such privatization deprives a free people of the inalienable public liberties and responsibilities of citizenship that alone dignify them as a people worthy of freedom (reasonably confronting the central issues of public conscience of their age and culture). For this reason, such indignation should, consistent with the values of free speech, express itself not in censorship but in creative forms of voluntary organization to rebut such arguments in the usual way. As we have seen, the principle of free speech is grounded in scepticism about the corruptibility of political power in the domain of the conscientious expression of public values; State judgments about the worth or value of speech in this domain fail to allow proper scope to the reasonable debate of morally independent and free persons about public matters of fact and value. Such reasonable scepticism extends as well to State abridgements of speech ostensibly grounded in protecting groups from disrespectful speech. The point is not that such speech is not sometimes disrespectful of groups and persons or that conscience is not sometimes corrupt; but that the prohibition of such speech by the State makes the State the improper enforcer of that respect as the arbiter of what counts as a good or bad conscience in a domain of public debate where enforcement of this kind contemptuously usurps the sovereign right of persons to be the ultimate critics of value in living. Respect for liberty of conscience requires of us the minimal civic courage of overcoming the fear of hearing views we detest and disallowing such fears of freedom as the basis of state censorship. Such a risk, if it is a risk, is reasonably borne if we, as free people, both understand and value the foundational role in a just polity of the sovereign public reason about issues of conscience it makes available to all on fair terms.

The interposition of the State in these matters enlists state power in the support and legitimation of what counts as a group identity and the proper respect owed that identity as the measure of what can count as reasonable public debate about such matters. But the State's judgments in this domain are no more impartially reasonable than they are in the area of religion or politics; the State here enforces inevitably crude majoritarian stereotypes of group identity on a par with similarly illegitimate enforceable State judgments about true religion and good politics. The relationship between individual and group identity must, in a free society, be open to the fullest range of reasonable discussion and debate on terms that allow persons to question, debate, and renegotiate their evaluative understanding of value in living on their own terms, including the relationship between their sense of themselves as individuals and as self-identified members of various groups. Perhaps the relationship between individual and group identity will be more reasonably contestable in a society as ethnically diverse and ideologically pluralistic as the USA than it is in more homogeneous societies; but even in more homogeneous societies, the terms of individual and group identity must, in those that are free societies, be open to broad and robust discussion and debate to allow the fullest range of public intelligence and imagination reasonably to be available to all on terms that respect moral autonomy and individuality. Otherwise, essential issues of public debate about value in living—the very terms of one's moral integrity—will be truncated to the measure of unreflective and often oppressive majoritarian stereotypes.

Much serious discussion of public values could, in virtue of the German rights of honour or dignity, give rise to state protection of persons who take offence at such discussion. The general structure of German constitutional argument imposes a duty on the State to protect rights.[49] In effect, the legitimacy of State power turns, like the comparable US Lockian constitutional theory,[50] on the way in which the State organizes and protects the basic rights of its people, including their basic rights of conscience, life, personal security, and the like. To this extent, the German constitutional theory is normatively appealing on grounds of its commitment to the protection of human rights. But the interpretation of this theory to include protection from offensive discussion rests on an inadequate understanding of the weight of free speech in such an overall theory of constitutional legitimacy. This interpretation does not take seriously the nature of the right of free speech in question, precisely because respect for this right requires a principled scepticism about abuses of State power in a certain domain. In short, the central concern of free speech is not protection by the State, but from the State. In the area of free speech, however, the German interpretation of this theory of the State as the positivistic source and protector of rights here subverts such protection by its legitimation of an improper State role, an illiberal moral paternalism in the domain of conscience directed at protecting people from offence to their convictions, in effect, from challenge and debate. Such 'protection', if carried to its logical extreme, might homogenize the complacencies of a public opinion that concurs on bromides and symbolic gestures of group solidarity; it does not empower people responsibly to understand, claim, and enforce their human rights as free and reasonable people.

There is a larger point worth making here, associated with the relationship of this view of free speech to the idea of defensive democracy. The protection of human rights, if it means anything, cannot be limited in its scope to those who, in the view of the State, support and do not subvert the constitutional order. A constitutional order, ostensibly grounded in the protection of human rights, must extend human rights to all subject to its political power. German constitutionalism undoubtedly espouses this general constitutional theory, and surely self-consciously means to transcend more traditional German national ideologies constructed around rights-

---

[49] For judicial elaboration on this point, see the *Princess Soraya Case* (1973), 34 BVerfGE 269, trans. in Donald P. Kommers, *The Constitutional Jurisprudence of the Federal Republic of Germany*, 131–6; *Abortion Case* (1975), 39 BVerfGE 1, ibid., 348–59; *Schleyer Kidnapping Case* (1977), 46 BVerfGE 160, ibid., 362–3.

[50] See, in general, Richards, *Foundations of American Constitutionalism*.

sceptical polarities of friends and enemies[51] often founded on retaining the purity of the nation's allegedly constitutive ethnic homogeneity.[52] But the German constitutional ideology of defensive democracy is in tension with its more fundamental commitment to inalienable human rights; indeed, its terms suggest the return of the repressed, the older ideology of friends and enemies that it surely means constructively to transcend. Correlatively, its limitation of the right to free speech (by rights of honour or dignity) is unjustifiable for the same reason. The protection of the right to conscience, as an inalienable human right, must extend to all persons within the scope of its principle, namely, those who conscientiously express views on matters of public value and fact. Respect is owed them as persons who originate views and claims and who have the right to authenticate themselves by speaking conscientiously in their own voice and their own terms. The principle of free speech requires that each person is guaranteed the greatest equal liberty to exercise this right in its proper domain consistent with a like liberty for all. It subverts the principled moral force of this right to truncate its protection in terms of some range of views that are politically or morally mainstream and others that are not. This makes ideological conformity, not respect for the human rights of all persons (whatever their convictions), the measure of membership in the constitutional community. As I earlier argued, respect for a right like free speech enjoys its greatest moral force when it extends its protection even to subversive advocates who challenge its authority; the same point applies here to group libel. Respect for the moral sovereignty of dissenters from mainstream views makes the best statement that could be made about the constitutive inner morality of a constitutional community based on respect for human rights.

[51] For a clear statement and defence of such a German national ideology, see Carl Schmitt, *The Concept of the Political*, George Schwab trans. (Rutgers University Press, New Brunswick, NJ, 1976). For an illuminating account of Schmitt's life and work, including his complicity with the Nazi regime, see Joseph W. Bendersky, *Carl Schmitt: Theorist for the Reich* (Princeton University Press, Princeton, 1983). Schmitt's complicity with the Nazis places him, like Heidegger, among the leading German intellectuals of their period now very much under critical scrutiny in Germany and elsewhere as part of a tradition that the new German constitutional order very much wants to repudiate. On Heidegger, see Victor Farias, *Heidegger and Nazism* (Temple University Press, Philadelphia, 1989). It would be paradoxical indeed if German constitutional doctrines like defensive democracy were, as I suggest, very much in unconscious thrall to such a now repudiated tradition.

[52] For a development of this idea as central to the modern idea of political democracy, see Carl Schmitt, *The Crisis of Parliamentary Democracy*, Ellen Kennedy trans. (MIT Press, Cambridge, Mass., 1985), 9.

There is legitimate political power enough to deal with those dissenters who would move beyond dissent to overt acts that threaten the rights of others (for further discussion, see below). Most dissenters do not do so, and many non-dissenters will threaten such acts. The principle of free speech insists that the mere offence taken at dissenting views cannot be the measure of a clear and present danger sufficient to justify the abridgement of speech. Jefferson's earlier cited point about religious liberty applies here as well: 'he [the civil magistrate] being of course judge of that tendency will make his opinions the rule of judgment', thus falsely and mischievously conflating ideological dissidence with overt acts that violate rights.

The issue of constitutional principle may be more abstractly stated. The principle of free speech arises from a historical scepticism, rooted in rights-based political theory, about the uses of State power to homogenize public opinion by the use of its coercive power to criminalize heresy or blasphemy or seditious libel and the like. In each case, criminal prohibitions of thought and speech were based on State judgments about the worth or value of thought and speech (on the ground of a putative corruption of conscience); such judgments both unreasonably limited the scope of thought and discussion to the measure of the dominant political orthodoxy and correlatively deprived persons of their inalienable rights reasonably to think and discuss public matters as free people. The principle of free speech, based on rights-based scepticism about such enforceable political judgments, must extend to all such judgments, including those based on the offence taken by persons to conscientious views expressed by other persons. Such constitutional concern must apply not only to group libel prosecutions but prohibitions analogously based on disrespectful thoughts and speech.

For this reason, obscenity prosecutions would raise issues of constitutional principle if these prosecutions are based, as they appear to be, on judgments about the disrespectful character of the putatively obscene materials and of the thoughts and experiences to which use of such materials leads. It does not dispel but only aggravates the issue of free speech principle to redescribe the putative evils, as some American feminists[53] and the Canadian Supreme Court

---

[53] See, in general, Catharine A. MacKinnon, *Feminism Unmodified: Discourses on Life and Law* (Harvard University Press, Cambridge, Mass., 1987); *Toward a Feminist Theory of the State* (Harvard University Press, Cambridge, Mass., 1989).

now do,[54] in terms of the degradation of women as such. That argument clearly places obscenity prosecutions in the framework of group libel[55] and, for that reason, renders them altogether more constitutionally problematic.[56] Why are certain pornographic images of women (as opposed to others) or pornographic versus non-pornographic images of women taken to express disrespect for women as such? The idea must be that these images (as opposed to others) morally degrade women as such from their status as full persons and as bearers of equal rights. But even to state the claim is reasonably to contest it. Pornographic images (in contrast to conventional group libel claims) make no such express claims. The view that they do make such claims is itself a controversial interpretive claim, ascribing to producers and users of these materials condemned moral attitudes (a kind of corrupt conscience), quite like the motivation for group libel laws. In fact, such materials may be, as some feminists argue they are, emancipatory of the unjustly stunted and starved sexual interests of women as well as men, an emancipation of interests that many persons of conscience (profoundly concerned with traditional injustices in the areas of gender and sexuality) take now to be central to a life well and humanely lived.[57] Indeed, non-pornographic material (not only advertising, but traditional religious views of women's nature and role) may be more degrading, more debilitating of the integrity and autonomy of women as creative moral agents. In this maelstrom of increasingly free and reasonable debate about the sources of the unjust

[54] See *Donald Victor Butler* v. *Her Majesty the Queen*, decided 27 Feb. 1992 (slip opinion). The Supreme Court of Canada also cites alleged arguments of harm from such material, largely depending on the highly controversial fact-finding of the Meese Commission in the United States. On the complete unreliability of this study from the perspective of the principle of free speech (its question-begging distortion by ideological motives of censorship), see David A. J. Richards, 'Pornography Commissions and the First Amendment: On Constitutional Values and Constitutional Facts', *Maine L. Rev.* 39 (1987), 275.

[55] MacKinnon quite clearly sees and espouses this analogy; see *Feminism Unmodified*, at 156–7.

[56] This argument assumes that group libel laws are or should be constitutionally problematic for the reasons already discussed in the text. The constitutionalism of nations like Canada, which accept the legitimacy of group libel laws, has at least been consistent in extending the analogy to obscene materials. The same cannot be said of the United States, whose constitutionalism rejects group libel laws but accepts anti-obscenity laws.

[57] See, in general, Varda Burstyn, ed., *Women Against Censorship* (Douglas & McIntyre, Vancouver, 1985).

subjugation of women, enforceable State judgments of the worthlessness or disvalue of certain thought and speech enforce intrinsically controversial *interpretive* judgments based on the dominant, sexually repressive, and now highly questionable political orthodoxy about issues of sexuality and gender; they do so precisely in the way (on the putative ground of a corruption of conscience) that, on grounds of free speech, we have good reason to suspect unreasonably to limit discussion and debate on these matters and deprive persons of their inalienable rights of thought, experience, and discussion. To deny that such laws abridge rights of conscience is unreasonably to circumscribe the scope of protected conscience to the measure of majoritarian views of the good life. Human rights, trimmed to the measure of such majoritarian judgments, lack their proper force precisely in the area where, as a matter of constitutional principle, they are most exigently required (namely, protection of the human rights of minorities).

Such majority judgments, if enforced through law in the domain of speech, mandate a kind of orthodoxy of appropriate tribalization in the terms of public discourse. Public claims disrespectful of groups are subject to State prohibition. But, as we have seen, this empowers the State to determine not only what discourse is properly respectful and what not, but what groups are entitled to such protection and what are not. But such State-enforced judgments introduce stereotypical political orthodoxies as the measure of human identity, thus removing from public discourse precisely the contest of such stereotypical boundaries that a free people often most reasonably requires. The identity of no moral person can be exhaustively defined by their ethnicity or race or gender or sexual preference or any of the other terms of common group identification familiar today. The social force such group identifications often have today unreasonably diminishes both the range of diversity and individuality that exists within such groups and the similarities between members of such groups and the groups with which they are contrasted. To enforce such identifications through law censors from public discourse precisely the kind of discourse that best challenges them. Such State censorship of a range of discourse stifles, in turn, the empowering protests of individuals to that discourse through which they express, demand, and define their individuality as persons against such stereotypical classifications.[58] Paradoxically, it is precisely the groups that the State may regard itself as most reasonably protecting from group libel (the most historically stigmatized groups, like blacks in the United States, or women and sexual minorities generally) that should, as a matter of free speech principle, most reasonably be constitutionally immunized from such protective State power. Ralph Ellison's *Invisible Man* pleaded for racial justice in America in these eloquent terms: 'Our task is that of making ourselves individuals. The conscience of a race is the gift of its individuals.'[59] If the struggle against the stereotypical indignities of racism (or sexism or homophobia) is essentially a struggle for individuality, free speech rightly requires that the terms of emancipation must be the empowering responsibility of individuals, including the voluntary organizations through which they define themselves and their struggle.

As I earlier suggested, these concerns may be most vivid for a pluralistic, largely immigrant culture like that of the United States. Generations of Americans have recurrently had to endure the ordeal of Americanization, encountering nativist prejudice against their ethnic or racial group and determining how, if at all, their identity as Americans would interact with their identity as an African-American or as an immigrant from Italy or Eastern Europe. In a constitutional culture as rights-based as the United States, Americans, whatever their ethnicity or race, reasonably strive to be individuals, but individuals enriched by the cultural depth of their diverse heritages or the struggle reasonably to construct their heritages (as reflected, for example, in the development of women's and gay studies[60]). A people, thus constituted, finds in the principle of free speech, as I have discussed it, the natural terms in which a diverse and robust public culture will afford them both the freedom and rationality to reflect critically on the values and disvalues of their American and their

[58] On the important strand of American free speech thought emphasizing expressive authenticity, see Steven H. Shiffrin, *The First Amendment, Democracy and Romance* (Harvard University Press, Cambridge, Mass., 1990). Unfortunately, Shiffrin wrongly isolates this romantic Emersonian strand of thought from the neo-Kantian theorists, like myself, who find in American neo-abolitionist transcendentalism a clear and enduring strand of Kantian thought, argument, and practice. See David A. J. Richards, *Conscience and the Constitution: History, Theory, and Law of The Reconstruction Amendments* (Princeton University Press, Princeton, 1993).

[59] Ralph Ellison, *Invisible Man* (Vintage, New York, 1989), at 354.

[60] For an important development in the latter genre, see Jonathan Dollimore, *Sexual Dissidence: Augustine to Wilde, Freud to Foucault* (Clarendon Press, Oxford, 1991).

immigrant identities and to weave together a sufficiently complex tapestry adequate to express the authentic moral identity of a free person. This is not the American bleached WASP, but the American who weds convictions of universal human rights to the cultural and human depth such rights, properly understood, make possible.

This constitutional argument does not, of course, disempower the State from taking a range of reasonable measures to attack constitutional evils like racism and sexism. The State has a public responsibility, consistent with the equal protection clause of the Fourteenth Amendment, to advance basic education in democratic values like toleration of minorities and anti-discrimination, including the forms of desegregation mandates required by *Brown* v. *Board of Education*.[61] The State also must and should aggressively protect citizens from actions threatening the rights of others (including inchoate crimes like conspiracy) motivated by irrational hatred and prejudice, including forms of sexual harassment.[62] The responsibility of the State in this arena must include the passage and enforcement of anti-discrimination laws applicable both in the public and private spheres. Finally, the unconstitutionality of group libel and similar laws leaves open, indeed stimulates and encourages the kind of rebuttal of racist and antisemitic speech so prominently part of the American political landscape through the activities of such organizations as the NAACP, the Anti-Defamation League, and many others.

The American constitutional objection to group libel laws is based on their failure reasonably to meet the standards set by the argument of principle that we call free speech. I recognize that there is venerable authority for not extending the principle of toleration to the intolerant[63] and that the modernist European nightmare of antisemitism[64] might be supposed to offer continuing contemporary support for such a view at least in circumstances comparable to those of Weimar

---

[61] 347 US 483 (1954).

[62] This would and should include, in my judgment, prohibitions and regulations directed against the *ad hominem* use of pornographic material in a work environment to intimidate women. Such a work environment is not in this case properly understood as a public forum for free speech purposes, and may therefore properly be subjected to forms of prohibition and regulation of speech that would raise constitutional issues of free speech in a public forum. On public forums, see Richards, *Toleration and the Constitution*, at 219–226.

[63] For useful discussion, see John Rawls, *A Theory of Justice*, pp. 216–21.

[64] See Raul Hilberg, *The Destruction of the European Jews*, 3 vols (Holmes and Meier, New York, 1985).

Germany (in fact, the Weimar democracy did not evenhandedly protect the free speech of the right and the left, and certainly did not use the legitimate powers it had to protect rights at threat from racist injustices).[65] Most contemporary constitutional democracies, including, as we have seen, Germany itself, understandably take the view that the institutions of constitutionalism must self-defensively protect themselves against the modernist demons of populist racism by refusing such groups certain constitutional liberties. On this view, limitations in free speech protection foster, against the historical background of the powerful role of populist racist fascism in European politics leading to World War II, a much needed public education in constitutional values, making precisely the kind of statement that must be made about the ultimate ethical values of respect for the human dignity of all persons.

American free-speech law undoubtedly has its grave critical defects;[66] but its view of group libel offers a plausible alternative interpretation of the principle of free speech to the common view elsewhere about group libel. American interpretive experience suggests that a sound argument of principle not only protects such anti-constitutional speech (for the reasons already examined at length), but, properly understood, renders such protection a more effective instrument of ultimate public education in enduring constitutional values, in particular, the place of the basic human rights of conscience and speech in a free and democratic society of equal citizens. In American circumstances, the principle of free speech— extended to blatantly racist and antisemitic advocates like the KKK[67]—has remarkably energized and empowered the battle for

[65] For useful discussion of those circumstances and their background, see Peter Pulzer, *The Rise of Political Anti-Semitism in Germany and Austria* (Harvard University Press, Cambridge, Mass., 1988); Jacob Katz, *From Destruction to Destruction: Anti-Semitism, 1700–1933* (Harvard University Press, Cambridge, Mass., 1980).

[66] The treatment by the United States Supreme Court of the relationship between free speech and economic power is one of the areas of the gravest doubt both as a matter of sound interpretation of American history and as an argument of democratic political theory. For elaboration of this view, see Richards, *Toleration and the Constitution*, at 215–19. In this domain, the German constitutional theory of the duty to protect rights, including economic rights, may be a much better interpretation of the theory of constitutional legitimacy that both Germany and the United States share. For a recent, often compelling critique of the Supreme Court's treatment of campaign financing and related matters along these lines, see Mark A. Graber, *Transforming Free Speech: The Ambiguous Legacy of Civil Libertarianism* (University of California Press, Berkeley, Calif., 1991).

[67] See *Brandenburg v. Ohio*, above; cf. *Collin v. Smith*, above (American Nazi Party).

racial justice and religious toleration under the rule of law, a story ably told by Harry Kalven in *The Negro and the First Amendment*.[68] An American constitutionalist, like Kalven, would defend our position as a matter of principle.[69] An argument of principle based on respect for conscience must understand the moral ground on which it stands, one which includes in its conception of what a community of principle is all persons who conscientiously exercise their moral powers and who recognize their ultimate responsibility to depend on themselves (not the State) to exercise their moral powers in defence of rights. The principle of free speech rests on the basic human right of each citizen, consistent with the like equal right of all, to be the ultimate critic of the legitimacy of State power. The principles of our tolerance are most in need when the dissent is most radical, not when it is most conventional. Our commitment to this kind of free testing of the legitimacy of our institutions will be measured by the degree to which we extend our right of free thought even to the radical dissent of moral barbarians who would provoke us to their immorally exclusive measure of insularity, parochialism, and faction. Our principles are, I believe, best and most reasonably affirmed when we resist the temptation to respond to bigots in kind and insist on embracing them in an inclusive moral community that recognizes in all persons that which some of them might wilfully deny to others, the equality of all persons as free and reasonable members of a political community of principle. Protecting the rights of the speakers and speech we hate affirms the deeper fraternal bonds of a political community based on universal human rights. In the case of the right of free speech, the response, as a matter of principle, to hate should be, if not the inhuman demands of universal love, at least the humane demands of tolerance and mutual respect.

[68] See Harry Kalven, Jun., *The Negro and the First Amendment* (University of Chicago Press, Chicago, 1965).
[69] See also, in general, Harry Kalven, Jun., *A Worthy Tradition*.

3. Freedom of Speech and Expression: A Libertarian View

JAN NARVESON

1 INTRODUCTION

It is widely supposed that there is such a thing as a 'principle of freedom of speech', and that it occupies, or ought to occupy, a special place in our, or any decent, society. The US constitution specifically protects it; the Canadian constitution's Charter of Rights and Freedoms proclaims as a 'fundamental freedom' that of 'thought, belief, opinion and expression, including freedom of the press and other media of communication'.[1] Our question here is whether such a principle is reasonable, and if so, why. It would seem to assert a general right, on the part of all, to speak what they will. Many questions arise. What sort of right would that be, and in what range of circumstances is it to apply? Just what would and what would not be protected by it? In any case, would it occupy a special place among the various freedoms we ought to be concerned about? Singling it out for specific mention in a constitutional document suggests that it does. Why is this?

The best way to answer any of these questions would be to produce a general rationale for such a principle, one that would both explain why we should have it and provide insight into any exceptions, qualifications, or limitations we might want to impose. I shall take a stab at that in these pages, appreciating that incompleteness and tentativeness are bound to dog one's footsteps in such a project. In the following pages, I will argue (1) that there is indeed a general principle of free speech, but (2) deny that it is 'special', or at least that it is *very* special, and (3) note that it is easy to misconstrue the thrust of a right of free speech in such a way as to make it protect what need not be protected, or to protect the right things, but to an absurd degree.

I undertake my discussion in the belief that there is a general principle of liberty about which we should be concerned, indeed,

---

[1] Canadian Charter of Rights and Freedoms, s. 2.

concerned above all, politically speaking. That general outlook will not be defended here, except rather incidentally. Instead, I will be especially concerned with the question of just when the restriction of speech activities would be permissible or possibly obligatory even if we do accept the outlook in question. The concept of free speech relates to the question: on which grounds may speech activities be suppressed or restricted? Absent some special reason for interference, people's speech activities are to be left alone, not just by governments but by all other parties. Unwarranted interference will be interference on any grounds other than those generated (hopefully) in our enquiry; such interference will be grounds for complaint by those concerned. Put in terms of rights, then, the question is, which rights can override the right to speak freely—once we know what that is? Interestingly, a principal such will be the right to free speech itself: we can often say, 'You may not say that on this occasion, because doing so interferes with other people's right to freedom of speech'. But we will not assume that that is always the answer. What we will assume is that the answer always is 'Because it interferes with someone else's legitimate liberty'.

2   THE LIBERTARIAN PRINCIPLE

The libertarian holds that the liberty of individuals is the only proper concern of the State, and that thus a general right to liberty is the fundamental principle of social morality. What would be its implications regarding the subject of speech and expression? That is the subject of this article. Some will have no sympathy with that idea. That is too bad for them, in my view, and also too bad for me and the rest of us, for in consequence they will feel free to do various things I think they do not have a right to. In the meantime, though, readers may wish at least to consider what is involved in the idea in question; they may view this as purely hypothetical and of mainly academic interest.

Since it is a matter easily misunderstood, we must begin by getting, however sketchily, a handle on this idea of a 'basic general right to liberty'. Rights, to begin with, *constrain*, and what they constrain is, of course, liberty. One individual's right to do x is (at least) other people's duty in respect of his doing x. More precisely, and here I agree, for instance, with Joseph Raz, to have a right is to have a property (usually an interest), possession of which is a ground for imposing a duty on others.[2] Which duties? Minimally, that others keep off— that they *let* the rightholder do *x*. Rights are, at least, requirements that others refrain from whatever acts would prevent the rightholder from doing what she has the right to do.

In particular cases, the 'others' on whom duties are imposed will be certain particular or specific individuals and not people in general. Those are the cases, in the liberty view, in which some particular understanding or transaction between the rightholder and those others has taken place: for example, a promise, or the specific assumption of that duty. Such understandings can also give rise to what are known as 'positive' rights: rights that some others not merely refrain from interfering with the rightholder, but that they also actively perform some service for him, e.g. supply some good or resource (such as a resource necessary for doing *x*). But *general* rights, that is, rights against other people in general, cannot, on the libertarian view, be positive. That we in general owe certain positive services to others is what the libertarian denies. For to owe them is to have one's liberty constrained still further than it need be; whereas to allow others negative rights and thus to accept the duty to refrain from forcing them to do things is the bottom line, in the absence of which there would be no morality at all. These last two arguments need emphasis.

If we have no duties, we may do as we like; if there are no duties at all, we may interfere uninhibitedly with each other's chosen activities. In such a situation, the 'state of nature' in the classic Hobbesian understanding of it, we *might* be described as being in a condition of 'unlimited liberty'. And what more could a 'libertarian' want? But in fact, the Hobbesian situation is the very negation of liberty. If others may at any time prevent me from doing anything, or even deprive me of my life, then I am *not* 'at liberty', except in the residual sense of being free from moral criticism. The purpose of rights is to help make it possible for each person to live the sort of life he or she prefers. No person can do that if others simply intervene at will, as they may well if they are free to do so.

One might, of course, also lack the means to do what one would like. Mightn't liberty be promoted by requiring others to supply those means? The libertarian's argument is that while, of course, that would indeed be nice for *me*, it is an imposition on the person who would

---

[2] Joseph Raz, *The Morality of Freedom*, (Oxford University Press, Oxford, 1986), 166.

have to supply them. It may be one that the other would not see *as* an imposition: he might be quite willing to do this thing for me, if I but ask. And my freedom to ask him, as will be argued below, is indeed my right, certainly part of what will be granted us in a libertarian society. But his freedom to refuse is equally basic. If some people end up helping others, it will have to be either out of the goodness of the hearts of the helpers, or due to some voluntary exchange between them, in which the helper receives from the benefited person something that he regards as making it worthwhile. What is forbidden is for anyone to use force for this purpose. Force is confined to dealing with the use of initial force on the part of others. *General* positive rights, at least of very substantial kinds, are not on the cards. If, of course, there is some possible agreement of everyone with everyone that would involve a general disposition to supply certain services in response to need or on demand of others, then we could perhaps get certain general positive rights off the ground. Issues involving this distinction between positive and negative rights loom rather large in some contexts of speech and expression, as will be seen.

Our various chosen lines of activity will sometimes bring us into conflict, nevertheless. Who then must give way? How in general are we to settle such conflicts? Here the libertarian will distinguish two sorts of cases. In one sort, the occasion of the conflict is that one person intentionally sets out to damage the other. Since respecting each other's liberty is the fundamental requirement of a libertarian view, such conflicts are resolved by ruling the aggressor in the wrong. However, that leaves innumerable cases in which the conflict is incidental to the pursued end. Suppose that I am in the middle of doing something which does not, so far as it goes, necessarily prevent you from doing what you wish, and similarly you are embarked on some programme of activity which has no necessary negative impact on me, yet it turns out that we cannot both succeed in our respective endeavours. Then what?

Our major conceptual resource for sorting such things out is that of *property*. Suppose that in order to do what I intend to do, I need to utilize a certain thing; and you, pursuing your purposes, would need to utilize the same thing. We can resolve such conflicts if we can reasonably assign the use of those things to one or the other of us. If there is sufficient reason to regard the thing as *yours*, then the conflict is easily resolved: I must then ask you whether I may use it, and if you say no, then I shall have to do something else. If it is mine, on the other hand, then just the reverse. In either case, the conflict is peaceably resolved.

Can we non-arbitrarily assign property rights? The libertarian says that we can. To begin with, we note, this general right of liberty is in fact nothing more nor less than itself a property right. To act is to utilize something, namely oneself (more precisely, one's body or mind). To be allowed to do as one pleases is to be allowed to do as one pleases *with* oneself. Liberty is self-ownership. The libertarian then proposes that we can extend that native dominion over certain bits of the world which is one's control of one's own personal assets, physical and psychological, to other things. First, it may be that one of us 'got there first': as it happens, you are already doing your thing, no one else having been around. Then if I come upon the scene, I am, in effect, an interloper and it is I who must give way, for what I am doing then interferes with what you are doing; which is what is forbidden by the view we are exploring. I must try something else, or try the same kind of thing somewhere else, or at some other time, or make arrangements with the others who did 'get there first'. Only in the exceptional case where both 'get there' at the same time would some principle of fair division be needed. From there on in, voluntary transfers of rights over various things, in the form either of gift or exchange, is the exclusive morally permissible method of dealing with others. This, for instance, makes every individual the proper owner of whatever he or she makes by unaided effort. In the case of aided effort, shares are settled by negotiation with the co-operating persons concerned.

But for various good reasons, perhaps not everything should be 'privatized'. To facilitate voluntary exchange, we need to be able to move about: streets, pathways, and so on might preferably be 'public', with certain general rights of access to all. There will be market-places, perhaps recreation areas, and so on. 'Public property', as one might call it, raises innumerable problems of its own.

Public property, however, is not owned by nobody, freely open to all. What we think of as 'public' places are in fact under the control of certain smallish groups. In Winesburg, Ohio, the rules for the utilization of certain parks will be set by the Winesburgians, and not by, say, the United Nations, the Government of Albania, or even the Government of the United States. Public property is actually the relatively private property, substantially speaking, of particular publics, each having power to make its own specific rules about how and when the items in question may be used, and, roughly, by whom. What limits there are to such a power, what necessary structures of permission must be built in to any reasonable use of it, is a difficult and important question. Most of our present inquiry concerns it.

With this rather quick general account of the background theory operative in this article,[3] let us now turn to our subject, speech and expression.

3   LIBERTY AND THE SPEECH SITUATION: FIRST APPROXIMATION

John Stuart Mill, in his famed *Essay on Liberty*, advocated something approximating the liberty principle as it has been described above. And he noted that while many of our acts are not immediately protected by such a principle, since they inherently involve other people as well as the agent, there are others which do not. Wherever an act has no effects on others, or affects them 'only with their voluntary consent', the liberty principle would come into play. He supposed that the 'realm of consciousness' was one major area in which that would apply.[4] If speech and expression occupied such an area, then we would have a clear and simple basis for asserting a general right to speak or express oneself. The principle of freedom of speech would go something like this. P1: *Anyone may perform any speech-act at any time.* On this principle, person A's wanting to say something would be *sufficient* reason for *allowing* A to say it.

But does speech fall readily into such an automatically protected 'realm'? Plainly not. To speak is, at least normally, to speak *to* someone; the 'expression' which a general right to express oneself would protect is interpersonal expression, the cases in which one person expresses himself *to* another person. True, we can talk to ourselves, and doubtless one could 'express' oneself in the absence of others. Perhaps private thought can be regarded as talking to oneself, in which case freedom of thought would be a special case of freedom of speech. Even if thought is private, many philosophers will reasonably argue that the language in which that thinking takes place is essentially public, and we need not dispute that here. It is sufficient just to regard these one-person cases of speech and expression as

[3] For a more thorough exposition, see Jan Narveson, *The Libertarian Idea* (Temple University Press, Philadelphia, 1989), Pt. I. Some discussion of the subjects of this article will be found there as well. Cf. 285–7.

[4] Mill, *On Liberty* (J. M. Dent: Everyman, London, 1926), 75.

residual; what we are really interested in are the normal cases, where speech and expression are communicative from one individual to another or others, involving a speaker (or more generally, an 'expresser') and an audience, which hears or otherwise witnesses the expressive acts.

Of course, what is communicated includes more than just 'propositions', speech-acts in perhaps the narrowest sense. We also communicate attitudes, emotions, values, orders, requests, enquiries, and so on. What is said below is intended to apply to all such acts, unless specific restriction is made or clearly implied in the context at hand. The terms 'speaker' and 'speech' are here used in this more general sense.

Speech is interpersonal in a further sense besides the obvious one noted above. Not only is it an activity in which A 'does something to' another person, B, something that at least minimally affects and involves B, impinging on B's sensory field and cognitive faculties; but there is also the philosophically interesting point that it relies essentially on structures of interpersonal rules. Potential for misuse of the rules in question creates a further arena for possibly negative effects, and thus possibly a further basis of legitimate restriction clearly within the bounds of the liberty principle itself.

The short route to a freedom of speech principle is therefore blocked at the outset. Being essentially interpersonal, the possibility that a first person's saying something to a second person contravenes some right of the second person looms. I shall go rather further here. If I say something to you, my intention is that my message will end up being received, digested, taken in, by the relevant parts of your cognitive/emotional faculties. But this will happen only if you *attend* to what I say. And attending is an act on your part, a use by you of some of your own perceptual and cognitive resources.

This sharpens up the issue posed by the question, Have we a general right to speak? The issue is this. If I have the right to speak to you, does this mean the right to complete the communicative act aimed at you, *including* its intended result that you hear me out? If so, then it is obvious, on the view we are exploring, that we have no such right. For that would have to be a *positive* right: the right on my part that you perform a certain service, namely of attending to my speeches. And the liberty view denies that we have any general duty to perform such services: the speaker's freedom to speak is inherently limited by the audience's freedom to hear. Also, the circumstances or the manner in which we express ourselves may violate rights of ambient persons.

The idea that you have 'freedom to hear' must not be misunderstood. There is no general right to have our perceptual faculties in one state or another. But the liberty view does, I hold, entail a general right that others do not *put us* in one perceptual state rather than another, that they may not *impose* themselves on us. A right to peace and quiet is a right against other persons that they refrain from effecting non-trivial marginal increments of sensory input in our acoustic (or visual) space. It is not a right that you do whatever you can to reduce the prevailing noise level from other sources, should that happen to be currently intolerable to me. That would, of course, be a positive right—just what the liberty principle generally denies.

The rights of hearers to hear or not hear as they choose may be defended on two grounds. First, one might simply appeal to self-ownership, our property in ourselves, which I have claimed is in effect what the libertarian view fundamentally asserts. Others may not utilize my property without my permission; my acoustic consciousness, as it were, is my property, and so you may not, prima facie, contribute unwanted marginal alterations to what goes on in that space. Second, one could point out that we would always have the right to block our ears or to go elsewhere when you speak. To suppose that we have a general right to be heard would be to deny that right. But since it is plainly a right we have by virtue of the general right of liberty, we again see that the 'general right to be heard' cannot be maintained.

4   PRIVATE PROPERTY AND SPEECH

Having clearly identified private property, of the familiar kinds, will take care of many speech situations. If I am occupying your property, then, prima facie, you set the rules and I may not speak without your permission (often obviously implicit, as when you invite me for dinner); if you are on mine, then it is the other way around. It may be in your interest to hear me out, or it may for various reasons be your duty. But once I am on your property, there can be no general case for requiring you to listen to me. If I own the space in which you propose to speak, my right of ownership permits me to make it a condition of your further occupancy that you speak only as I wish you to: for instance, not at all, or only on certain subjects and in certain manners.

(This is assuming full ownership; more restricted rights may or may not include the strongest one just noted.)

What about my speech rights when you are on my property? Must you then hear me out? Again, you may always leave; and I could make it a condition of your staying that you listen, just as you might make your staying conditional on your also having a turn to speak, or whatever. Certain rules of speech etiquette arise in civilized society, and it is a reasonable presumption that they apply no matter where we are. But the presumption can be revoked, with notice, and the owner of the spaces in which speech exchanges take place has, clearly, the right to do so.

Does this mean that the rights of private property are superior to our right of freedom of speech? The short answer is Yes. But a subtler answer is that on the liberty view, they are really both cases of the same thing. Ownership is the right to dispose at will of the owned thing. In the one case, what we own is our houses, businesses or whatever; in the present case, it is our organs and powers of speech and expression.

When we are on 'public' property, however, things are more complicated. Which is to take precedence—your right to speak, or my right to peace and quiet? Or suppose we both wish to speak at once? If we do so, that would frustrate both of us, since the resulting cacophony would leave both of us with no actual audience (but only sufferers from our noise output). The indicated solution is to take turns, if indeed we each wish to hear the other. But what if we do not? If one wishes to hear and has no interest in speaking, there is no problem about the other's speaking. If both prefer silence to hearing the other's speeches, then both, I suggest, should be quiet. But if both prefer the combination of talking but not listening? Then both will talk, though it won't be normal *speech*, but instead mere gabbling.

The question arises whether anyone is prima facie in the wrong in such cases. Are there rights to speak and rights to silence, both equally balanced? No. Silence, I believe, is the indicated baseline, just as having the air in one's lungs in its normal, unpolluted condition is the baseline for smokers in the vicinity.[5] The would-be speaker who encounters someone and proceeds to speak invades the other person's

---

[5] The baseline relative to any given smoker is its prevailing condition before the smoker comes on the scene. If that is a polluted condition already, and his addition to the air would not produce a marginal worsening, then he may have no duty not to smoke.

condition in a way that the quiet person entering a roomful of speakers does not. That person's marginal contribution to the condition of the others is not negative, for he leaves them in the same state they would have occupied in his absence; whereas the speech-maker, S, leaves the quiet person, Q, worse off than Q would have been had S not shown up at all. Obviously S can say things that Q wants to know or enjoys. A pleasant greeting to a stranger indicates that he's in company that wishes him well. Or if S conveys news important to Q, this too will be welcome. But talking 'just to pass the time of day' is not, for Q, an improvement on the status quo.

What's needed in public spaces are reasonable rules, and sometimes there can be such rules, made reasonable from all points of view, because they provide spaces for all to do as they variously prefer. In Hyde Park Corner, speeches of unlimitedly critical nature are the order of the day, and Q can go elsewhere in the park to avoid them. But if he cannot, then there is a problem, and a prima facie violation of rights.

It is tempting to suggest that all problems of the kind we are dealing with can be resolved by appropriate privatization. We may consider the segmentation of Hyde Park for different purposes as amounting to an approximation to privatization in the public realm: people over *here* may do *x*, but not over *there*. In that sense, privatization strategies are indeed what will be pursued on the following pages. But I do not suppose that there should literally be no public spaces, though some libertarians have gone to that length. We must rather see what reasonable principles, somehow capable of accommodating all, can be found for speech in the many public and semi-public arenas where our problems mainly lie.

5   THE PRINCIPLE OF FREEDOM OF SPEECH: SECOND VERSION

Let's now have a second try at formulating the Principle of Freedom of Speech. It might, in view of our discussion so far, go like this: P2: *Everyone has the right to say anything he or she wishes, at any time, to anyone who is willing to hear that speech-act at that time.*

More generally, P2 says that people have the right to send messages to receivers of those messages who are willing to receive them from those senders and by those means. (The last condition is essential. They might object in various ways to the packaging, the medium, as much as to the message. If you send me a cheery 'Happy Birthday' at 135 decibels, leaving my eardrums bleeding, I may not regard this as a favour, however welcome the message.) A speaker must be respectful of any restrictions his audience could, in the circumstances, reasonably be expected to want imposed. But, says P2, if a speech-act by person A meets those conditions, then that is sufficient for allowing A to say on.

We can state the idea in this way. We each have what we might call an 'information space', which in the case of speech in the narrowest sense of the term is an acoustic space: the space such that speech sounds penetrating it will reach one's perceptual faculties and, probably, register on one's mind (which in turn is one's ultimate resource, being, in fact, one's psychological self). Freedom of speech is freedom with respect to two things: (1) one's information-conveying faculties—larynx, chest, and so on; and (2) one's information-receiving space. The completely free person in these respects says whatever he wishes to say, and hears whatever he wishes to hear.

The idea has complications of its own, in fact. What is it to 'want to hear' what another says? Antecedently, after all, we normally don't quite know what the other is going to say, and if we did, a main point of speech, which is to add to one's stock of information, would be defeated. But what if you do not like it when it arrives? You would prefer, let us suppose, not to have heard that particular speech. Not all unwelcome speeches are wrongful to make, after all.

We can help matters out here by modifying a concept from the performing arts. Let us say that there are admission tickets to the speech performance, issued by potential speakers *and* listeners. Speeches are performances, and audiences have (or lack) tickets to these performances. The modification is that would-be performers also need tickets from their audiences, licensing the performer to say his piece. For simplicity, we may say that the one who needs to 'buy' is whoever prefers the speech to the *status quo*. That could be either the potential speaker or his potential audience.

Attending to others who speak in one's presence is consequent on 'buying' a sort of 'ticket' to that performance. Most such tickets are free, of course, in the monetary sense. However, there is always a price of some kind: at a minimum, one devotes time and attention to the expected speech-act, valuable resources which one might have expended in some other way. In receiving speeches, one licenses the other to engage in a performance of assorted speech acts. It is not plausible to think that when one signs up for such a performance, the licence you issue to the performer gives him *carte blanche* to say just absolutely anything.

To pursue the analogy: if I have acquired a ticket to what is billed as a performance of two Beethoven Quartets, and what I get instead turns out to be twenty-three old Beatles tunes arranged for string quartet, then I have a complaint. There must be some kind of antecedent understanding of the approximate range of performances which I have lent you my ears to hear. Between friends, this is usually no great problem. Between strangers, it can easily be: one may not tell off-colour stories to just anybody; you are not welcome to come to my door and berate me with the doctrines of your religion. Not even on the public subway system may you do that, insisting on a right to my attention. Public performances have titles and perhaps abstracts or advertisements to let the potential purchaser of tickets know what he will be getting into, enabling the potential audience to refuse.

This shows the fundamental objection to Justice Holmes's celebrated comparison of political speech to calling 'Fire!' in crowded theatres. The correct objection is that that speech-act does not fall within the range of what we paid our money to come and hear. In the case where the call is false, that is particularly obvious. Note that falsehood *per se* is not the point: in a narrow but recognizable sense, most of the statements made by participants in a dramatic performance will, after all, be literally false. But even where the building really is on fire, so that the call is 'true', the uncontrolled shouting of 'Fire!' may be out of order for a related reason: we come to the theatre neither to hear irrelevant speeches nor to get burned to death, nor yet to be trampled by persons attempting to avoid that fate.

In fact, Holmes's proscription of certain incendiary speeches on the ground that to make them was like the shouting of 'Fire!' in a theatre drew an analogy that was, in its setting, wholly inapposite. For in the first place, the speaker at a political rally opposing a national policy says things that *do* fall into the relevant range of utterances expected by the audience. Most likely, and certainly in that case, it was just the sort of thing they came to hear. And second, the USA at the time was not, in any conceivably relevant sense, a crowded theatre whose unwitting members might be trampled in a mad rush to the exits from its war policies. Holmes's reasoning was a travesty and was offered in support of what could hardly be a clearer case of wrongful suppression of freedom of speech. Yet had it been, say, the scene of the Los

Angeles riots, police might very properly suppress the speech of someone leading a mob against a store-owner. No one bought a ticket from the hapless store-keeper to despoil his goods.

The principle of freedom of speech as it thus far stands, then, certainly permits many restrictions on acts of speech. Indeed, it does so in all sorts of cases where the reasons for the restrictions are hardly 'grounds' at all: if I want you to pipe down because I simply don't feel like listening, that is quite sufficient, so long as you speak in places under my control, or in a public area where you have no special right to speak.

Are we concerned that we be free in the respects I have described? If so, how seriously? I propose that we are indeed, and that the grounds in question are as basic as we can get. Persons of different persuasion to mine will insist that the sort of justification achieved merely by the consent of those concerned is not enough: we must also look to the welfare of their souls, for instance. In some cases, this concern would justify forcing people to hear what they don't want to hear; in others, it would justify forcing people to refrain from saying what they want to say. I would insist that the sort of 'grounds' permitted by liberty are necessary, and that the welfare of the souls of participants is a separate, though no doubt important, topic which must be left to the possessors of the souls in question—for better or worse so far as their own welfare goes.

6 THIRD PARTIES

In any case, we are plainly not through as yet, for thus far we have attended only to first and second parties—speakers and their intended audiences. The intent of our second try at a principle of free speech is, in effect, to require that all costs and benefits to the speech exchange be fully internalized among *all* participants in speech acts. No one is to have a cost imposed on him that he does not voluntarily pay for the benefits he gets. If this general position is accepted so far as it goes, then our focus must now shift to the concerns of third parties, non-participants. Their situations are not covered by P2 as it stands. We need to move to a final formula that takes them into account: P3: *Everyone has the right to say anything he or she wishes, at any time, to anyone who is willing to hear that speech-act at that time and by those means,* provided *that (1) no third parties are thereby made unwilling recipients of unwanted messages,* and *(2) that the speeches in question are not in context means to visiting uncompensated costs on any third parties.*

The question is, then: when may we intervene in free speech transactions out of a concern to protect those who are not parties to them?

One way to deal with this would be to expand the notion of 'audience' in such a way as to include any who are in any way affected by A's speech to B, thus eliminating third parties as a category. But this trivializes the idea and makes unworkable the application of what is normally a quite restricted term. Many who are in no ordinary sense of the term part of a speaker's intended audience may be affected by A's discourse, and adversely so, in some way or in some respect. We need to know which of such effects count, and matter enough to recognize as reasonable grounds of restriction.

We might put P3 in these terms: that speech-acts between consenting parties are legitimate, *so long as they impose no significant negative externalities on others.* Then the questions are: what constitutes a 'significant negative externality'? And what is it for a speech-act, as such, to do that? I will treat these cases under the following four general categories: (1) 'noise pollution'; (2) the 'academic' interest: in the promotion and dissemination of human knowledge (this, of course, can also be a first- or second- party interest), and/or correction of error; (3) the 'political' aspect: speech-acts having a special relation to the political life of the community, e.g. as it affects the process of electing persons to political offices, or of getting political actions and policies effected; and (4) the 'personal liability' aspect: insult, libel, slander, exploitation, and violation of privacy.

I will discuss them, briefly, in that order.

7   NOISE POLLUTION

Much of what violates P3 comes under the heading of what we may call 'communicatory noise': propositions conveyed to persons who do not actually want such propositions to be conveyed, either at all or by such means, or at the times or in the circumstances in question, and conveyed by persons who may or may not have intended that those particular persons receive the information in question. The concept of 'noise' here is much wider than the normal one in which it is a purely acoustic matter and has no conceptual content. Some noise does convey propositions. The advertising on TV which interrupts the programme I came to see and hear, loudspeakers droning out propaganda to random citizens in some totalitarian countries, and Muzak in the mall may all qualify. Cognitive noise is another matter: A communicating to B, in dulcet tones, the articles of a religion of no or negative interest to B also qualifies.

There are two dimensions to consider under this heading. First, how *annoying*, how unwelcome, is it? Second, how *avoidable* is it? That is, how easy or difficult is it to avoid?

Both are matters of essentially continuous degree. So if we suppose that at some level things are permissible and at others not, then we need some plausible principle for setting the relevant standards.

It also seems plausible to suggest, as a general rule, that these two factors interact: restrictability is proportional to unavoidability multiplied by annoyingness. This is analogous to (in fact, a case of) expected utility: the overall utility of an act for an agent is the probability that a certain outcome will occur, given the act, multiplied by the amount of benefit or harm of the outcome if it does occur. Similarly, we may say, the expected nuisance value of noise is its relative unavoidability multiplied by its relative intrinsic noisomeness.

Thus, large billboards may be very annoying, but if they are only seen in places which it is extremely easy to avoid being in, their annoyingness if seen will not be much of a problem. But if they are erected in the market-place where we all must go for our daily bread, or by the public highways over which we all drive, then they are quite definitely a problem. Even highly offensive magazines, on the other hand, may easily be avoided, by non-purchase or by not entering the store that sells them. But if placed right next to the bread counter where all must go, their covers will not easily be kept out of the field of view, and then those to whom the sight is unwelcome have a complaint on that score, even though ease of non-purchase is perfect.

Roughly speaking, then, we may hypothesize that given a relevant threshold of noisomeness, the more unavoidable the exposure to the items in question, the more control over the content should be put in the hands of involuntary observers. Conversely, the more easily avoided, the less control those parties have. In general, those who hold that speech should be in principle unlimitedly free are assuming, I believe, that the noise-pollution aspect of the speeches in question is zero. And that is very often true, but by no means always.

Now suppose that there are several observers who differ in their degree of dissatisfaction from the exposure in question, some minding scarcely at all, others deeply unhappy about it? A fairly plausible conjecture here might be to invoke a maximin principle: those who would be most unfavourably affected should have most control over the content, in respect of those properties unavoidably encountered by those persons.

Thus advertising on TV, it is reasonable to suggest, does not violate my rights because whether I view it or not is up to me: one can, after all, readily turn off the offending box (a 'mute' button makes this still easier). Muzak in the mall is more of a problem: I need not shop at that mall, of course, and that helps. And if the next mall has it too? Eventually I may be out of luck: in Iran you may be quite unable to escape the voice of the mullahs intoning evening prayers. Either you stay away or you endure. In several awful countries citizens had effectively no choice whether to hear government propaganda at high volume. How much control must I have before the present but uncalled for information ceases to violate my rights regarding information?

8   NOISE AND OFFENCE

Does the sheer fact that I do not agree or that I, in other respects, object to what you have to say constitute a relevant kind of 'noise' for our purposes? Notice that it certainly would, if the speech is made on my property, while if it is made on yours, then I have, prima facie, no complaint. The snag is that a speech made on your property might nevertheless come to my attention. Part of the idea of 'noise' here is that the way in which it might thus come to my attention is crucial. If you set up loudspeakers on your property to intone the doctrines which offend me, my objection may be to *what is said* over them and not, or not just, to the sheer acoustic level of the signal. But this would be a legitimate ground of complaint, nevertheless.

Our principle, however, takes care of many of these cases. If I can hear your preaching loudspeaker no matter what I do, you violate my rights. If I have to go out of my way to receive the signals in question and nevertheless choose to do so, you do not. The point here is that the sheer fact that you believe, or are inclined to utter, the offensive items is not enough to justify your conveying them to me uninvited.

This considers only the 'pollutive' aspect of possibly offensive speeches. We will consider other aspects when we come to the fourth category: insult, libel, and so on.

9 THE ACADEMY AND FREEDOM OF INQUIRY

John Stuart Mill, notoriously, defended the rights of freedom of speech as being necessary to the promotion of human knowledge. But it is surely questionable, on the one hand, that people have a general duty to promote human knowledge. If the reason why they ought to allow people to speak freely is that general knowledge will be thereby enhanced, then it is not clear why we should protect the right to gossip across the back fence, say. No 'advancement of human knowledge' there, I daresay! As a defence of free speech, this is much too narrow to cover everything that needs to be considered. Nevertheless, there are those who do make a point of trying to promote knowledge, and the utility of having accessible repositories of general knowledge is for most of us very high. Thus most of us will be glad that there are institutions devoted to this end.

Note, by the way, an aspect of the academy that almost inherently satisfies the strictures of the preceding section: its knowledge, recorded in books and the like, found in libraries and developed in classrooms and laboratories, is *very readily avoidable*, so those who object to the contents of books or of classroom discourse may easily take the option of not reading them and not attending the classes. In that regard, the academy is a benign institution from the perspective of liberty.

There are institutions billed as having this same end of 'promoting human knowledge', where some significant qualification of the rubric is called for. Consider, for instance, religious educational institutions, especially at the level of higher learning. They wish to promote human knowledge, perhaps; but they are committed to a particular view of what can be 'known'—namely, only doctrines logically compatible with the religious teachings of the institution in question. Such institutions, provided that they are privately funded, are in my view perfectly legitimate; but they are not exactly 'academic' in the full sense of the word. The same sort of qualification would apply to institutions dedicated to certain other general ideologies. What they pursue is not simply truth, but truth *provided* it is consistent with the central tenets of the ideology in question. In what I shall call 'pure academies', on the other hand, the end really is truth—truth, whatever it may turn out to be, rather than 'truth', provided that doctrines P, Q, and R are accepted as being among the truths.

Even in the 'pure' academy, though, it will not be just any old truths we seek. There are far too many of those, most of them quite devoid of serious interest. We hope to identify certain interesting ones, rather than just any. Today's universities are, at least by intention, 'pure' in the sense defined, of being devoted to seeking out the truth no matter where it lies.[6] Even so, Mill's doctrine now runs into a different problem. For when there is an interpersonally conducted search for knowledge, it is far from true that *just anything goes* in the way of expressions. Quite the contrary. When knowledge is our goal, many restrictions on speech activity are automatically relevant. Here are three.

(1) There are, in the first place, rules of good order in regard to the making of speeches (or indeed, the reading of scarce books). The meeting of open minds requires that most mouths be closed at any given time. Vocal chords may not be exercised *ad libitum*: we must wait our turn, concede turns to others, and so on. And unlike the rule in situations unstructured by this special end, it is, correspondingly, often our duty to listen. There are things which we simply must read if we are to have any chance of being on top of our subject. The college could rightly impose on all students the duty of reading Plato and Shakespeare before they emerge, BA in hand.

(2) What may we say when we do get to speak? Definitely not just anything. The academic's right to speak at an academic gathering, when one's turn comes, is a *positive* right, entailing a duty on the rest to hear what the speaker has to say. Such a right can only reasonably be granted on the assumption that it is fairly likely that the individual in question will say something worth their attention. One may not just chatter away: to do so wastes the valuable time of colleagues by taking advantage of their willingness to lend an ear, using that time for speech activities that have no probable bearing on the end being sought, namely, knowledge in the area. Such activities may justifiably

---

[6] Sectarian institutions, I should note, nevertheless *may* be purely academic. Convinced *a priori* that *p*, *q*, and *r*, but utilizing impartial standards of assessment of putative knowledge, they nevertheless find that, luckily, no new knowledge disconfirms their favoured beliefs. But if it did? If their view is that in that case, it's tough cookies for those beliefs, then they would certainly rank as true academies.

be suppressed, for example by the chairperson of the session, or the teacher in the class; if worse came to worst, force might even be employed. For at some point, those activities violate the rights of those who came under the impression that they were attending a session devoted to the project of promoting knowledge in the particular area under investigation. Invoking my earlier metaphor, we may say that the irrelevant drivel from the unwanted speaker simply is not what they 'bought their tickets' to hear.

(3) Nor is that all. As time goes on, we get a better understanding of some subjects than we had before. When we do, there are theses, claims, views, which though plainly *relevant* to the subject, as being theories in the domain in question, are nevertheless ones we do *not* have a duty to hear (any more). In the sort of cases I have in mind, what we can say is that we have been through this before: the view in question is simply not worth listening to, or at least not in the absence of new evidence or argument—of which, suppose, the speech in question is singularly devoid. Yet if we do not welcome such speeches, it is not a case of 'suppression' in the usual sense of that term. My esteemed but dotty colleague is welcome to publish—at his own expense—whatever nonsense he likes. What he is not welcome to do is to use up valuable research money, or the valuable time of serious students, colleagues, and support staff, trying to get it discussed, let alone accepted.

Conversely, of course, those who are competent to speak productively on a subject must have extreme freedom to speak on it. Hecklers shouting down learned speakers with interesting ideas who have been invited to present them have no place in institutions of learning. It is one thing for those at the frontiers of knowledge to conclude that Mr X should not be invited because his ideas are not interesting; it is quite another for him to be shouted down without ever getting a hearing, by those who have decided that they know the truth of the matter, and that dissent is not to be tolerated. Whenever mob rule or violence prevails over the communication of cognitively important ideas and its testing by rigorous standards of reasoning, the goal of knowledge has been abandoned, and the free society along with it.

Nor should 'tenure' be deemed incompatible with losing one's position for non-accomplishment over a lengthy period. When that is so, as it can be, then valuable and scarce academic resources are being wasted and should be put to better use by hiring someone else. You cannot have an institution coherently devoted to the pursuit of anything if judgments of achievement are not allowed to be made, or if no one is deemed capable of making them. Some do seem to construe academic freedom in those terms: as involving the right to do anything (or nothing) and not even have it judged on its merits at all, or the curious view that one's right to say it should not be contingent on its having any merit—or of judgments of merit being reserved exclusively to the person 'doing' it. So long as we are in the serious business of advancing knowledge, rather than passing the time of day in a pleasant way (warm, comfortable, secure), such ideas are entirely absurd.

What I have just said licenses the making of what are quite clearly value judgments in academia. The point is that we must make such judgments, and must take such actions, if we are to proceed effectively with our project of advancing human knowledge. Some activities, we can judge with virtual certainty, have no chance whatever of doing this, and we should not expend scarce academic resources to support them. Others must be heard, and the right of those who press them to do so defended, perhaps even to the death.

But when we leave the halls of the academy, forcibly preventing cranks from speaking their piece before willing listeners in the public square is quite another matter. Persons sunning themselves on the beach, scurrying down to an ice rink in hot pursuit of a puck, absorbed in religious contemplation, or chattering over the back fence, need not lend an ear to a learned professor's discourse on the theory of the syllogism in the fourteenth century, even if he earns the Nobel Prize for it. What the chatterers and the rest have to say does not measure up to academic standards, true. But that is quite beside the point. For, J. S. Mill to the contrary notwithstanding, society *is not an academy*. The right to express oneself to those willing to hear, provided that it is not done in such a way as to pose threats to others beyond one's immediate audience, does not rest on society's valuing the truth. It rests on something more general and more fundamental: the right to be who you are and do what you want, whatever others may think.

10   POLITICAL SPEECH

In a recent book, Gary Madison argues that

Only a constitutional society is a *rational society*, if one understands reason not in a narrowly technological sense ... [which] can exist only when people behave reasonably, that is, when they renounce dogmatic beliefs and ideologies and enter into free and unrestricted discussion, a discussion in which each person is, in principle, as qualified to a hearing as any other and in which the 'expert' ... counts for nothing. What the 'good life' consists in is something that can never be scientifically determined but only agreed upon through unlimited discussion and peaceful persuasion.[7]

Here Madison eloquently expounds a familiar and important theme: that free discussion plays a central role in the political theory of liberalism. But it also illustrates the point I wish to make next: namely, that the protection of free speech plays two very different roles in the free society, and that we may rate these very differently in different connections. Moreover, they can have strikingly different implications for policy. Let me call these the 'political' role and the 'civil', or non- political, role.

The *political* role of free speech lies, obviously enough, in the area of discussion of matters of political interest. Democracy is that political system in which the fundamental political power in the society is to be divided equally: everyone is to have as much as anyone else, neither more nor less. If citizens do not exercise this power intelligently, democracy may not be worth having. But if they are to do so, they must know what the issues are, what the different candidates are likely to do if elected, and therefore what those candidates have to say, how they see the issues, and how likely they are to do what they claim, if elected. To the extent that the citizen's information is slanted, controlled, manipulated, funnelled, and otherwise restricted, we may expect things to go worse, both for him and for us. The citizen needs a free press as well, so that the ideas of others in addition to politicians—who after all have a vested interest in politics—may be available to the voter as well.

By contrast, the *civil* role of free speech has no special connection with politics. When you and I chat about composers and hi-fi systems, and the people next door talk about how their daughter is doing at school, we are simply pursuing our several interests, utilizing assorted speech activities in the process. Some of us may also utilize speech activities to ponder the good life, hoping by exchange of ideas to arrive at a clearer and more satisfying conception thereof. But whether or not we are engaging in that rather sophisticated and philosophical activity, we are normally just working away at living

[7] Gary Madison, *The Logic of Liberty* (Greenwood Press, Westport, Conn., 1986), 141.

our lives, as well as we can manage. Perhaps, as Madison says, what the good life is 'can never be scientifically determined'; but in these very fundamental respects in which I am now discussing the subject, there is scarcely any reason to think that the good life can be 'agreed upon through unlimited discussion and peaceful persuasion' either.

But there is also no *need* to agree—for that matter, there may be no 'truth' here to seek or to reach agreement on, tentative or otherwise. Ordinary people doing their own thing do not require as their justification for doing so that when the last word is in, their versions of the good life will have been confirmed in some ultimate high court of rational judgment. They are entitled to that degree of protection which consists in the rest of us forbearing from interference in those activities, regardless of any such consideration, provided only that they in turn refrain from interference in the lives of others. And this is true whether or not their particular patterns of speech-usage do anything whatever to forward the efficacy of governments, liberal or otherwise.

The divergence in policy implications between these two functions is fundamental and may also be substantial. If we are to have democratic government, we positively must have political discourse, and it positively must be relatively uninhibited. Citizens need information, and from the public's point of view it is not sufficient that others are merely not prevented from trying to supply them with it. This is particularly true as regards information concerning the doings and deliberations of the government itself. Only extraordinarily should the doings of the legislature be secret, for example; only in very extreme cases, if any, could it have any right to delude or mislead the citizen. We need to know what our government is doing for reasons that require a positive flow of information, as complete as readily possible, regarding what it is up to. In so far as we lack it, our liberal polity is likely to function less well.

But the same is *not* true regarding our flow of information about the ballet, or the price of eggs, or the doings of famous persons. Naturally, when we have an interest in some matter, then in so far as that interest is served by information, it is also our interest, prima facie, that it be accurate, reliable, and so on. But then, the style in which the subject is discussed, and the quality of the associated graphics, are at least as important to typical readers or viewers as the substance of the speech-acts in question, if not more so. Readers of sensational tabloids do not particularly expect the truth, but they do expect to be cognitively and otherwise titillated—amused, flabbergasted, and so on. The TV advert that amuses while endeavouring to sell us a second-rate hamburger may reasonably hold our attention despite its paucity of 'relevant information about the product'.

Now, democratic institutions, in the narrowest sense of the word, will survive intact if the flow of such stuff is arbitrarily restricted. And—who knows?—possibly the reader of such trivia would live a better life were he instead to read *The Economist* or some other sober journal of public opinion. Fine. But if that isn't what he wants to do, even on the basis of extremely modest consideration, we have no business cramming him with our superior wisdom. Taking a broader and, I think, more intelligent view of democracy, we might go further and suggest that a 'democracy' that could survive only by cramming its unwilling citizens with political information does not deserve the name.

11 PRIORITY OF THE CIVIL RIGHT OF EXPRESSION

If we ask which of these two functions of freedom of speech is more *important*, from the public point of view, then we can understand those who think it is the political one. If we must have government, then we certainly don't want it to fall into the hands of tyrants, and avoiding that perhaps takes precedence, even over getting the latest news from the Rialto.

Perhaps—but if we instead ask which of these two functions is more *fundamental*, then that is quite another matter. For clearly the *civil* function is. Democratic institutions, or any political institutions, are means to ends, not ends in themselves. Not, that is to say, necessary ends for everyone. Some people—some politicians, I suppose, and a few highly extroverted civilians—take the sort of interest in politics that connoisseurs take in fine wines. For them, perhaps, it is appropriate to describe politics as an end in itself. But most of us are not like that, and it is impossible that we all could be. A nation consisting exclusively of politicians, apart from the fact that it would not survive long, would have nothing to be political *about*. For politics to make any sense, there must be ground-level activities in which people engage for *non*-political reasons, indeed, ultimately for their own sakes—or, if you prefer, for the sake of 'realizing their view of the good'. But the interest that those activities remain untampered with and contravened by others is intrinsic to them. If we want to accomplish goal G, then we must, in so far forth, also want that nothing, and therefore no one renders it impossible for us to accomplish G. This is so whether G is political or not; and as said, it usually is not.

Speech acts are integral to a very large proportion of those assorted, and often very humble, activities. To interfere with the speeches we make to each other in the course of them is to interfere with those activities themselves. In many cases, one could hardly even say that speech was merely causally efficacious or an indispensable means to the ends pursued: often enough, it's part of their very essence. A bridge game, a religious service, a picnic, shorn of its communicative aspect, is unrecognizable. To clamp down on our available repertoire of expressions is to interfere; and we should object to the idea that such interference is justified by the mere fact that those activities are, after all, mundane and trivial. So they are: so are we, if it comes to that. Nevertheless, here we are and those are the things we want to do. And if you see nothing wrong with intervention at this mundane level, then you are no friend of human freedom.

Is there anything special about freedom of speech? In the political realm, the answer is undoubtedly in the affirmative. Democratic institutions have their problems, and the need to be protected from the whims of majorities is urgent in any such. But still, they are the best we can currently do to avoid the worse evils of outright dictatorship: the tyranny of the majority is somewhat preferable to that of the minority. And democratic institutions are indeed in peril if we disallow, say, political speeches on the ground that what they say is false and what they advocate evil. Normally those are merely reasons not to vote for the candidate in question.

But what if millions are likely to vote for that candidate— and as a result, the Nazis take power? In a proper democracy, no doubt, such a party would not be able to do most of what it did, with no matter how large a majority. But in a weak or improper one, the question of forcibly suppressing a party whose speeches are nothing but running derogations of fellow citizens and advocate what have to be violations of rights of those and other citizens reasonably arises. Within a strong democracy, whose constitutional protections are in good order, the case for suppressing any political speech is virtually nil. Freedom of the individual comes first, and democracy is subordinate to it—not the other way around. Any polity that clearly understands that has no fear from any political party, however shoddy. But with any number of polities that aspire to democracy but fall significantly short, things may be quite otherwise.

When we look merely to the civil realm, however, the short answer to the question whether principles of free speech are of *special* importance is basically in the negative. Speech activities do not loom *above* other activities; they simply are part and parcel of a lot of those activities. Whether my life has been more seriously interfered with when someone keeps me from saying what I wish to say to someone than it would if instead, say, my car were stolen or my leg broken, plainly varies. Usually, either of the latter would be more serious, but in some cases the former would be. It is a matter of judgment in the particular case, and by the persons concerned. This outcome is, I think, an advantage of understanding all civil rights to be specifications or applications of one single principle of general liberty.

We must also distinguish between obstacles to one's speaking that are adventitious and occasional and those that are directed and on-going. The latter, institutional blocks to speech activities that would otherwise be possible, is plainly more serious. A possible need to quell a particular speech likely to incite uncontrollable riot is one thing; permanent denial of occasion to say the sort of thing that individual had to say is quite another. There the institutions in question deprive the speaker of something likely to be highly valuable, both to himself and to others. To justify such blocks, we need very good evidence that the speech-acts in question clearly and directly cause harm to others, and that enabling the harmed individuals to make their case in a civil court is not an adequate remedy. Which brings us to the vexed question of how and whether speech may be said to cause harm.

12 SPEECH AND HARM TO PERSONS

Fundamental to liberalism is the imposition of limits to the liberty of the individual when what he does may preclude exercise of the liberty of others. Most express this in terms of 'harm' to those others. On the view being explored here, what makes a 'harm' to others eligible for restricting liberty is that it *consists* in such a preclusion, as with the exercise of violence. But speech activities, even 'violent' ones, do not obviously do this. Sticks and stones can plainly break bones, but how do words possibly 'harm' us? They can be delivered at painful volume levels, or the speech of A can render inaudible the speech of B, say; but we are concerned now with the idea that the conceptual content, the messages delivered in speech, might 'harm'. How is this to be understood? There would seem to be two fundamental ways:

a) directly: by offending, derogating, demeaning, or in general verbally abusing; and

(*b*) indirectly: by *inducing hearers to act* in such a way as to bring physical or other independently definable harms upon some persons: A's words induce B to break C's bones.

Case (*a*) is, I think, in principle taken care of by my freedom-to-hear clause. If those who hear do so without having been, as it were, invited, then their offence is irrelevant. They listen out of turn, and they hear at their own risk. If on the other hand they heard upon suitable invitation—they had a 'ticket' to the 'performance' in question—then so long as the offending matter lies within the range that falls within the description under which they acquired their right to listen, they have no complaint. On the other hand, if the speech-performer exceeds his terms of reference, he is at fault and may be held liable. Determining just what these terms are in a particular case is, of course, often difficult.

Is the sheer fact of offensiveness sufficient ground for suppression? Have we the right to think evil of others? Clearly we must here make what may be a fine distinction. We ought not to think evil of others—unless, of course, there is evidence that they *are* evil. This is a matter of morals in its 'inward' aspect. The soul of one who cavalierly thinks evil of others is in an objectionable condition. But the power of the State may not be exercised with a view to curing such maladies.

On the other hand, when we not only think but speak the evil in question, redress, as in the exaction of apology, may be in order. The category of 'noise pollution' invoked earlier may be invoked here as well. Your unreasoned negative opinion of me is something the expression of which I do not need, and with which you may not clutter up my acoustic space.

But what if it *is* reasoned? If I am subject to well-founded criticism in respects that matter to me, it is presumably in my interest to know this. What we have then is still unpleasant, but it can hardly 'offend' or be regarded as mere abuse, except in respect of the manner in which it is phrased or delivered. Still, here we may invoke a public duty of civility: even when justified, criticism should not be harsh, or grate on the ears (or the soul). We should keep a 'civil tongue in our heads'.

Case (*b*) is very much trickier, for various reasons. And we must certainly bracket off one subset of cases that offer no fundamental analytical problems. Those are the cases in which the speeches in question are part of a larger train of activities, aimed at some independently wrongful objective. The bank robber communicating with his partner in planning or executing the crime is not engaging in the sort of activity that a principle of freedom of speech protects. Such activities violate the institution of speech itself, by utilizing it for the defeat of just the sort of ends speech is intended to enable us to perform, such as peaceful commerce, mutually enjoyable activities such as the arts, or the advance of interesting knowledge. One who gives an order or intentionally contributes, by verbal means, to actions that violate rights is clearly culpable. But what is wrong is not just that he says certain things, but that in saying them he is in effect doing or participating in the doing of independently wrong actions.

Culpable *inducement* is a much more problematic notion. Human activity is, after all, normally subject to rational controls. If A 'induces' B to harm C as a consequence of some speech performance of A's, we can ask why B was persuaded, why he did not consult his own judgment, failed to resist the inducement. That is one reasonable question to ask. Some answers would make A culpable, others would leave the responsibility within B's hands. In particular, if A provides false information which, if true, would *justify* B's assault on C, then A is blameworthy and perhaps punishable, at least additionally to and perhaps instead of B. For after all, if A's argument is a sound one, then B's assault *is* justified. The common soldier obeying his superior's order to fire reasonably presumes that the target is the enemy rather than an innocent civilian. When the superior knows that this presumption is false, he is at fault. But how contrary to appearances may things be before the soldier should cease to follow this presumption? At *some* point, he must not simply obey.

What of the case where what A says to B is not an 'argument' at all, but an inducement in some more visceral sense? But it is not clear how this works. Does A's speech sever connections in B's nervous system? Does it short out his decision-making facilities? Such characterizations, often enough invoked in these contexts, are surely not normally applicable. But if they are, as perhaps where B is insane or a (not very well brought up) child, then again A would indeed bear some responsibility; still, we may also say that we no longer have a 'speech act' in quite the usual sense of the term in such cases. The question where rational and responsible adulthood leaves off and states functionally equivalent to childhood begin is obviously an extremely difficult one. But the bearing of the distinction presupposes that being a rational adult *matters*, which is to say, that there are distinctive considerations holding in that domain, the absence of which, as (perhaps) in children and the insane, accordingly makes a serious difference in the relevant modes of reacting. When dealing with the totally irrational and irresponsible, different categories are appropriate.

Yet the difference cannot lie in the fact that adults do nothing but process information in a magisterially aloof way. On the contrary: adults may be offended, verbally assaulted, their sensibilities ruffled, egos wounded, and so on. We must somehow separate those things from action taken upon considered judgment; and we may demand that actions *be* considered. Thus, take the Nazi rabble-rouser who in fact succeeds in what he intended to do—rouse the rabble in question, to acts of violence against innocent persons (say, Jews in 1934). He plays on the ignorance of his audience, for one thing. He also perhaps triggers base motives in the audience, fanning rather than dousing the flames of evil passion. Here, I suggest, it is important to distinguish between the *falsehoods* he supplies them with and the aspect of *triggering* independently objectionable passions.

For the former, the speaker may indeed be held responsible. When we speak, we imply, in the absence of clear indications that what we say is unreliable, that we are to be taken seriously. 'P', as the theorem has it, is equivalent to ' "p" is True'. Where the speaker in fact knows p to be false, the act of so speaking is directly wrong, and certainly may be punishable. Where he does not, but the question of p's truth is of major importance by virtue of its capacity to figure in an argument that would justify actions which would normally be wrong, the evil is irresponsibility, and could justify a call for retraction or perhaps outright suppression.

Even here, though, we must also appreciate that general fallibility is part of the human condition. Audiences need to check their facts before embarking on campaigns of violence. The fact that some bloke with a strong voice has just intoned 'p' is *not* sufficient reason to believe that p. There are circumstances in which someone's saying 'p' is adequate reason to accept p, and the more nearly this is so, the more blameworthy is the speaker, as compared with the hearer, when p turns out to be false. The commanding officer in my previous case who says 'That man is the enemy! Fire!', knowing perfectly well that the man is nothing of the sort, may be *entirely* to blame.

Next, if our speaker knows that his audience is liable to act on p without due thought, then again he must share in the blame if they proceed so to act. 'What did you expect?' we may reasonably ask. Beyond some point the model of unleashing the dogs becomes appropriate. For humans, it should not be so. The 'dogs' have a primary share in the blame. Even so, one who is well aware of these tendencies in his audience, and yet encourages rather than criticizing them, acts badly.

The upshot would seem to be this: where judgment on the part of the individual should plainly have countered the tendencies to act which may have been triggered by some speaker, the legal blame for acting falls on the agents of the harmful action. The speaker, for his part, is also due for some moral blame, and where he speaks knowingly falsely, the blame is severe. But where what the speaker says is independently false, and moreover intended to stimulate those very actions, then he is criminally liable.

In all this, of course, I am assuming that there are some knowable general principles about right and wrong action—not only knowable, but generally known. In the academy, where our duty is to question everything and not take things on faith, this is not a safe assumption. But beyond its doors, it is, if not a 'safe' assumption, yet our only assumption. It can break down, of course, in two familiar ways: by there being no operational standards at all on which we can rely, and by there being different ones from those we think are right. In the former case, it is a little difficult to see how anyone could properly be blamed for saying anything to anyone. In the latter, on the other hand, we must have a caution. If we blaspheme against Allah, as our audience might well suppose we are doing, then it might be worth our life; or if we accuse another of doing so, it might be worth *his*. The religious fanatics who kill on this ground are certainly in the wrong; but it would be imprudent in the extreme to be guided only by that fact.

The question, I think, is this: what is the proper moral modality, as we may call it, of such considerations? To speak the wrong things to the wrong people is imprudent, certainly. But in the end, if those who seize upon what someone says to do evil can wholly blame the speaker, then a good deal—in the end, all—of civilized life is at an end. For there is surely nothing that cannot be misinterpreted or turned to wrong ends by sufficiently misguided persons. The law must side against the actor rather than the speaker whenever the intentions of the speaker are not plainly blamable on a publicly sustainable canon of criticism. This, I think, is the largest part of the principle of freedom of speech. But it is clear enough how fragile, and how dependent on the existence of a generally civilized and peaceable community it is, in practice.

There are also the conceptually rather difficult problems of gossip and the like which are mixed cases of direct and indirect harm. Perhaps these succumb to our general treatment if we keep in mind the following distinctions.

First, false information damaging to reputation or otherwise is always, prima facie, culpable.

Second, even where true, some information we might convey about someone is not ours to convey: obtaining it or broadcasting it may involve a violation of privacy.

Third, information passing both tests may nevertheless be easily misconstrued, or those who pass it on will distort it from malicious motives, and so on.

But beyond this, we must leave these things to the judgment of those concerned. A fair amount of most people's lives, I would guess, involves personal appraisals, of friends, enemies, public figures, business associates, and so on. This activity is largely harmless, though on the other hand, it is often very significant for the subjects of those appraisals. Irresponsibility in them can lead to major alterations in the lives of those concerned. Yet if we were to try to impose strong controls on such things, with a view to protecting rights, it would amount to an intolerable imposition on freedom of association; for such association is often primarily in the mode of speech. Part of the risk we run in associating with people is that we create the potential for misinformation that adversely affects reputation, and much else also depends on it. But intervening by force of law to try to reduce that risk to zero at source is misguided. Here again, freedom to live our lives implies freedom to talk, even if the consequences are sometimes unfortunate.

As a case in point, consider the affair of Zundel, who has been criminally punished for publishing a book proclaiming that the Holocaust was a hoax. This, it is said, inspires hatred, etc., of the concerned group, in this case the world's Jews as a whole. And what was the offence? Was it a claim that the Jews (and a large number of others) were *lying* about the holocaust? If so, a suit in civil courts is indicated, and not a trial at criminal law (which, as has been widely noted, served greatly to increase the amount of publicity for Zundel's book, which certainly deserved the fate it would otherwise have received, namely, near-total obscurity). If someone publishes a tract maintaining that certain extremely well-documented, and in this case extremely horrific, events did not in fact take place, he will certainly lose a case at law if that's where it goes; and of course has already lost out in the 'market place of ideas'—so far as its central thesis is concerned, Zundel's book ranks somewhere below Creationism in its claims on the attention of serious scholars.

Beyond that, Zundel's book does not even advocate violence or restriction of rights of the people offended by it. Where, then, is the case for criminal restriction? It is difficult to see that this is anything but itself a violation of Zundel's right to say what he thinks. That *what* he thinks is absurd is not sufficient ground of suppression, and even had he advocated plainly immoral action, our ground for that is slim, at least unless it could be shown that in the circumstances, there was a high probability that people would be moved by it to perform harmful actions which, in turn, could not be adequately dealt with by the appropriate methods of criminal law.

The matter of probability is clearly important. John Stuart Mill himself agreed that a speech before an angry mob, denouncing some innocent potential target of their violence, might rightly be suppressed. A published leaflet can hardly have such an effect. The appropriate remedy is always refutation, of course, though how easily 'refuted' a racist diatribe may be, to an audience not steeped in or even capable of academic standards of assessing arguments, is a difficult question.

Refutations of this kind would be more frequent if the costs of the refutation were borne by the original publishers and authors. Suppose that Zundel was required to fund a publication of similar scope, pointing out all the evidence against his absurd thesis? This might have a salutary effect. Putting him in jail, on the other hand, will do nobody any good, starting with Zundel himself. The most appropriate immediate remedy is to spread truth sufficient to counteract any damage that might be done by the spreading of falsehood.

It might be asked why we should think that people have a right to good reputation. The reply is simple. To be prone to evil, or to be untrustworthy, are properties of character that are justifiably responded to by shunning or worse: the potential for fruitful interaction with such persons is diminished by comparison with the norm of honesty and reliability which all may and should presume, in the absence of good evidence to the contrary. The spreading of bad reputation is therefore a liability to its subject; and if this is ungrounded, then those who spread it do its subject damage. Often this damage can be translated into dollars and cents, as when someone loses a contract or a job offer because the potential contractor believes the malicious claims spread by our slanderer.

Hitler effectively circulated the message that Jews were enemies, guilty of assorted crimes, and the like. To what degree his acceptance was motivated by hysteria and paranoia is not easy to say, but certainly avenues of attempted rebuttal were soon closed to the victims, and it would surely not have been so easy for so many people to participate enthusiastically in their extermination were they adequately exposed to rebuttal. Speech is not riveted to action, but its connection is too firm to allow us to be comfortable with a policy of always waiting for overt evils before any effort is made to counteract the messages which occasioned those evils.

13   CONCLUDING REMARKS

The gist of this investigation is that if we take a principle of free speech to be a theorem stemming from a sweeping principle of liberty as our sole fundamental political premiss, then we nevertheless see many ways in which there can be legitimate restrictions on speech and expression, stemming from their very essence, which is interpersonal in nature. Communication among free beings is an important matter, both in respect of its bearing on political activity, narrowly understood, and more fundamentally as a basic and substantial component of our lives as social beings. The onus of justification is always on those who would suppress or prevent an expressive act from taking place. But it can often be met. Speech activities have enemies, as it were, from without and within; they merit protection from both.

4. Freedom of Commercial Expression

ROGER A. SHINER

1 INTRODUCTION

'There is no sound basis on which commercial expression can be excluded from the protection of s. 2(b) of the Charter.' Thus spake the Supreme Court of Canada in *Ford* (618), sentiments which the Court repeated in *Irwin Toy* (608) and has adhered to ever since. This essay is written in the belief that no articulate and principled justification has been provided for the Court's so holding, and from the perspective of some scepticism as to whether such a justification can be provided. As I shall show, major issues in the foundations of political morality are raised by the topic of freedom of commercial expression. It would be a major project to lay them out coherently,[1] and the present discussion does not pretend to be more than a preliminary statement of the issues and of plausible lines of argument.

The paper depends heavily on some initial philosophical assumptions which I will not here independently defend. I will first lay these out, together with some initial clarifications of terms.

1.1 The meaning of 'commercial expression'

First, what do we mean by 'commercial expression'? The Supreme Court of Canada has not defined the concept very clearly. The Court said in *Ford* (610):

While the words 'commercial expression' are a convenient reference to the kind of expression contemplated by the provisions in issue, they do not have any particular meaning or significance in Canadian law, unlike the corresponding expression 'commercial speech', which in the United States has been recognized as a particular category of speech entitled to First Amendment protection of a more limited character than that enjoyed by other kinds of speech. The issue in the appeal is not whether the guarantee of freedom of expression in s. 2(b) of the Canadian Charter should be construed

---

[1] The project is currently work in progress, and a book-length manuscript will hopefully be its outcome.

as extending to particular categories of expression, giving rise to difficult definitional problems.

I am in this essay largely concerned with Canadian adjudication and Charter jurisprudence. I will not be attempting any detailed analysis of the US case law. It is very much in flux. None the less, a working definition for this essay may be extracted from US jurisprudence. To quote from a recent decision,

> the [US] Supreme Court has identified three characteristics of commercial speech, while being careful to note that none is necessary or sufficient for speech to be classified as commercial. According to the Court, speech that is *concededly* an advertisement, refers to a specific product, and is motivated by economic interest may properly be characterized as commercial speech.[2]

The emphasis seems to be on advertising, whether promotional or informational,[3] although it is clear that many other aspects of commercial life take place through the medium of language and significant acts like hand-shaking or programme waving yet, so far at least, have not been the occasion for litigation under s. 2(b) of the Charter. I have in mind statutory regimes for contract, securities law, labour law, and the like.

1.2 'Coverage' versus 'Protection'

There is also a distinction[4] to be drawn between the *coverage* afforded to some person or act by a constitutional provision and the *protection* so afforded. To state what is covered by a constitutional provision is to state what actions etc. come within its scope, what actions raise or implicate the issues embodied in the constitutional provision. To state what is protected is to state what actions, for example, one may appeal to the courts to enable one to perform or what restrictions one may appeal to the courts to lift as a final holding in a case. This

---

[2] Silberman J., in *Wall Street*, at 372.

[3] There is an important set of issues here which will have to be ignored in this essay. The question really only concerns *truthful* advertising. No defender of freedom of commercial expression objects to restrictions on false advertising. However, what about simply misleading advertising? Or manipulative advertising? What about so-called 'lifestyle advertising', which relies on associational techniques, not on giving information, and thus has neither truth-value nor truth-conditions? If, as is standardly argued, the value underlying freedom of commercial expression is true information, do these non-assertoric forms of advertising still deserve protection, and if so, why? For considerable scepticism on the point, see Moon, 'Lifestyle Advertising'.

[4] Due to Schauer: cf. *FSPE*, 89–90.

distinction is conveniently institutionalized in the Canadian Charter of Rights and Freedoms in the relation of s.1 to s.2 of the Charter. These sections read as follows:

1. The *Canadian Charter of Rights and Freedoms* guarantees the rights and freedoms set out in it subject only to such reasonable limits prescribed by law as can be demonstrably justified in a free and democratic society.
2. Everyone has the following fundamental freedoms: ... (b) freedom of thought, belief, opinion and expression, including freedom of the press and other media of communication.

Section 2(b) simply states that any actions which constitute the exercise of freedom of expression are covered by the section. However, one will not know for any such specific action whether it will indeed receive constitutional protection, or for any such Government regulation restricting such action whether it will be struck down, until the court has considered whether or not some restriction on that action is demonstrably justified in a free and democratic society.

In this essay, I am primarily concerned with whether commercial expression should be covered by s. 2(b). I shall often talk of 'protection', because clearly, if constitutional coverage is to amount to anything worthwhile, most of the actions, for example, covered must also be protected. But I am not here much concerned with what conclusions the Supreme Court has reached about the actual protection of various cases of commercial expression through its s. 1 analyses; I am concerned only with their reasons for thinking that commercial expression is covered by s. 2(b) of the Charter—that is to say, their reasons for thinking that commercial expression as understood above is an activity which implicates the reasons a society has for having a provision like s. 2(b) in its constitution.

The value of this terminological stipulation (for that is really all it is—the distinction is not underwritten by lexicography) can be seen from a recent Supreme Court case, Re *s. 195.1(1)(c)*. Lamer J. (as he then was) argues (at 108–11) that s. 2(b) should be interpreted so as to have the widest possible scope and a very narrow set of exclusions, with the consequence that the vast majority of putative restrictions on freedom of expression will be justified, if at all, under s. 1 analysis. He therefore makes remarks such as: 'I am of the view that s. 2(b) of the Charter protects all content of expression irrespective of the meaning or message sought to be conveyed'; and 'While the guarantee of free expression protects all content, all forms are not, however, similarly protected' (at 108). He summarizes his discussion thus: 'All content of expression is protected while the set of forms that will not receive protection is narrow and includes direct attacks by violent means on the physical liberty and integrity of another person' (at 112). He thus concludes that the speech at issue in the case, the speech of a prostitute soliciting, is expression 'protected' by s. 2(b). However, when he turns to s. 1 analysis, Lamer J. is in no doubt at all that s. 195.1(1)(c) of the *Criminal Code* of Canada constitutes a reasonable limit on freedom of expression within the meaning of s. 1 of the Charter. Now, there is a real conceptual oddity to declaring solicitation for commercial sex, for example, 'protected' by the Charter, but also that the government can legitimately restrict such expression by making it criminal. In the proposed terminology, this oddity disappears. Solicitation is *covered* by the Charter through s. 2(b) in that it is not regarded as an expression which raises no constitutional issues at all. Yet it is not protected by the Charter, because restriction of it is a limit justifiable by s. 1 analysis.[5]

1.3   The Need for a Theoretical 'Architecture'

Whether it is possible, or even desirable, to give a hard-edged definition of 'commercial expression' I leave aside. The enterprise of characterization must needs be an issue of jurisprudence, of 'top-down' theory, not an issue of the stable meaning of a term in ordinary language. The terms 'expression' or 'speech' to denote a category of behaviour covered by constitutional provisions such as s. 2(b) of the Charter or the First Amendment of the US Constitution are terms of art. To put the matter in extensional terms, there are many instances of 'expression' which are not regarded as covered by the Charter— cases of fraudulent expression, for example, and the Supreme Court in *Irwin Toy* says the same of violent expression (607). There are many offences under the *Criminal Code* of Canada where speech constitutes all or the major part of the *actus reus*.[6] There are many examples of expressive behaviour which are covered and are not linguistic. The Canadian Charter's use of 'expression' rather than the US First

---

[5] I shall not in what follows tinker with the wording of quotations where the author uses 'protect' and cognates but where I would use 'cover' and cognates. The meaning should be clear from the context.

[6] For a list, see Lamer J. (as he then was) in *Re s. 195.1(1)(c)*, at 110.

Amendment's term 'speech' is presumably designed in part to ac-knowledge this fact.[7] The term 'expression' in s. 2(b) of the Charter is 'theory-laden'. It therefore does not follow merely from the fact that some piece of behaviour, linguistic or not, is 'expression' in some plain extra-legal sense that it is constitutionally covered by s. 2(b). Instead, the argument that some behaviour is covered by s. 2(b) must be 'top-down' or, to use Schauer's valuable term, 'architectural'.[8]

The point is a general one, whatever the kind of speech or ex-pression at issue. But it is particularly sharp for commercial ex-pression simply because commercial expression is in part a matter of economics. Economic activity as a human activity cannot be carried out without the use of speech; that is a transcendental point, given that humans are language-users. Yet at first sight the right of govern-ments to regulate the economy through statutory or other regimes is unquestioned. Commercial expression pits a form of behaviour which is paradigmatically non-regulable—expression—against one which is paradigmatically regulable—commercial activity. Initial in-tuitions clearly divide. Ever since *Virginia Board* and *Irwin Toy*, the Supreme Courts of Canada and the US have claimed that the econ-omic character of commercial expression or speech is less funda-mental from the point of view of constitutional jurisprudence than its character as expression or speech. Commentators have not always agreed: Strauss writes:

Commercial speech has no especial importance to the political process ... The First Amendment does not protect commercial activity generally. And there is little about commercial *speech* that distinguishes it from other com-mercial activity. (50)

As intuitions, neither one has precedence over the other. A theory is needed to defend either one. One who denies that last assertion faces

[7] I follow here the position taken by Fred Schauer in *FSPE*, followed by Barendt in *FS* and Jackson and Jeffries. The Supreme Court explicitly acknowledge Schauer's work in *Irwin Toy* (606). None the less, they there define 'expression' very broadly indeed—'Activity is expressive if it attempts to convey meaning. That meaning is its content'. This characterization is far broader than Schauer's 'narrow concept of "speech"': see *FSPE*, ch. 7.

[8] See 'Commercial speech and architecture', *passim*. I do not believe that the recent decisions of the Supreme Court in *Ford* and *Irwin Toy* are 'architectural' in the required way. They do not rest on any articulate theory of freedom of expression. Rather, they are intuitive responses to particular fact-situations. I will return to this issue towards the end of the essay. In *Re s. 195.1(1)(c)* at 108 Lamer J. (as he then was) quotes Schauer on the role of a Free Speech Principle in s. 2(b) jurisprudence, but he signally fails to provide a theory of the required kind.

the following dilemma. The Supreme Court of Canada has a choice, as the Charter is constituted, between regarding some regulated example of commercial expression as not covered by s. 2(b) and so not protected, or as covered by s. 2(b) but its regulation as justified by s. 1 analysis. If it chooses the first option, then it needs a theory to say why something which is intuitively expression is none the less not covered by s. 2(b). If it chooses the second option, then it needs a theory of the justification in political morality of the limitation on freedom of expression. Either way, a theory is needed. The particular approach that the respective Supreme Courts have chosen to take is not forced on them by the very ideas of speech or expression themselves. The approach is a political choice, and it needs a justification by a theory in political morality.

1.4   Rights and Freedoms

Another preliminary clarification is to underline the neo-Hohfeldian aspects of the Charter's conceptual framework. Hohfeld distinguished between (*a*) 'right' in the proper sense as 'claim right' with the jural correlative of 'duty' and the jural opposite of 'no-right', and (*b*) 'liberty' or 'privilege' with the jural correlative of 'no-right' and the jural opposite of 'duty'.[9] The Charter likewise distinguishes systematically between 'rights', which in some form create directly and correlatively duties on the part of government, and 'freedoms', which create directly and correlatively only a 'no-right' on the part of government to interfere with the enjoyment of such a freedom. Section 2 defines the fundamental freedoms, of which freedom of expression is one. These freedoms create rights and duties indirectly, through the need to create what Hart has called the 'protective perimeter' within which the freedom can be exercised.[10] Despite the importance of this distinction, I want to underline that when we also draw, as we must, a theoretical distinction between rights and utilitarian goals (even if we wish to say that, at another level of analysis, rights are very special utilitarian goals),[11] or rights and interests (even if we wish to say that, at another level of analysis, rights are specially protected interests), both rights in the Hohfeldian/Charter sense and

[9] *FLC*, ch. 1.
[10] Cf. *EB*, 171. Cf. also Rand J. in *Saumur* and his famous remark about 'the residue inside the periphery', at 670.
[11] This view is defended by Wayne Sumner, *MFR, passim.*

freedoms in the Hohfeldian/Charter sense are *rights*, not interests or utilitarian goals.[12]

1.5   Rights, Persons and Organizations

My next piece of preliminary stage-setting is to wheel in, again without independent justification, some distinctions and claims made by Meir Dan-Cohen.[13] First, he considers the extent to which corporate organizations may be considered as real or natural persons. He identifies two strategies towards the goal of assimilating corporations to natural persons, which he calls 'personification' and 'aggregation' (pp. 15–16, 26–30). *Personification* takes seriously the unity of an organization:

It conveys the triple insight that organizations are commonly the objects of meaningful predication; that this predication is possible and meaningful apart from and in the absence of any detailed knowledge pertaining to individual constituents of the organization; and that in many cases the same predication is equally appropriate for organizations and for individuals. (26; Dan-Cohen's emphasis)

The predications in question—for example, 'manufactures', 'lobbies', 'plans', 'proposes', 'opposes', 'resents', 'negotiates', 'hires', 'appoints', 'discriminates', 'treats properly', etc., all are verbs of agency and *ceteris paribus* imply intentionality and mentality. If intuitively they apply straightforwardly and meaningfully to organizations, then isn't the obvious explanation for this that organizations are (paradigm) persons? *Aggregation* assumes 'the normative status of any collective entity is identical with the normative status of the individuals that compose it' (p.15). Thus, intentional predicates are properly applicable to organizations because organizations are aggregates of persons to whom such predicates are properly applicable.

Dan-Cohen rejects both personification and aggregation. In doing so, he tells a story familiar in recent organization theory. Organizations are in Dan-Cohen's terms 'large, goal-oriented,

---

[12] It has been pointed out to me by Rex Martin that Hohfeld's scheme includes as basic legal relations powers and immunities, liabilities and disabilities, and that freedom of expression may perhaps be more plausibly seen as an immunity, creating a disability on the part of governments ('Congress shall make no law ... '). I take the point, though whether it will make any substantive difference to the force of the argument developed in this paper I do not at present know. I leave that hostage to fortune.

[13] Cf. *RPO*, esp. Pts I and II. Cf. also my Critical Notice.

permanent, complex, formal, decisionmaking, functional structures'
(p.31). Many of these features render absurd personification—
persons are not large (not in that sense), permanent, complex (not in
that sense), formal (or not in that 'Weberian' sense), or (*pace* Aris-
totle, but that is a whole different story) functional. Aggregation is
eliminated by the fact that formality produces 'impermeab[ility]'—
'events and actions, directed at and affecting the organization, may
have [difficulty] in "getting through it" and affecting in similar ways
particular individuals' (p.35). Complexity produces 'opaque-
ness'—'it [is] hard to "see through" [the organization]: it is difficult to
trace the decisions and acts of the organization to particular individuals' (p.36). Even goal-orientedness is accompanied by 'goal displacement' (pp.36–7) and 'recalcitrant instrumentality' (p.37). I shall
assume the failure of the strategies of personification and aggregation
in what follows.

Second, Dan-Cohen presents a useful four-fold taxonomy of
rights. There are two paradigms in the law for the justification of legal
decisions—the paradigm of social utility and the paradigm of individual autonomy. A distinction may be drawn between original rights
(rights A has out of concern for A: ORs) and derivative rights (rights
A has out of concern for B: DRs) (p.58). A may also rest a claim on
a right without himself or herself having one—A may rely on B's
right, as in subrogation in insurance litigation, or invoke B's right,
as in guardianship cases (ibid.). The two classifications of rights cut
across each other. To explain that, Dan-Cohen introduces alongside
autonomy rights (ARs) the notion of a 'utility right' (p.79: UR), 'a
legal right justified by considerations of utility' (ibid.). A legal right
may thus in theory be one of four kinds—OAR, DAR, OUR, DUR.
At the risk of taxonomical overload, I should say that each of these
rights may be a right or a freedom in the sense of the Charter
distinction.

1.6   The Standard Objection to Freedom of Commercial Expression

With all of this background in place, let us then turn to the standard
objection to the inclusion of commercial expression within the coverage of s. 2(b) of the Charter. The classic Canadian statement of the
objection comes from Estey J. in the *Jabour* case:

The freedom of expression with which the court is here concerned of course has nothing to do with the elective process and the operation of our democratic institutions, the House of Commons and the provincial legislature. We are indeed speaking about the right of economic freedom of speech, the right to commercial advertising. It can hardly be contended that the province by proper legislation could not regulate the ethical, moral and financial aspects of a trade or profession within its boundaries. (pp.44–5)

Rehnquist J. (as he then was) of the US Supreme Court has expressed the view more pungently:

The Court insists that the rule it lays down is consistent even with the view that the First Amendment is 'primarily an instrument to enlighten public decision-making in a democracy'. I had understood this view to relate to public decision-making as to political, social, and other public issues, rather than the decision of a particular individual as to whether to purchase one or another kind of shampoo. (*Virginia Board* 787)

Nor do I think that those who won our independence, while declining to 'exalt order at the cost of liberty', would have viewed a merchant's unfettered freedom to advertise in hawking his wares as a 'liberty' not subject to extensive regulation in the light of the government's substantial interest in attaining 'order' in the economic sphere. (*Central Hudson* 595)[14]

On this view, constitutional coverage and protection for expression have their historical and doctrinal roots in a relation to individual autonomy and the democratic process, neither of which have anything to do with advertising and economic activity generally. We may deploy the vivid metaphor of the 'market-places of ideas', but that market-place is constitutionally different from the economic market.[15]

[14] Mill made the same point: 'The so-called doctrine of Free Trade ... rests on grounds different from ... the principle of individual liberty' (*On Liberty*, Everyman, 150–1). Callaghan J. in *Klein* (539), Rowles J. in *Griffin* (335), and McKay J. in *McLean* (184–5) are other Canadian judges to have expressed the same sentiments. It needs to be noted that Rehnquist J.'s primary motive in phrasing the objections is quite different from mine. He is concerned to defend strenuously states' rights against interference from the federal Government. The same motive is evident in Higginbotham CirJ's dissent in a liquor advertising case. He votes to uphold a Mississippi restriction on such advertising because 'I would not have thought it the role of the courts to quarrel with a state legislature's regulatory pushes and shoves of its own economy' (*Dunagin*, at 755).

[15] As Lorraine Weinreb has aptly said: 'Like a snake swallowing its tail, the reality of market relationships is validated through its own metaphorical image. The metaphor invites us first to understand the role of expression through certain presuppositions about the market and then to apply that understanding to the market itself. The weakness of this procedure is that those presuppositions about the market are no longer unquestioned.' ('Does Money Talk?', 341)

I believe this objection is fundamentally sound, and the remainder of the paper is an attempt to give it some philosophical support.

2 COMMERCE AND ORIGINAL AUTONOMY RIGHTS

The Supreme Court has approved by incorporation into its decision in *Ford*[16] a three-fold account of the values served by the constitutional coverage and protection of freedom of expression:

1. Freedom of expression is essential to intelligent and democratic self-government.

2. Freedom of expression protects an open exchange of views, thereby creating a competitive market-place of ideas which will enhance the search for truth.

3. Expression is valued for its own sake, seen as an aspect of individual autonomy. Expression is to be protected because it is essential to personal growth and self-realization.[17]

The first and third of these values seem to me to be obviously functions of what are in Dan-Cohen's scheme Original Autonomy Rights, paradigmatically possessed by natural persons. Individual autonomy underlies the first, Meiklejohnian value of participation in the democratic process. The 'people' by whom and for whom there should be government are natural persons. Those for whom growth and self-realization are fundamentally valuable are also natural persons. 'Personal growth' does not refer to physical increase in size, but expansion and enrichment of intellectual and emotional faculties and capacities. The liberty to participate in an open exchange of views also seems to me primarily a value for natural persons, although, since it figures prominently in the rationale for constitutional coverage of commercial expression, it will need (and will have) fuller discussion of its underlying logic. Given the failure of the aggregation and personification strategies, it is not possible for corporations, the

16 At 617, reaffirmed in *Irwin Toy* at 612.

17 The wording is taken from R. J. Sharpe's recent article on commercial expression, and is a variation on the well-known four-part analysis of T. Emerson. The four 'values' that freedom of expression protects—maintenance of a system of free expression is necessary (1) as assuring individual self-fulfilment, (2) as a means of attaining the truth, (3) as a method of securing participation by the members of the society in social, including political, decision-making, and (4) as maintaining the balance between stability and change in society. Cf. 878–9. As Dale Gibson has recently argued ('Case Note', 344–5), there are plenty of reasons for disquiet about the Court's adoption of these official values without getting near the issue of commercial expression. I do not consider those issues here.

prime purveyors of commercial expression, to argue for an OAR to constitutional coverage of their commercial expression based on the values of self-government and self-realization.[18]

Peculiarities of the fact-situations in the litigated cases blur this point, and the issue is worth some analysis.

2.1 Professional Advertising

A large number of the key cases in the area of commercial expression have been constitutional challenges to statutes regulating the professions, which typically have put restrictions of some severity on the ability of such professionals to advertise their services.[19] Lawyers, dentists, optometrists, and pharmacists all have litigated such cases. These cases all involve corporations of a quite idiosyncratic kind— the individual natural person who for pragmatic reasons of taxation status incorporates himself or herself as a professional corporation. Part of the way in which an autonomous natural person may promote self-realization is through the choice and pursuit of a career, especially one as intellectually complex and financially profitable as a traditional profession. There is a lot of not wholly misplaced hand-wringing in the *Klein* decision about the travails of a struggling young lawyer and the need to advertise to obtain a foothold in the profession.[20] All the same, the underlying issue is still thoroughly economic: advertising regulation of the kind impugned is a very effective entry-barrier for new professionals, and as such serves considerably to reduce the level of competition for the services provided and thus to reduce economic efficiency.[21]

[18] In *Re RJR–MacDonald*, the challenge in Quebec to the Tobacco Products Control Act (S.C. 1988, C. 20), the cigarette companies in fact do seem to be claiming an OAR to self-expression: 'The applicants complain that the Tobacco Products Control Act deprives them of their right to communicate with their consumers and to compete among themselves' (479; see also 495). I find the claim extreme. I note also the fallacy of Chabot J.'s reasoning in striking down the Act in quoting Dickson CJC in *Big M Drug Mart*, Wilson J. in *Jones* and *Morgentaler* as sources for the doctrine that commercial expression is a form of self-fulfilment. The first two are freedom of religion cases; the latter has to do with criminalization of abortion. Each of these issues are central issues of self-fulfilment for natural persons, and the use of them as precedents for commercial expression by tobacco companies is wholly question-begging.

[19] In Canada, *Klein and Dvorak, Grier, Griffin*, and *Rocket* have all come within this category. The list in the USA is equally long.

[20] Contrast the Ontario Court of Appeal in *Rocket*; they are rudely dismissive of the crude self-promotion of the principals in that case, despite upholding their appeal. The advertisements in question 'serve no public interest' (Dubin ACJO at 659); they are 'distasteful, pompous and self-aggrandizing' (Cory JA at 679).

[21] Cf. Strauss, 52; McChesney, 360–5, 374–8.

None the less, if the paradigm of self-expression and self-realization is, as it traditionally is, the artist, then these professional advertising cases are misleadingly borderline. Compare the status of an individual professional corporation with an ordinary business, small or not, which has the taxation status of a sole proprietorship. Valerie Ford, after whom the celebrated case is indexed, operated a wool shop as a sole proprietorship. However much sympathy one may have with her personally, and no matter how much personal satisfaction she derived from running her wool shop, the wool shop is still a commercial business, and part of the economic market-place, not the 'market-place of ideas'.[22] And so it is with the professional corporation. The personally expressive aspects of the professional corporation are contingent. The situation in the case of the artist is the reverse. Artistic expression is intrinsically non-commercial, and becomes so only by choice. In fact, the more that art becomes commercialized, the more suspicious folks become of its artistic status. We forgive Margaret Atwood her material success, because her art seems in no way to have suffered. We do not forgive the successful lawyer his or her material success; we give them our business.

2.2   Newspaper Vending Box Cases

In two recent cases, the US Supreme Court in *Lakewood* and the BC Court of Appeal in *Victoria* have reached opposite results in cases concerning restrictions imposed by cities on the erection of newspaper vending boxes on city property. It is a commonplace that the fact that a newspaper company makes a profit from selling newspapers in no way interferes with any constitutional right it may have to freedom of expression or of the press. But does it follow that any restriction on the sale of newspapers is a restriction on freedom of expression, it not being disputed that the freedom to publish is in part

---

[22] Likewise, it seems from the US Supreme Court case report in *Prune Yard* (77) that, in one of the classic shopping-centre leafletting cases in the USA, the PruneYard shopping centre is a sole proprietorship of one Fred Sahadi. No matter how much personal satisfaction Mr Sahadi gets from being the owner of a suburban shopping-centre, it does not seem to me that the corporate status of PruneYard Shopping Center Inc as an artificial and not a natural person is the slightest bit affected by the nature of its taxation status. Jim Weinstein pointed out to me at the conference that Lochner, whose case in the US Supreme Court is regarded as the paradigm of judicial intervention into the economic process, was a baker and a small business-person. Protection of small businesses was a concern of the US Court at the time.

the freedom to have one's publications purchased and read? The majority in *Lakewood* decided that indeed the periodic licensing requirement imposed by the City of Lakewood for the establishment of newsboxes on city property 'was sufficiently threatening to freedom of expression to invite judicial concern'. White J. in dissent vigorously rejected this claim, arguing that 'the placement of newsracks on city property is not a protected activity under the First Amendment'. The BCCA in *Victoria* paralleled this reasoning. Although the court noted that, after *Irwin Toy* it can no longer be claimed, as it was by the trial judge in the instant case, that 'the Charter was not designed to protect the economic interests of a large national newspaper', the court also warned that 'it is important to consider carefully the scope of the freedom of expression as it applies to this case since failure to do so may have the effect of trivializing this fundamental freedom' (p.7). While a complete ban on newspaper circulation clearly would be an infringement of freedom of expression, restrictions like those of Victoria and Lakewood seem to affect only, if at all, the economic interests of the newspaper publisher. While the presence of a profit motive cannot be a bar to constitutional coverage, since many political speakers, for example, are paid for speaking, none the less the distinguishing feature of these cases is that the only motive is the profit motive of increased circulation.[23] To talk about the autonomy right to self-realization on the part of the *Globe & Mail* being infringed by the Victoria restriction seems grotesque anthropomorphism, however strong the coverage and indeed protection needed for editorial decision-making.

2.3　Corporations and Political Advertising

Corporations through campaign contributions and through the expression of opinion can become major players in the political game. It might seem that simply because the opinion being expressed is political it must be constitutionally covered; in the nature of the case any participation in the political market-place of ideas is a locus for the freedom of expression value of self-government. However, despite the majority decision in *Bellotti*, the assertion is not obviously true. Again, the point is not that any accompanying economic motive

---

[23] Paradoxically, the Victoria ordinance with its outright ban seems less expression-threatening than the Lakewood ordinance with its discretionary licensing. As Brennan J. for the majority in *Lakewood* argued (781–3), the control exercised by a licensing authority may amount to prior restraint.

disqualifies the expression from coverage. Rather, the case of corporate political expression, as White J. in dissent in *Bellotti* well realized, raises in acute form aggregation problems for any claim of an autonomy right. He wrote:

The Court holds that the First Amendment guarantees corporate managers the right to use not only their personal funds, but also those of the corporation, to circulate fact and opinion irrelevant to the business placed in their charge and necessarily representing their own personal and collective views about political and social questions. I do not suggest for a moment that the First Amendment requires a State to forbid such a use of corporate funds, but I do strongly disagree that the First Amendment forbids state interference with managerial decisions of this kind. (p.803)

There are circumstances under which association in a corporate form may be viewed as merely a means of achieving effective self-expression. But this is hardly the case generally with corporations operated for the purpose of making profits. Shareholders in such entities do not share a common set of political or social views, and they certainly have not invested their money for the purpose of advancing political or social causes or in an enterprise engaged in the business of disseminating news and opinion. (p.805)

Rehnquist J. adds: 'Although a newspaper corporation must necessarily have the liberty to endorse a political candidate in its editorial columns, it need have no greater right than any other corporation to contribute money to that candidate's campaign.' (p.825) I find these comments persuasive. Not only do corporations lack any original autonomy right to the expression of political views; they also cannot derive one by aggregation from the views of the individuals in the management, nor in the shareholders.

I am no more impressed by *Pacific Gas*. Pacific Gas was required to provide a forum for views opposing those which it had for some time itself been expressing in flyers mailed along with its bills. The US Supreme Court found that, notwithstanding property rights to relevant space, 'compelled access' penalizes and deters the expression of ideas and forces speakers to tailor their speech to opponents' agenda, thus infringing Pacific Gas's freedom of expression. The anthropomorphism is again extraordinary. Corporations, in fact, have their cake and eat it. As White J. points out (p.819), the common law was generally interpreted as prohibiting corporate political participation. As a result, the SEC's rules permit corporations to refuse to submit for shareholder vote any proposal which concerns a general economic, political, racial, religious, or social cause that is not significantly related to the business of the corporation or is not within its control.[24] It is illogical to allow an appeal to the non-political nature of corporations to permit them such a refusal, and then to accept them as fully autonomous participants in the political process with full constitutional coverage of their political freedom of expression.

2.4   Corporations and Language Rights

The Supreme Court was misled by the mixed case which started it down the road to s. 2(b) coverage of commercial expression, the Quebec Language Charter case of *Ford*. There are palpable reasons in Canada why there should be both covered and protected freedom of expression in our two official languages. A law which proscribes the use of one of those languages in the public arena is therefore immediately, and rightly, suspect. The Court rightly remarked that 'language is a means by which a people may express its cultural identity. It is also the means by which the individual expresses his or her personal identity and sense of individuality' (p.604). But note that we are here again thinking primarily of natural persons. I find it hard to see how a shoe store, a wool shop, a tailor and dry cleaner, a florist, or a cheese distributor each have 'a personal identity and sense of individuality' which gives them an OAR to advertise in the language of their choice. It is hardly a coincidence that the *Ford* factual narrative refers to these businesses impersonally (as we say) as 'it'.[25] The political demands to strike down a repudiation of one official language have seduced the Court into an unjustified extension of constitutional coverage to commercial expression under s. 2(b).

In short, in all of these kinds of case, there are concomitant elements which drive in the direction of constitutional coverage and protection—the professional as individual; the newspaper as contributor to political expression; the political nature of some corporate expression; the corporation as user of an official language. But, however acceptable the actual behaviour in question, it does not follow, either from any one of these cases alone or from some set of them collectively, that a commercial corporation has an original autonomy right to freedom of commercial expression.

---

[24] As noted by White J., *Bellotti* at 825.
[25] The report does make a point of referring to 'Valerie Ford, carrying on business under the firm name and style of Les Lainages du Petit Mouton Enr.' (p.583); I have, however, commented on the sole proprietorship issue already: cf. p.102, n.22 above.

3   COMMERCE AND DERIVED AUTONOMY RIGHTS

The previous section talked about original autonomy rights. What about derived autonomy rights, the case where A has a right based on a right of B? 'In order for an organization to have a DAR, it must have the protection of some OAR as a goal, and the DAR must be thought conducive to the pursuit of that goal' (Dan-Cohen, 74). There are some well understood paradigms for a DAR to freedom of expression. A journalists' association may invoke the right to free-dom of expression of one of its members. The organization here plays a purely procedural role (Dan-Cohen, 62). A university, or a uni-versity staff association, may have a DAR to academic freedom in the name of protecting the OAR to academic freedom of its staff.[26]

There are decided cases of freedom of expression which are like this. In civil rights era cases in the USA, the NAACP won two important decisions. The Supreme Court had ruled in 1886 in *Santa Clara Co* v. *So Pac RR* that corporations were 'persons' for purposes of the due process and equal protection clauses of the Fourteenth Amendment, but denied that corporations were 'citizens' for pur-poses of the privileges and immunities clause. The principle was specifically applied in *Grosjean* in 1935 to freedom of the press under the Fourteenth Amendment. The Court had also clearly ruled in 1938 in *Hague* that, while an ordinance forbidding the distribution of printed matter and the holding of public meetings violated the rights of individual union members to freedom of speech and of association, the CIO, as a corporation, could claim no such rights. None the less, in 1958, the Court ruled in *NAACP* v. *Alabama* that the NAACP had standing to assert the personal rights of its members under the Fourteenth Amendment to carry out lawful activities, and thus that it was constitutionally protected from having to hand over its member-ship lists. In 1963 in *NAACP* v. *Button*, the NAACP benefited from a ruling that 'although petitioner is a corporation, it may assert its right and that of its members and lawyers to associate for the purpose of assisting persons who seek legal redress for infringement of their constitutionally guaranteed rights'.

---

[26] But caution must still be exercised: 'The multiplicity of organizational goals, the phenomenon of goal displacement, as well as organizational tendencies toward self-aggrandizement, all complicate the task of maintaining full correspondence between an organization's DAR and its underlying individual autonomy right' (*RPO*, 77). I ignore these complications here.

Another plausible source of derived autonomy rights in the context of freedom of expression are unions and picketing. Canadian courts have held that picketing can be covered by s. 2(b) of the Charter. Hutcheon JA's dissent in the BCCA hearing of *Dolphin Delivery* thought that peaceful picketing is an exercise of the right of freedom of expression: 'in this case', he said, 'the picketers would be expressing the opinion that they do not approve of Dolphin Delivery performing work for Purolator Courier' (p.203), and that 'picketing of an ally would be an exercise of the right of freedom of expression guaranteed by the Charter' (p.205). Esson JA for the majority upholding the injunction against picketing was more cautious:

Not all picketing is a form of expression. The facts of each case must be examined to determine whether it is, in substance, a form of expression or something else ... From the evidence which is before us, it appears that the picketing was not of a kind which had as its purpose or object the conveying of information or opinion, or of persuading anyone to a point of view, or any purpose or object which could reasonably come within the term 'expression'. (p.212)

The Supreme Court as far as concerns s.2(b) agreed with Hutcheon JA:

In any form of picketing there is involved at least some element of expression. The picketers would be conveying a message which at a very minimum would be classed as persuasion, aimed at deterring customers and prospective customers from doing business with the respondent ... The injunction against the picketing has imposed a limitation on a Charter freedom. (pp.186, 189)

However, the union's appeal was dismissed after s. 1 analysis. Both of these kinds of case turn on issues very different in substance from commercial expression—the political aspirations of blacks in the USA, and of workers to form protective associations. Commercial advertising is only contingently advertising to form an association; most cases are nothing of the kind.

A third sort of case where DARs are arguably involved is freedom of information litigation. An individual may have the right to know what is being said about him or her in some repository of personal information. Citizens may also have some more diffuse 'right to know' concerning matters of political relevance. It is at least plausible to suppose that such an OAR may transfer over to an investigative journalist, although the weaker any explicit principal/agent-type relation, the weaker the derived right. Such cases deserve a fuller discussion than being merely noted, but I move on anyway. The new element that these cases introduce is the right to *receive* an expression of some kind—the information about oneself, for example. We will come shortly to consider how far cases of freedom of commercial expression may be based on a right to receive information.

4　COMMERCE AND UTILITY RIGHTS: THE SEARCH FOR TRUTH

I have said nothing so far about the second of the three approved (by the Supreme Court of Canada) values supporting freedom of expression, the value of the search for truth. Freedom of expression, recalled, protects an open exchange of views, thereby creating a competitive market-place of ideas which will enhance the search for truth. This approved value raises in a sharp form issues which will preoccupy us for the remainder of this essay. The search for truth value is different from the other two in that it does not fit the autonomy paradigm; it is an instrumental value. Truth is a good, and activities are valued because they are instrumental towards that good; they do not in themselves express that good as self-expressive activity in itself expresses the good of self-expression. Thus in terms of Dan-Cohen's distinction between autonomy rights and utility rights, the search for truth value will yield utility rights, not autonomy rights.

This fact has one immediate advantage—the conceptual barriers to corporations as possessors of such rights are low. Organizations in principle clearly may have DURs just in case they contribute to social welfare. What of OURs? Can only persons have them? One might think so, because the individual's happiness is what gives that individual a OUR, and organizations cannot be 'happy' in that sense. Dan-Cohen argues, however, that this individualism is misleading. In classical maximizing utilitarianism, A's increased happiness is not valuable as such, but valuable because of its contribution to overall social welfare. Classical maximizing utilitarianism is thus, as its critics have pointed out, not a respecter of individual persons. In that case, the OURs of a person have a derivative quality to them, and therefore the status of organizations within the paradigm for utility 'is not essentially different from that of individuals' (p.81). In short, for Dan-Cohen,

There is nothing in the paradigm of utility that would necessarily, as a matter of principle, limit the range of rights given to organizations and prevent the law from assigning to them utility rights that are coextensive with, or indeed even broader than, those given to individuals. (*RPO*, 82)

The only aspect of the search for truth value that is interestingly relevant to freedom of commercial expression will concern cases that do not overlap with the other two values. That is to say, if freedom of commercial expression in some actual legal decision would already be underwritten by one or other of the freedom of expression values identified, the decision is of less jurisprudential interest. However, I have been trying to argue that the other two values provide only conceptually shaky support for the constitutional coverage of commercial expression. The reliance of corporate expressers on the search for truth value is therefore crucial to the case for freedom of commercial expression, and an appreciation of the jurisprudential issues the value raises equally crucial. In fact, the decided cases reveal that this value is relied on extensively as the ground for requesting constitutional coverage for commercial expression. Let us then turn to considering the cases in more detail.

5   THE PROTECTION OF THE RIGHTS OF LISTENERS

The standard argument for the thesis that the search for truth value yields both constitutional coverage and constitutional protection for commercial expression is to claim that the commercial speaker or expresser relies on the listener's right to receive the information in question. Where, as is typically the case, the commercial expression is an advertisement, the right of the listener is conceived of as a right to have the informational content of the advertisement. This right is a utility right, resting on the claim that the listener has a valued end to which the information contributes, that end being the chooser's own welfare. The classic statement of the argument in Canadian constitutional adjudication is by Cory JA (as he then was) for the majority of the Ontario Court of Appeal in *Rocket*.

Advertising permeates to an almost overwhelming extent the daily life of the community ... Advertising must play a significant role in the choice of products purchased ... The consumer has a right to as much helpful information about the products offered as he or she can get ... [The] choice of products or a method of their utilization can have important consequences not only for the consumer but for the environment and thus for all members of the community. Governments and public-spirited organizations may wish, by means of commercial messages, to warn the community of the dangers of polluting the air and water by the use or misuse of certain products.

Every aspect of living from the acquisition of food and drugs to transportation and shelter requires the consumer to make choices. The lower the income of the consumer the greater the importance of the choice and the greater the need for information and guidance. Frequently that guidance can only come from advertising messages. The right of the consumer to receive information is important in today's society.

So long as a free market for goods exists in our society then truthful and factual commercial messages will have an important role to fulfil. They are important enough to warrant protection under s. 2(b) ... The useful information society may obtain from commercial messages is so important and the potential benefits so great that they must come within the protective ambit of s. 2(b). (pp.664–5, 671)

The same theme runs throughout the case law and academic commentary where freedom of commercial expression has been upheld against restrictions on advertising and further quotation would be otiose.

It is important to keep track of terminology here. There is a three-fold distinction between: (*a*) a general Hohfeldian right to be treated with respect and not lied to, a right which has as its correlative a general duty to be truthful; such a right may secure restrictions on false or fraudulent advertising, for example: (*b*) a specific Hohfeldian right to know certain information, which creates upon the part of the information-holder a duty to disclose, as in contracts *uberrimae fidei* where a full duty to disclose material facts overrides the normal principle of *caveat emptor*: and (*c*) a Hohfeldian liberty or freedom to participate in an exchange of information with a correlative 'no-right' on the part of some other party as regards the exercise of the freedom, which freedom may require as part of its protective perimeter a duty not to restrict such participation and a correlative (claim-)right that there not be such restriction; the freedom of neighbours to disagree over politics on a street corner is an example of such a liberty, and rights to specific amounts of time for party political broadcasts come in this latter protective category.

The woolly nature of the language in Cory J.'s opinion about the 'right of the consumer to receive information' do not make me confident that the distinction between (*a*), (*b*) and (*c*) is being observed. None the less the distinctions are extremely important: the soundness of any argument for freedom of commercial expression based on listeners' rights depends upon them, as I shall now show.

Under the regulation of the Royal College of Dental Surgeons of Ontario impugned in *Rocket*, dentists were not permitted to advertise either office hours or languages spoken. Suppose a native speaker of Gujerati with limited English; such a person has a definite interest (I purposely use a non-committal word) in knowing whether there are any Gujerati-speaking dentists in their neighbourhood. A dentist now attempts to claim that they have a right in the general sense (we do not yet know which specific Hohfeldian right it is) to advertise that they speak Gujerati, a right denied them by the College, and they seek to have the College regulation declared covered by s. 2(b) of the Charter. How can one translate the interest on the part of the citizen into the specific freedom of commercial expression on the part of a dentist, a freedom to advertise derived from some original right possessed by the postulated native speaker of Gujerati?

In Hohfeldian terms the story must go as follows. The Hohfeldian right the citizen possesses, on the usual account, is a freedom to make informed economic choices. This freedom must in part be protected by a general right to truth in advertising (right (*a*) above), with a correlative duty on the part of the advertiser to be truthful and not misrepresent (not to say that they speak Gujerati when they do not). But that general duty and right are not enough to ground a right to access to the information about languages spoken: the general right and duty are conditional—if the dentist chooses to advertise the languages spoken, the advertisement must be truthful; no saying 'Gujerati spoken here' when command of the language is restricted to a few simple sentences. In order to yield a right sufficiently strong to be borrowed by a commercial advertiser to cover their freedom of commercial expression, the right of the listener must be a claim-right to have the information. Only if the citizen has the right to have the information will it be wrong for the government to forbid the possessor of the information to give it to the citizen.

But now there are serious difficulties. In the first place, the standard conception among economists of the role of information in the free market is that information, too, is and should be a commodity. It is a part of free market theory based on the principle of *caveat emptor* that governments should regulate at best minimally the provision of information, leaving the market itself to generate the pressure to provide information in terms of the efficient functioning of the market. In such a spirit free-marketeers strenuously object to what they see as overregulation on the part of the SEC in the USA with its precise and detailed disclosure requirements with regard to the launching of new issues. There is, in short, a fundamental incoherency here. Supporters of freedom of commercial expression object to restrictions on their advertising on the grounds of a listener's right to receive information. But if listeners really do have such a claim-right, then the advertising corporation possesses, not a liberty to provide the information, but a *duty* to disclose information, a duty of the kind which in other circumstances supporters of the free market wholly repudiate. In order to mean what its supporters want it to mean, the supposed *freedom* of commercial expression can be derived only from a listener's right to have information which is strong enough to negate that very freedom by imposing upon it a duty to provide information. A listener's right to receive information cannot coexist with a speaker's freedom to provide information only when and where they wish.

This argument may seem far too narrow. It relies on attributing to the listener a right to have a specific piece of information. But, it may be said, such a reliance is question-begging. First, the interest of the listener on which the corporation's freedom of commercial expression is based may not be a set of specific rights to specific pieces of information, but simply a general and diffuse interest in having all the information necessary to make informed economic choices.[27] Doubtless consumers do have such a diffuse interest. But it is too weak an interest for the structure to be erected on it; if the interest were a genuine claim-right, the burden of disclosure that would then be placed on corporations would be enormous. Society's diffuse interest in a well-functioning market allows various kinds of withholding of commercial information, to do with plans for company development, for example, information on results of mineral surveys, information on the state of research projects, information on the reasons for departures of personnel, and so forth. Argument for disclosure of information is always argument for disclosure of specific information in specific circumstances—if research indicates a particular product, a pharmaceutical drug for instance, is harmful and the manufacturer withholds the information from users, the users' right to have the information is well grounded. The majority in *Dunagin* makes a relevant argument here:

[27] I owe this objection to Susan Feagin.

The commercial speech doctrine was created primarily out of concern in protecting consumers and the information they receive. If it were true that consumers are now being inundated with commercial information about liquor in contravention of the state's interest, the values behind the commercial speech doctrine would not be very much threatened. (per Reavley CirJ, at 751)

That is, if I understand the argument aright, too much, or the wrong kind of, information may impede enlightened economic choices as much as too little. Thus, if the value promoted by commercial expression is the capacity to make enlightened economic choices, it does not necessarily follow that a non-regulated market in information is the proper regulatory regime.[28]

Second, it may be argued[29] that the main argument for freedom of commercial expression is a 'get government off the peoples' backs' argument. Restrictions on advertising are unwarranted interferences in what should be the free exchange of information between corporation and consumer. Thus to think in terms of a right to know and a duty to disclose is wrongheaded. The matter is one of a liberty on the part of the corporation to provide the information if it wishes, and an equal liberty on the part of the consumer to listen to the information if they wish, or to present incentives to the corporation to provide the information if the corporation is reluctant to do so. This is of course one picture of how a market in information can operate, and regulation of advertising certainly is incompatible with it. But the picture is not responsive to my present argument; it is a *petitio principii*. It assumes that the corporation is a possessor of liberty rights of equal standing with the individual consumer. But the truth of that claim cannot be assumed, for precisely what we are presently investigating is the possibility of an argument from listeners' interests to exactly that claim as a conclusion. If we already know that a corporation is a bearer of an original liberty right to give or withhold information, then regulation of advertising or forced disclosure are interferences with that liberty. But *ex hypothesi* we do not know this. We are seeing whether such a liberty right can be founded on listeners' interests of

[28] Feary (p.56) represents the interest in making enlightened economic choices as a kind of welfare right to basic goods—a curious argument for an avowed libertarian to present. While such an argument is attractive in a case like *Virginia Board*, where the availability of pharmaceutical drugs is at issue, it seems most implausible for, e.g., tobacco or hard liquor. The right to inflict lung cancer, heart attacks, or cirrhosis of the liver on oneself, whatever kind of right it may be, is surely not a welfare right.

[29] Cf. Rotunda, 'Commercial Speech', *passim*.

some sort. A liberty on the part of a listener, for example to watch or turn off a TV advertisement, once the advertisement may be permissibly shown, does not bear at all on whether the advertisement may be properly regulated in the first place. One cannot get from my liberty to turn off a beer advertisement directly to the wrongfulness of regulations on how beer may be advertised. Only if I have a claim-right to know that drinking such-and-such a beer will increase my rate of success in singles' bars is it an unjustified interference with the breweries' freedom of commercial expression to restrict them from telling me so.

As Burt Neuborne has rightly said in a recent paper, the listener is a new player in the First Amendment/s. 2(b) game.[30] Traditional freedom of expression theory has concentrated on the speaker or expresser. Neuborne gives a much more plausible interpretation of the supposed listener's right to receive information. In the standard argument as used by Cory J. described above, in Neuborne's words, 'a hearer-based interest is borrowed by a commercial speaker lacking any personal toleration-based First Amendment [or s. 2(b)] interest'. The result is 'a form of derivative First Amendment [or s. 2(b)] protection', which is 'quite different from the traditional speaker-centred doctrine. ... The commercial speaker relies solely on the hearer's purely instrumental interests in receiving information that is of help in making efficient choices' (26). As Neuborne emphasizes,

the interests of the newly recognized participants in the speech process are predominantly instrumental. Under existing theory, hearers have an instrumental First Amendment [s. 2(b)] interest in receiving information that will inform them and/or help them operate systems based on choice more efficiently. (25)[31]

If Neuborne's descriptions are correct, and I think they are, then the right of the listener at issue here is an original utility right, and the right of the advertiser which is based on borrowing that UR is a derived utility right, subject to the qualification in section 4 above on the very notion of an OUR. But if that is so, then some crucial jurisprudential questions have to be faced. The primary one is the

[30] 'Capital Markets', 24–5. He also identifies as other new players the bystander (for example, the woman whose rights are infringed by pornography), the conduit (the broadcaster, for example), and the government regulator. These latter complications are not adressed here.

[31] In fact, Neuborne writes 'efficient *and autonomous* choices', 'more efficiently *and autonomously*'. I consider below the significance of these additions.

question, to which I shall now turn, of whether utility rights are the kinds of rights which should enjoy constitutional coverage at all.

6   UTILITY RIGHTS AND CONSTITUTIONAL JURISPRUDENCE

In the judicial opinions and the academic literature supporting constitutional coverage for commercial expression, one argument appears over and over again. It is well put in Henry J.'s spirited dissent in *Klein*:

> It is still policy in this society to encourage the operation of underlying market forces to bring about the best allocation of economic resources in the interests of producers, consumers and labour alike . . . It is inconceivable that the system can work without advertising by entrepreneurs. (p.505)

The argument boosts the importance of advertising to the economic market-place. Advertising fosters two market goals—aggregate economic efficiency and consumer opportunity to maximize utility. As has been remarked by US critics of recent US Supreme Court decisions, the policy of encouraging advertising *qua* economic policy is certainly intelligible. But, as an argument for constitutional coverage of commercial expression, the argument is broken-backed. From the fact that aggregate economic efficiency and consumer opportunity to maximize utility are important, and even paramount, *policy* values, it simply does not follow that they deserve constitutional coverage, let alone constitutional protection. Nor does it follow that the criteria of economic efficiency and utility maximization are central to constitutional jurisprudence.

One must not give the impression that the specialists are unanimous in their support of recent court decisions on economic grounds. Here are some of the issues that economists have debated as relevant to whether this case or that case was rightly decided—whether advertising restrictions are inefficient by obstructing market entry; whether economic considerations support a worthwhile distinction between solicitation and advertising; whether information is something that can be suitably commodified, so that it makes sense to address issues of the delivery of information in economic terms; whether government regulation is inevitably and inefficiently stifling of entrepreneurship; the problems of agency capture and consequent market failure in a regime of government regulation; the fact that excessive control of securities information has produced a black market in information which allows even more opportunity for manipulation by the insider than would weaker actual regulation; whether the predominance of the sophisticated investor in capital formation renders tight regulation of the primary capital market inappropriate; the difficulties of the verification of fraud in primary capital markets; and so on.

These are all of course issues of primary social importance. But, I submit, they are not the stuff of constitutional jurisprudence. Constitutional coverage is paradigmatically the coverage of non-instrumental rights, values which are, in Dworkin's famous metaphor,[32] trumps over considerations of utility. If the determination of a constitutional right is left up to the market, and questions of economic efficiency and utility maximization determine the outcome of constitutional adjudication, we will have violated the heart of a right to constitutional coverage. The roots, both historically and conceptually, of constitutional jurisprudence lie in non- instrumental values and reasoning. To quote Neuborne again:

One dividing line between totalitarian societies and free societies is the noninstrumental approach adopted towards toleration in free societies. The toleration of behaviour associated with respect for human dignity does not have to pay its way in a free society. (p.15, n.46)

Constitutional coverage of expression, the fundamental freedom of expression, both are functions of human autonomy and human dignity, paradigm non-utilitarian notions. The standard arguments for freedom of commercial expression know nothing of such values. The point is well put by Dickson CJC, in fact, in the *Slaight* case, decided subsequent to *Irwin Toy*:

There are many diverse values that deserve protection in a free and democratic society such as Canada, only some of which are expressly provided for in the Charter. The underlying values of a free and democratic society both guarantee the rights in the Charter and, in appropriate circumstances, justify limitations on those rights. (p.427)

A further argument against constitutional coverage for what are fundamentally utility rights is the argument contra *Lochner*ism, or, as we should perhaps now call it in Canada, *Irwin*ism. This is the argument that constitutional decision-making is inherently

---

[32] 'Individual rights are political trumps held by individuals' (*TRS*, ix); cf. also 85.

antimajoritarian. If a question is submitted for constitutional adjudication, it must be a question which admits in principle of an antimajoritarian solution. If the issue is whether a supposed right I have to criticize publicly some policy of the government is genuine and is genuinely mine, then whether I have such a right cannot be determined by whether the majority will ascribe such a right to me. Questions of economic efficiency and utility maximization are not such questions. Jurisdiction over such questions is properly exercised by the legislature, as the seat of majoritarian political authority.[33] When courts, under the specious cover of deciding constitutional questions, decide what are in fact policy questions on policy grounds, they commit the eighth deadly sin of the substitution of the court's own views for those of the legislature on matters of public policy. The point is made in just this form by the District Court which heard Klein's original complaint (cf. *Klein* 538), and the Supreme Court itself in both *Edwards* (44, 51–2) and *Irwin Toy* (625–6).[34] Of course, if one is convinced that the issue of freedom of commercial expression is simply an economic or utilitarian issue, then *Irwin*ism is not as such a systematic deadly sin. The sinfulness is particularized to the question of whether the Supreme Court has done its economics homework, and has got the utility calculation correct. If one has the intuition that *Irwin*ism is a deadly sin in principle in constitutional jurisprudence, then one has appreciated precisely the distinction I am trying to make between economic policy and principled constitutional adjudication.

7   UTILITY RIGHTS AND THE CHARTER

The previous section canvassed general doubts about the position of freedom of commercial expression in s. 2(b) or First Amendment jurisprudence. In this section I look briefly at the Canadian context in particular. I shall suggest that there are plenty of resources within Canadian law for taking a different view from that of the Supreme Court about the Charter's coverage of commercial expression; and

[33] 'Properly' here means 'in accord with principle'. I am not asserting that in any, or even some, given case a legislature is justified in imposing a restriction. Such an assertion would be a matter of the economics of the given fact situation, and I say nothing about such issues here.

[34] It is also the burden of White J.'s dissent in *Bellotti* (804), and Rehnquist J.'s dissent in *Central Hudson* (584).

therefore that the decision of the Supreme Court to take the line that it has taken is a disquietingly political decision.[35]

Whatever may be true about the constitution of other jurisdictions, the Canadian Charter of Rights and Freedoms is not an efficiency-oriented, instrumental document. In the first place, it is a commonplace that s. 7 of the Charter, unlike the Fourteenth Amendment of the US Constitution, contains deliberately no mention of property rights. The Supreme Court in *Irwin Toy* ruled quite explicitly that a corporation cannot avail itself of the coverage and potential protection offered by s. 7 of the Charter. A corporation cannot be deprived of 'life, liberty and security of the person'. The Court, however, does go on to express a reluctance to rule out 'economic rights' altogether from Charter coverage, a wise reluctance in view of its holding in that very case. The Court also in *Amway* turned down a corporation's attempt to invoke the privilege against self-incrimination under s. 11(c).[36] The Ontario High Court in *Aluminum* has also indicated that s. 15 does not apply to corporate entities. I have no knowledge of the extent to which in any actual case a claim for s. 2(b) coverage of commercial expression has been challenged through its conflict with s. 7 and s. 15, but the potential seems there.

Second, also a commonplace, the Charter is not a committedly individualistic document. There is plenty of attention addressed to group rights, in s. 23 about minority language education rights, s. 25 about aboriginal rights, s. 27 about multiculturalism. Section 15(2) concerning affirmative action can also be read as giving rights to the wider community, as can even s. 1 and s. 33, the override clauses. Again, it seems inappropriate to think that the correct position in

---

[35] Somewhat the same line of analysis appears in Lorraine Weinrib, 'Does Money Talk?' Our papers for two different Freedom of Expression conferences in Spring 1990 were written quite independently, despite the overlap of argument. Arguments along a similar line that other sections of the Charter than s. 2(b) may override s. 2(b) have been developed for pornography (cf. Mahoney, 'Canaries in a Coal Mine') and hate literature (cf. Cotler, 'Racist Incitement'). See also the general line of argument in Hutchinson, 'Money Talk'.

[36] On the other hand, in the recent *Wholesale Travel* case, the Court rules that a defendant corporation both has standing to impugn the constitutionality of a statute on the basis that it infringes the rights of a human individual, and is entitled to remedial benefit from a finding that the statute is unconstitutional. Tollefsen (see 'Case Note: *Wholesale Travel*' and 'Ideologies Clashing', 726 ff.) sees this ruling as part of a general drift in the Supreme Court of Canada towards greater protection under the Charter for corporations, and notes that the *Wholesale Travel* ruling goes further than comparable rulings by the US Supreme Court despite the absence of any reference to property rights in the Charter.

cases of freedom of commercial expression must be to protect market individualism.[37]

Finally, there is the complex question of the difference between the Charter and the US Constitution in that there is in the US. Constitution nothing comparable to s. 1. It seems to me that we have to take this difference seriously. The US Supreme Court is inevitably forced to regard First Amendment adjudication as a complex exercise in interest-balancing. It cannot represent First Amendment adjudication as a contest between individual right and public policy, with all the resultant tilt towards individual right, because the prevailing climate of individualism invites decisions which cut a wide swathe through any attempt on the part of a legislature to promote the common good. The US Supreme Court must adjudicate by balancing, and to do that with intellectual integrity it has to pretend that all there are to balance are interests. This is true even if a right within an institutionalized normative system is not an interest to be weighed against other interests in the balance of reasons, but a protected normative position giving courts an exclusionary reason for upholding it.[38] Constitutional adjudication is exactly about the relation between the rules of an institution, and so the protected normative positions or rights they subtend, and the background societal values which the constitution enshrines.

The Supreme Court of Canada, however, can afford to take rights seriously. As Lambert JA said in *Cromer*,

It cannot be correct that the substantive rights and freedoms should be given their most expansive meaning on the ground that all control is supposed to lie in s. 1, while, at the same time, s. 1 is to be construed stringently because it is overriding an infringement of a substantive right or freedom. (p.652)

It is proper to make s. 1 a stringent test, just because it is *rights* under other sections of the Charter that would be overthrown when a putative restriction passes the test of s. 1 analysis. But that does mean that s. 2 must be kept as a section, covering and going a long way

---

[37] There is evidence of such opinions now in the USA. In *Ragin*, provisions of the Fair Housing Act prohibiting indications of racial preference in housing advertisements were held not to violate the First Amendment. Publication of such advertisements indicating racial preference was said not to be protected commercial speech. No reasoning, however, appears in the case report.

[38] For the important distinction between exclusionary reasons and reasons in the balance of reasons, and the role of the former in institutionalized normative systems, see Raz, *PRN*, *passim*, but esp. chs. 1 and 4.

towards, protecting autonomy rights. An expansive interpretation of the section, one which lets in a variety of utility rights as covered and potentially worthy of constitutional protection, will reduce the distinct provisions of the Charter to an amorphous mass. Utilitarian considerations will take over both reasoning about whether some activity is covered under s. 2(b) and whether it is protected by s. 1. As has been noted:

To limit the right or freedom expressed in absolute terms outside s. 1, that is to say, by not according it a scope coincident with the absolute language in which it is expressed, places no onus on the party seeking to uphold the limitation. To view the right or freedom as unqualified and limitations thereon only justifiable under s. 1, on the other hand, forces the party seeking to uphold the limitation to justify it in accordance with the criteria there set out and upon no other basis.[39]

If the thought behind the design of the Charter is that s. 1 has a different role to play in constitutional adjudication from the other sections, then intepreting the other sections so broadly that little is regarded as falling outside their scope makes such a different role impossible, and thus subverts the inherent design of the Charter.

I have tried to argue that freedom of commercial expression can only be interpreted as a utility right in Dan-Cohen's sense. It is true that, as such, it may as easily be possessed by a corporation as by an individual. The problems that there are in attributing autonomy rights to corporations do not arise for utility rights. But the result is a severe weakening of the case for constitutional coverage for commercial expression. Economic efficiency and utility maximization are not either historically or conceptually paradigm constitutional values. To admit them into constitutional jurisprudence invites architectural difficulties of both a formal and a substantive kind. In particular, it does violence to the unique character of the Canadian Charter of Rights and Freedoms to say that such economic and individualistic values are enshrined within it.

8   THE POLITICS OF THE CHARTER

Let us consider one last attempt to establish a jurisprudential basis for the coverage of commercial expression through the Charter. It may

---

[39] Watt J. in *Smith*, at 421.

be thought that I am misrepresenting the instrumentality of the supposed constitutional coverage for freedom of commercial expression. Consider the following passage from Henry J.'s dissent in *Klein*, which we may call the Yuppie Argument:

The proper functioning of the market therefore requires that the best possible information be communicated by producers and distributors to users of their products who are seeking the best combination of price, quality and volume. But the matter does not end there. The health of the economy is of critical importance to all members of a society whose access to products is essential to their life-styles, and whose very livelihood depends in the long run on a healthy economy. (p.506)

The idea embodied in the Yuppie Argument is not merely that utility maximization deserves coverage as a proper consequentialist goal. The idea rather is that the ability to make selective purchases in a free market is a basic freedom of choice which is as essential to individual autonomy as are any others of the expressive acts traditionally closer to the core of constitutional coverage of freedom of expression. The Argument assumes the fundamentality of *homo consumens* over *homo cogitans*. If thinking or reasoning are the fundamental human activities, then reason might well in principle conclude that controls on advertising are rationally preferable to no regulation. The Yuppie Argument pre-empts any such possibility by arguing for a fundamental right to consume.

The importance of the Yuppie Argument is this. In so far as a corporate advertiser borrows from a listener to the advertisement this right to autonomous economic choice in a free market, it is borrowing an autonomy right. From such a borrowing, the corporation would thus possess for itself, not a disparaged DUR, but a DAR, thus making significantly stronger its claim for freedom of commercial expression. Moreover, the case for such a view on traditional grounds is powerful.

When the ground rules are changed by the introduction of hearer-centred freedom of speech protection, the government may not deny certain hearers access to information of use to them in making informed and autonomous choices in order to protect the lowest common denominator of potential hearers, at least not in the absence of an overwhelming showing of necessity.[40]

[40] Neuborne, 'Capital Markets', 55.

To interfere with the free market in order to protect the weak is an unacceptably paternalistic taking from the strong: or so it is argued.[41]

The point of mentioning the Yuppie Argument is not because I think it is a sound argument. The Argument's value is that it brings out for even the blind to see what underlies the thought that commercial expressers have a derived autonomy right to freedom of commercial expression, derived from the autonomy right of listeners to information that will promote their ability to make choices in the market. What underlies that thought is quite clearly a libertarian political morality.[42] Again, the issue is not whether such a political morality is philosophically acceptable, though I clearly have views on that topic. The issue is whether constitutional adjudication in general, and Charter adjudication in particular, can or should adopt such a political morality as a guiding light.

Here is Rehnquist J. again in dissent in *Virginia Board*, a well-known passage:

The Court speaks of the importance in a 'predominantly free enterprise economy' of intelligent and well-informed decisions as to allocation of resources. While there is again much to be said for the Court's observation as a matter of desirable public policy, there is certainly nothing in the U.S. Constitution which requires the Virginia Legislature to hew to the teachings of Adam Smith in its legislative decisions regulating the pharmacy profession. (p.784)

It is not possible to escape the political consequences of the recognition of freedom of commercial expression, and the Yuppie Argument makes them clear. As Allan Hutchinson has recently argued:

The current legal system protects corporate commercial speech through the fictions that corporations are people and that corporations are private. People speak, corporations do not; they are the artificial mouthpieces of accumulated power ... Through the sanctioning by [*Ford*] and its

---

[41] Cf. again here Rotunda, 'Commercial Speech and the Platonic Ideal'; he relentlessly hammers away at the paternalism inherent in regulation of advertising, even regarding the decision on advertising to children in *Irwin Toy* as unacceptably paternalistic.

[42] This is quite evident in the discussions of freedom of commercial expression by Feary, Rotunda, and McGowan. I note here my debt to the latter's careful and thorough analysis of the US case law and academic commentary.

predecessors of the idea that economic fictions are rights-carrying entities at least as deserving of protection and concern as human beings, law constitutes a particular social and normative reality ... By positing corporations as having a similar status as citizens, it ignores the exercise of enormous power by corporations over the lives of citizens ... The state cannot claim that its refusal to regulate is a neutral act. Corporations are creatures of the state and any redistributive consequences attributable to corporate activity implicate the state.[43]

But the libertarian world view is only one view. As Callaghan J. in *Klein* acknowledges, 'the "free market" is itself only an idea, one particular idea, about how goods should be distributed in society ... there is nothing to prevent society from deciding some other method of allocation is better' (p.535). Supporters of the free market face the following dilemma. Either constitutions are not political documents, and stand outside the political process as embodiments of all that is fundamental and universal about the rights of natural persons: in which case there are insurmountable problems in granting to free market interests constitutional coverage and protection. Or constitutions are irretrievably political documents: in which case, while a libertarian view of a constitution is now a fully qualified player in the interpretative game, it cannot claim any right to be the correct interpretation; any political interpretation is, just so far, on a level with and in principle as good as any other political interpretation. The dilemma does not of course refute libertarianism, and is not intended to do so. It is intended only to reinforce a constant theme of this paper, that theoretical argument is required to justify constitutional protection for commercial expression: such protection is not an automatic consequence of the fact that political morality extends to individual human persons the freedom of expression. It is intended also to show that the obstacles to such an argument are higher than is typically acknowledged.

As before, in addition to these general points, there are specific points to be made about the Charter and the political morality inherent in it. I said very early on that Dickson CJC's remarks about purposive interpretation of the Charter were belied by the Court's practice in commercial expression cases. We can now see why this is

---

[43] 'Money Talk', 16–17. Similar sentiments are expressed by Wayne MacKay, 'Talk', 741, 745, 763–4.

so. He speaks in *Oakes* about 'the inherent dignity of the human person' and 'commitment to social justice and equality' (p.225). In the recent *Slaight* case, which, as noted, post-dates *Irwin Toy*, there is more of the same:

It cannot be overemphasized that the adjudicator's remedy in this case was a legislatively-sanctioned attempt to remedy the unequal balance of power that normally exists between an employer and employee. Thus in a general sense this case falls within a class of cases in which the governmental objective is that of protection of a particularly vulnerable group, or members thereof. (p.423)

Dickson quotes himself in *Edwards* to the effect that 'in interpreting and applying the Charter the courts must be cautious to ensure that it does not simply become an instrument of better situated individuals to roll back legislation which has as its object the improvement of the condition of less advantaged persons' (p.49). 'The courts must be concerned to avoid constitutionalizing inequalities of power in the workplace and between societal actors in general', he continues in *Slaight*. 'On the facts of this case, constitutionally protecting freedom of expression would be tantamount to condoning the continuation of an abuse of an already unequal relationship' (p.424) And he quotes himself again, from the *PSERA (Alberta)* reference case, at 199: 'a person's employment is an essential component of his or her sense of identity, self-worth and emotional well-being.'

All these remarks represent a very different conception of the values inherent in the Charter from the insouciant coverage of commercial expression in *Ford* and *Irwin Toy*. It will of course be pointed out that these values came into play in *Slaight* as part of the s. 1 analysis and not in the determination of the extent of s. 2(b). The Court in *Slaight* is quite clear that the administrator's order does interfere with the radio station's freedom of commercial expression. But is it not odd to load the whole task of respecting these values on to s. 1? Also, should not the court take cognizance of the fact that to advocate an unregulated market when inequalities of power are already in place is indeed to perpetuate those inequalities? The decisions in *Irwin Toy* and *Slaight* represent a jurisprudential schizophrenia, with *Irwin Toy* representing a set of values that appears hardly anywhere else in the Charter and in particular not among the values that the Court really regards as finally dispositive of cases. The defects of the Court's purposive approach in the commercial expression cases is that it does not follow the Court's perfectly proper articulation of the purposes of the Charter.

9   THE 'ARCHITECTURE' OF COMMERCIAL EXPRESSION REVISITED

9.1   The 'Contextual' Approach

I have indicated already that I think the constitutional coverage of and protection for freedom of expression, and *a fortiori* freedom of commercial expression, must have an architecture. It must be rooted in a principled theory of freedom of expression. There are important consequences of this point for the adjudication of freedom of commercial expression cases. In *Edmonton Journal*, a freedom of the press case concerning reporting restrictions in matrimonial cases under Alberta law, Wilson J. distinguishes between two general approaches to applying the Charter to actual cases. The first she calls the 'abstract' approach; it begins from general historical and jurisprudential principles and works down to the particular case before the court. She refers to Cory J.'s opinion in the same case as a paradigm of the 'abstract' approach. The other approach she refers to as 'contextual'. The virtue of such an approach, she claims (pp.583–4) 'is that it recognizes that a particular right or freedom may have a different value depending on the context ... a right or freedom may have different meanings in different contexts'. She exemplifies this approach in her opinion in *Edmonton Journal*, and in general she argues for the superiority of the 'contextual' approach. I believe this thought is deeply mistaken.

There are two particular reasons, if one regards constitutional jurisprudence as an 'architectural' structure of principles, for being sceptical about freedom of commercial expression. The first concerns the danger of excessive subdivision. In the USA, as Schauer has pointed out,[44] offensive speech, child pornography, defamation, invasion of privacy, as well as commercial speech, all have separate standards within First Amendment jurisprudence for the upholding or not of legislative restrictions on speech. Moreover, the level of protection accorded to commercial speech by the US Supreme Court

[44] 'Architecture', 1198.

is significantly lower than for other forms of speech.[45] Schauer properly objects to the U.S. approach as follows:

In the most profound sense, the First Amendment stands as a barrier to excess subdivision. It is opposed to particularized decision-making ... The First Amendment, if it is to be more than a platitude, must operate to preclude what would otherwise be, taken particularly, reasonable judgments to restrict. Thus, rendering impermissible certain otherwise permissible distinctions in speech value is central to understanding both how and why the freedom of speech operates. (pp.1198–9)

In Canada, the institutionalized separation in the Charter of coverage issues under s. 2(b) and protection issues under s. 1 means that the danger of excess subdivision is great. However, not only does the Supreme Court not see the danger coming. It even glorifies contextualization and fragmentation. In *Rocket*, the Court's actual holding is unremarkable; it follows consistently the precedent of *Ford* and *Irwin Toy*. McLachlin J.'s *obiter* commentary, signalling as it almost certainly must how the Court intends to proceed in future cases, is remarkable. Her objection to the US Supreme Court's categorization approach is exactly not that of Schauer's: her objection is that the US Court does not go far enough. She fully embraces Wilson J.'s 'contextual approach' from *Edmonton Journal*, quoting approvingly the above remarks about different values and different meanings in different contexts.

I submit that the contextual approach in fact evinces a serious misunderstanding of the nature of constitutional rights and freedoms. In principle the aim seems laudable—to tailor the decision in the case to the particular circumstances of the facts of the case. Such contextualized decision-making is often associated with making judgments in equity. But the whole point about a court of constitutional law is that it is not a court of equity. Constitutional protections represent broad and impartial protections extended to every citizen as such and as of right, in virtue of their equal dignity as persons. A

---

[45] In *Bates*, the US Supreme Court held that the overbreadth doctrine of the First Amendment did not apply to commercial speech. In the recent *Blue Cross of Philadelphia* case, the 3rd Circuit court held that allegedly defamatory statements made in comparative advertising campaigns were commercial speech to which the heightened protection of the First Amendment's actual malice standard did not apply. In a recent holding on commercial speech, the *Fox* case, the Supreme Court has held that any restriction on commercial speech no longer has to meet even a 'least restrictive means' test. It is sufficient if there is a reasonable 'fit' between the Government's ends and the means chosen to accomplish those ends. This is a low hurdle indeed.

constitutional protection in the nature of the case, unlike the substantive guidelines for an administrative tribunal, for example, is not something which should be applied to greater or lesser degrees according to the circumstances of the case. We do not think, for example, that there are some groups of people which deserve more protection under s. 7 or s. 15 than others—if the idea of differing degrees of constitutional protection under s. 15 were perfectly palatable, the argument that discrimination by sexual orientation should also be included in s. 15 would not even get off the ground. Yet it clearly does, whether or not it is in the end a sound argument. The fact that we might intuitively want to claim that the advertising of a professional corporation should be treated differently than the advertising of a large multinational conglomerate should clue us in to the fact that we are really not here dealing with constitutional coverage and protection of fundamental individual freedoms at all, but something much more akin to perfectly unproblematic regulation of a market economy in the general public interest. If I am right in these latter remarks, then the points made above about the impropriety of using constitutional law to substitute the court's own views for those of the legislature on issues of regulating the economy are weighty.

9.2   The Danger of Dilution

The second danger concerns the real possibility of the dilution of s. 2(b) coverage by allowing almost anything to count as 'expression'. The danger is well put by Taggart JA in *Victoria*:

It is important to consider carefully the scope of the freedom of expression as it applies to this case since failure to do so may have the effect of trivializing this fundamental freedom. It is all too easy to accept all suggested infringements and limitations as incursions on fundamental freedoms and democratic rights and then to justify them through the application of s. 1 of the Charter. If that easy course is followed it will give s. 2 and perhaps other sections of the Charter a penumbra of trivia which will obscure the real substance of the freedoms and rights.[46]

Similarly, Callaghan J. argued in *Klein*:

If commercial speech serves a function completely different from that associated with non-commercial speech; if its too-close association with political

[46] At 7–8. The danger is also recognized by the US Supreme Court in *Ohralik*, at 456.

speech threatens to devalue the latter and the First Amendment; if it is of less moment; if it is entitled to less protection, and to regulations formulated with less precision, than that to which non-commercial speech is entitled; then surely the question arises, why protect it at all?

As Schauer has remarked, the 'problem comes when resistance to change is diminished by new applications, and has the effect of weakening the rule even with respect to the old applications'.[47] In this context, the essentially open invitation issued by Lamer J. (as he then was) in *Re s. 195.1(1)(c)* at 110 to challenge under s. 2(b) any provision of the *Criminal Code* of Canada which makes speech or expression part of the *actus reus* of an offence is disturbing.[48] Furthermore, one cannot help feeling that the enthusiasm with which McKinlay J. in the Ontario H Ct hearing of *Edible Oil* accepted the argument that to choose the colour of margarine was an exercise of freedom of expression covered by s. 2(b) suggests there is some force to the dilution or devitalization argument. The argument, grantedly, is not knock-down. As McGowan has pointed out, 'the argument must still hinge on the notion that the speech causing the [diluting] (here commercial speech) is somehow demonstrably less 'valuable' than the speech we seek to protect. The argument is thus irrelevant until one proves that the speech at issue is less valuable' (p.443). Again, we have brought forcibly before us the need for a proper theoretical rationale for constitutional protection for commercial expression, and the impropriety of quick arguments from the fact that commercial expression is expression.

In short, the lesson of recent opinions in freedom of expression cases is that the Supreme Court of Canada is contemplating fragmentation and subdivision of constitutional coverage and protection to a degree far beyond that contemplated by even its opposite number to the south. I am entirely behind the attempt not to follow slavishly the Supreme Court of the USA or the House of Lords, and to create a 'made in Canada' jurisprudence for our particular social context. But to attempt to outdo the US in the fragmentation and dilution of constitutional protection is a bankrupt way to carry out the project of the Canadianization of Canadian law.

[47] 'Architecture', 1194.

[48] Particularly so, in that in all likelihood virtually all the challenged sections are likely to survive s.1 analysis. The Court's work will then be all philosophical. I will be the last to deny the value of philosophical analysis. However, the public costs of leaving it to philosophers are far less than leaving it to Supreme Court litigants and judges.

10 CONCLUSION

I want to end with an objection and an acknowledgment of a (and surely there are more) glaring omission.

The above remarks have proceeded on two different levels. On one level I have been making a series of remarks about Canadian institutional history and what it signifies. On another level I have been arguing more generally about constitutional jurisprudence. The objection may be urged[49] that this latter discourse is 'essentialist' in an odd way. It supposes that there are *a priori* principles of such jurisprudence, whereas the truth of the matter is that citizens can put into their constitution anything which as a matter of fact they want to put there. No such *a priori* principles are available. I acknowledge the objection, but I think that it raises issues which fall outside the scope of the present paper. The view defended here, in so far as it is not a view simply about institutional history, is a version of 'legal formalism' in Ernest Weinrib's sense.[50] The objection is a version of legal positivism. The issue between my view and the objection is a special case of the general conflict between positivistic and anti-positivistic theories of law. It is as appropriate for me here to ask the objector for a defence of positivism as it is for the objector to ask for a defence of my 'legal formalism'. Neither is appropriate.[51]

The omission is at the level of political theory. I have indicated that I do not believe the foundational political morality for the Charter to be frontier libertarianism. But I have not said what I believe it is. I appealed at one point to Hutchinson's dialogic communitarianism. But it seems to me that other forms of communitarianism less socialistic might be appealed to, as might perfectionist liberalism. The task of working out the deep jurisprudential underpinnings in political philosophy for a Charter doctrine of commercial expression must be undertaken on some other occasion.

[49] It was by Les Green at the conference.

[50] 'Legal formalism claims that juridical relationships can be understood as embodying ... an "immanent moral rationality" ... Juridical relationships so conceived are intelligible by reference to themselves and not solely as the translation into law of an independently desirable political purpose.' ('Formalism', p.957). The 'purpose' of course may be as well the protection of individual autonomy as it may be aggregate economic efficiency.

[51] For the extent to which I believe antipositivism is plausible as a theory of law, see *Norm and Nature: The Movements of Legal Thought*, Clarendon Law Series (Clarendon Press, Oxford, 1992).

I have argued in this paper, first, that there can be no OAR to freedom of commercial expression on the part of commercial express-ers, since OAR's belong to natural persons and commercial express-ers are not natural persons. I then considered the possibility that commercial expressers may have an OUR to freedom of commercial expression, but raised doubts about the very idea of constitutional coverage for utility rights. I also argued that Canadian law itself, consistently with my view of constitutional law, gives plenty of evidence that the primary function of the Charter is to cover and protect autonomy rights, not utility rights. I went on to consider an argument that, if sound, would seem to give to the commercial expresser a DAR from the listener's right to exercise autonomy by making informed economic choices in a free market system. I pre-sented such an argument as the prescription of a libertarian political philosophy. I questioned whether it is the proper purpose of the Charter to defend a libertarian political theory, and I argued that in any case there is plenty of evidence that the Charter is not so designed. Finally, I raised the twin dangers with respect to constitutional rights and freedoms of fragmentation and dilution. I argued that the Su-preme Court's present commitment to a contextual approach to freedom of expression exposes Canadian citizens to both these dangers, and is therefore to be repudiated.

In short, it seems to me that the Supreme Court's present position on freedom of commercial expression not only has no sound basis in the theory of political morality; it also involves distorting the legal realities of the Canadian Charter. Each of these reasons are sufficient to express deep regret at the Court's continuing posture.[52]

Table of Cases

Canadian Cases

Attorney-General of Quebec *v.* La Chaussure Brown's Inc. *et al.* [Indexed as: Ford *v.* Quebec (Attorney-General)] (1988) 54 DLR (4th) 577

Attorney-General of Canada *v.* Law Society of British Columbia (the *Jabour* Case) (1983) 137 DLR (3d) 1

[52] I am grateful for helpful comments subsequent to the Conference from Jack Iwanicki, Charles Silver, and Fred Schauer, and especially the students in my seminar on Freedom of Expression and the Charter at the University of Alberta, Fall Term 1990.

Attorney-General of Quebec *v*. Irwin Toy Ltd.; Moreau *et al*., Interveners [indexed as Irwin Toy Ltd. *v*. Quebec (Attorney-General)] (1989) 58 DLR (4th) 577

Dolphin Delivery Ltd. *v*. Retail, Wholesale & Department Store Union, Local 580 *et al*. (1984) 10 DLR (4th) 198 (BCCA)

Edmonton Journal *v*. Attorney-General for Alberta *et al*.; Attorney-General of Canada, Intervener (1989) 64 DLR (4th) 577

Jones *v*. R (1986) 28 CCC (3d) 513

R *v*. Amway Corp. (1989) 56 DLR (4th) 309

R *v*. Big M Drug Mart Ltd (1985) 18 CCC (3d) 385

R *v*. Edwards Books & Art Ltd. (1986) 35 DLR (4th) 1

R *v*. McLean (1986) 28 CCC (3d) 176

R *v*. Morgentaler (1988) 37 CCC (3d) 449

R *v*. Oakes (1986) 26 DLR (4th) 200

R *v*. Smith (1988) 44 CCC (3d) 385 (OHC)

R *v*. Wholesale Travel Group Inc (1991) 84 DLR (4th) 161

Re Aluminum Co. of Canada Ltd. and the Queen in right of Ontario; Dofasco Co., Intervener (1986) 29 DLR (4th) 583

Re Canadian Newspapers Co. Ltd. and City of Victoria *et al*. [indexed as Canadian Newspapers Co. *v*. Victoria (City)] (1989) 63 DLR (4th) 1 (BCCA)

Re Cromer and BC Teachers' Federation (1986) 29 DLR (4th) 641

Reference re Public Service Employee Relations Act (Alta) (1987) 38 DLR (4th) 161

Reference re ss. 193 and 195.1(1)(c) of the Criminal Code (Man) (1990) 56 CCC (3d) 65

Re Grier and Alberta Optometric Association *et al*. (1987) 42 DLR (4th) 327 (ACA)

Re Griffin and College of Dental Surgeons of British Columbia (1988) 47 DLR (4th) 331 (BCSC)

Re Griffin and College of Dental Surgeons of British Columbia; Attorney-General of British Columbia, Intervener [indexed as Griffin *v*. College of Dental Surgeons of British Columbia] (1989) 64 DLR (4th) 652

Re Institute of Edible Oil Foods *et al*. and the Queen (1987) 47 DLR (4th) 368 (OHC)

Re Institute of Edible Oil Foods *et al*. and the Queen; Ontario Milk Marketing Board, Intervener [indexed as Institute of Edible Oil Foods *v*. Ontario] (1989) 64 DLR (4th) 380

Re Klein and Law Society of Upper Canada: Re Dvorak and Law Society of Upper Canada (1985) 16 DLR (4th) 489 (OHC)

Re RJR-MacDonald Inc. and Attorney-General of Canada; Attorney-General of Quebec, Intervener; Re Imperial Tobacco Ltd. *v*. Attorney-General of Canada; Attorney-General of Quebec, Intervener 82 DLR (4th) 449 (1991) (QSC)

Re Rocket *et al.* and Royal College of Dental Surgeons of Ontario *et al.*
(1988) 49 DLR (4th) 641 (OCA)
Retail, Wholesale & Department Store Union, Local 580 *et al.* v. Dolphin
Delivery Ltd. (1986) 33 DLR (4th) 174
Royal College of Dental Surgeons of Ontario *et al.* v. Rocket *et al.* [indexed as
Rocket v. Royal College of Dental Surgeons of Ontario] (1990) 71 DLR
(4th) 68
Saumur v. City of Quebec and Attorney-General of Quebec [1953] 4 DLR 641
Slaight Communications Inc. (Operating as Q107 FM Radio) v. Davidson
(1989) 59 DLR (4th) 416

US Cases

Bates v. State Bar 433 US 350 (1977)
Board of Trustees of the State University of New York *et al.* v. Todd Fox *et
al.* 109 S Ct 3028 (1989)
Central Hudson Gas & Electric Corporation v. Public Service Commission of
New York 447 US 557 (1980)
City of Lakewood v. Plain Dealer Publishing Co. 100 L Ed 2d 771 (1988)
Dunagin v. City of Oxford, Mississippi 718 F 2d 738 (1983) (USCA, 5th Cir.)
First National Bank of Boston *et al.* v. Bellotti, Attorney General of Mas-
sachusetts 435 US 765 (1978)
Grosjean, Supervisor of Public Accounts of Louisiana v. American Press Co.
Inc. *et al.* 297 US 233 (1936)
Hague, Mayor, *et al.* v. Committee for Industrial Organization, *et al.* 307 US
496 (1939)
Lochner v. New York 198 US 45 (1905)
National Association for the Advancement of Colored People v. Alabama ex
rel. Patterson, Attorney General 357 US 449 (1958)
National Association for the Advancement of Colored People v. Button,
Attorney General of Virginia *et al.* 371 US 415 (1963)
Ohralik v. Ohio State Bar Association 436 US 447 (1978)
Pacific Gas & Electric Co. v. Public Utilities Commission of California 106 S
Ct 903 (1986)
Posadas de Puerto Rico Associates, dba Condado Holiday Inn v. Tourism
Company of Puerto Rico *et al.* 478 US 328 (1986)
PruneYard Shopping Center v. Robins 447 US 74 (1980)
Ragin v. New York Times Co 923 F 2d 995 (1991) (USCA, 2nd Cir.)
Robins *et al.* v. PruneYard Shopping Center *et al.* 592 P 2d 341 (1979) (SC Ca)
Santa Clara County v. Southern Pacific Rail Road 118 US 394 (1886)
Securities and Exchange Commission v. Wall Street Publishing Institute Inc.
dba Stock Market Magazine 851 F 2d 365 (DC Cir. 1988)

U.S. Healthcare *v.* Blue Cross of Greater Philadelphia 898 F 2d 914 (1990) (USCA, 3rd Cir.)

Virginia State Board of Pharmacy *et al. v.* Virginia Citizens Consumer Council Inc. *et al.* 425 US 748 (1976)

References

Barendt, Eric, *Freedom of Speech* (Clarendon Press, Oxford, 1987).

Cotler, Irwin, 'Racist Incitement: Giving Free Speech a Bad Name', in David Schneiderman, ed., *Freedom of Expression and the Charter* (Thomson Professional Publishing, Toronto, 1991), 249–57.

Dan-Cohen, Meir, *Rights, Persons and Organizations: A Legal Theory for a Bureaucratic Society* (University of California Press, Berkeley, 1986).

Dworkin, Ronald M., *Taking Rights Seriously*, 2nd edn. (Harvard University Press, Cambridge, Mass., 1977).

Emerson, T., 'Toward a General Theory of the First Amendment' *Yale Law Journal* 72 (1963), 877.

Feary, Vaughana Macy, 'Taking the Right of Freedom of Commercial Communication Seriously', *Journal of Business Ethics* 11 (1992), 47–59.

Gibson, Dale, 'Case Note: *Attorney-General of Quebec* v. *Irwin Toy*', *Canadian Bar Review* 69 (1990), 339.

Hart, H. L. A., *Essays on Bentham* (Clarendon Press, Oxford, 1982).

Hohfeld, Wesley, *Fundamental Legal Conceptions*, ed. W. W. Cook (Yale University Press, New Haven, Conn., 1923).

Hutchinson, Allan, 'Money Talk: Against Constitutionalizing (Commercial) Speech', *Canadian Business Law Journal*, 17 (1990), 2–34.

Jackson, Thomas H. and John Calvin Jeffries, Jr. 'Commercial Speech: Economic Due Process and the First Amendment', *Virginia Law Review* 65 (1979), 1.

MacKay, A. Wayne, 'Freedom of Expression: Is It All Just Talk?' *Canadian Bar Review* 68 (1989), 713.

Mahoney, Kathleen, 'Canaries in a Coal Mine: Canadian Judges and the Reconstruction of Obscenity Law', in David Schneiderman, ed., *Freedom of Expression and the Charter* (Thomson Professional Publishing, Toronto, 1991), 145–79.

McChesney, Fred S., 'A Positive Regulatory Theory of the First Amendment', *Connecticut Law Review* 20 (1988), 355.

McGowan, David F., 'A Critical Analysis of Commercial Speech', *California Law Review* 78 (1990), 359.

Moon, R., 'Lifestyle Advertising and Classical Freedom of Expression Doctrine', *McGill Law Review* 36 (1991), 76.

Neuborne, Burt, 'The First Amendment and Government Regulation of Capital Markets', *Brooklyn Law Review* 55 (1989), 5.

Raz, Joseph, *Practical Reason and Norms* (Hutchinson, London, 1975).

Rotunda, Ronald D., 'Commercial Speech and the Platonic Ideal: Libre Expression et Libre Enterprise', in David Schneiderman, ed., *Freedom of Expression and the Charter* (Thomson Professional Publishing, Toronto, 1991), 319–35.

Schauer, Frederick, *Free Speech: A Philosophical Enquiry* (Cambridge University Press, Cambridge, 1982).

——'Commercial Speech and the Architecture of the First Amendment', *University of Cincinnati Law Review* 56 (1988), 1181.

Sharpe, Robert J., 'Commercial expression and the Charter', *University of Toronto Law Journal* 37 (1987), 229.

Shiner, Roger A., 'Critical Notice of Meir Dan-Cohen, *Rights, Persons and Organizations*', *Canadian Journal of Philosophy* 19 (1989), 661–84.

Strauss, David A., 'Constitutional Protection for Commercial Speech: Some Lessons from the American Experience', *Canadian Journal of Business Law* 17 (1990), 45–54.

Sumner, L. W., *The Moral Foundation of Rights* (Clarendon Press, Oxford, 1987).

Tollefsen, Chris, 'Ideologies Clashing: Corporations, Criminal Law and the Regulatory Offence', *Osgoode Hall Law Journal* 29 (1991), 705.

——'Case Note: *R* v. *Wholesale Travel Group Inc'*, *Canadian Bar Review* 71 (1992), 369.

Weinrib, Ernest J., 'Legal Formalism: On the Immanent Rationality of Law' *Yale Law Journal* 97 (1988), 949.

——Lorraine E., 'Does Money Talk? Commercial Expression in the Canadian Constitutional Context', in David Schneiderman, ed., *Freedom of Expression and the Charter* (Thomson Professional Publishing, Toronto, 1991), 336–57.

5. Freedom of Expression and Choice of Language

LESLIE GREEN

1 THE PROBLEM

In linguistically divided countries, governments often regulate the use of language; they make some languages official, they restrict others, they impose linguistic requirements on educational or professional qualifications, and so on. My question is this: Do sound principles of free expression direct or constrain such regulation?

The issue is a familiar one to Canadians whose federal government requires the use of French and English for certain purposes, and whose provincial governments have often restricted one or the other. Historically, French and languages other than English bore the brunt of deliberate repression, but nationalist governments in Quebec have recently turned the tables and banned, in certain contexts, the use of English and other languages. Quebec's Charter of the French Language, for example, made French the sole official language of that province, and prohibited non-French commercial publicity, firm names and, with certain exceptions, public signs.[1]

In a series of important and highly controversial judgments, the Supreme Court of Canada struck down some of these provisions as inconsistent with the guarantees of free expression found both in the

This paper was first published in *Law &Policy* 13 (1991), pp. 215–229. Versions of this paper were read to a conference on freedom of expression at McMaster University, Hamilton, Ontario, and at the Boalt Hall School of Law, University of California, Berkeley. I am grateful to the participants, and to the editors and referees of *Law and Policy* for helpful criticism.

[1] The Original Act, R.S.Q. 1977, c. C-11, provides that 'Except as may be provided under this act or the regulations of the *Office de la langue française*, signs and posters and commercial advertising shall be solely in the official [i.e. French] language'. Similarly s. 69 prohibits non-French firm names. Section 58 exempts publicity carried in publications circulating in languages other than French, and religious, political, ideological, or humanitarian communications provided that they are not of commercial character (s. 59). Nor does it apply to small businesses of less than four employees, to publicity for the cultural activities of non-French ethnic groups, or to business specializing in foreign or ethnic goods.

entrenched Canadian Charter of Rights and Freedoms and also in
Quebec's provincial human rights statute. These decisions were generally admired by English Canadians and, not surprisingly, deplored
by the Quebec French. In consequence, the government of Quebec
used its power under the Charter to derogate from the free expression
guarantees, a decision that they may, in retrospect, have regretted.
That action quickly polarized public sentiment and was among the
factors making it impossible for Quebec to secure the agreement of all
the majority-anglophone provinces on constitutional amendments
which would have given it more control over its cultural affairs.
Perhaps the linguistic division of opinion on the cases was to be
expected. More surprising, however, was the political division, for the
decisions did not attract much support from liberal and left-wing
academics either. They were disappointed to see the Court protecting
commercial expression and to see it assisting a historically powerful
group (English Quebeckers) against a historically weaker one
(French Quebeckers). Groups who are normally friends of free expression were thus surprisingly hostile to the Supreme Court's defence of it in these cases.

Part of the puzzle is explained by the fact that these cases involved
commercial signs and that there are many liberals whose commitment
to free expression does not reach that far. But it is, I think, quite
wrong to let one's views about commercial expression occlude the
broader issue here. First, some of the grounds on which Quebec
defended its legislation (for instance, that its government enjoyed
'democratic legitimacy', i.e. was elected) would permit the restriction
of non-commercial expression as well. Second, some Quebec
nationalists thought—and still think—that the impugned legislation
did not go far enough in restricting English. Finally, the will to
regulate more broadly was in any case manifest in the proposal of the
Montreal Catholic School Commission to ban languages other than
French from the playgrounds and corridors of their schools. None of
this is resolved by one's views about commercial expression, so by
focusing solely on that aspect liberals lost the opportunity to test their
views more fully.

Still, it is not *obvious* that a sound view of free expression should
protect choice of language. (And here I mean morally, and not
just legally, sound.) Indeed, some Canadians regard that suggestion
as a kind of legalistic joke, rather as if one argued that the
Oleomargarine Act, in requiring margarine to be dyed orange,

wrongfully discriminates on grounds of colour. But I want to suggest that this is mistaken and that free expression does properly extend so far as to protect choice of language.

Principles of free expression protect expressive acts by imposing disabilities or duties on people, and they do so *in order to* protect such acts. The question whether freedom or expression protects choice of language thus needs to be distinguished from a broader question: Are there *any* principles of political morality that direct or constrain the regulation of language?

The questions are importantly different. Governments should not, for instance, act irrationally. Since there is no evidence that Quebec's restrictions on external commercial signs would do more good than harm that is enough to impugn them, at least morally and perhaps constitutionally as well. But that is not an argument derived from free expression. Likewise, it is wrong to pay English-speaking workers more than French-speaking workers when language is irrelevant to the job. But the wrong is one of discrimination, not the violation of freedom of expression. Again, it would be wrong to punish people for speaking French at home. But the evil here is just that in prohibiting a harmless activity it restricts their personal liberty.

Principles of rationality, non-discrimination, and personal liberty will in such ways often protect language use indirectly, as fallout from their central aims. Free expression plays an independent role only if it enhances these protections, if it protects language beyond what can be expected from other principles of political morality (Greenawalt 1989: 9–10). That is the sort of principle I want to explore here.

I follow Scanlon in regarding an expressive act as 'any act that is intended by its agent to communicate to one or more persons some proposition or attitude' (Scanlon 1972: 206). Expressive acts are thus all those that bear the communicative intentions of some agent, whom for sake of simplicity we shall call the speaker. This must not, however, be taken to imply that all expressive acts are speech acts: writing, signalling, playing music, painting, etc. can all be expressive, as can some criminal acts, including acts of terrorism and civil disobedience. Much fruitless debate in political theory is inspired by the narrow language of the First Amendment to the American Constitution which protects 'freedom of speech, or of the press'. This has given rise to many unedifying attempts to distinguish speech and action. In contrast, section 2 of the Canadian Charter, like many other human rights documents, casts the net more broadly to catch:

'freedom of thought, belief, opinion and expression, including freedom of press and other media of communication' (Canadian Charter,
1982). That is, I think, a better way to demarcate the territory. Such
unity as exists in the area flows, not from the fact that these are all in
some obscure sense forms of 'speech', but rather that they are all
expressive.

Generally, an act counts as expressive only if it attempts to get
others to understand or share some proposition or attitude, and only
if it does this communicatively, that is, by trying to get them to
recognize that it is done with that intention.[2] I say, 'proposition or
attitude', because it would be a poor and excessively rationalistic view
of human communication to think that it only serves the communication of truths. The contents of communicative acts are quite diverse: we attempt to communicate to others, not only propositions or
ideas to be believed, but attitudes and values to be shared. In the case
of artistic expression, for example, communicative intent is hardly
ever propositional. Attitudes, values, and dispositions all enter into
our common life in important ways and are transmitted in part
through their expression. In any case, so far as the Charter is concerned, the cognitive and the affective are both accommodated by the
language itself which distinguishes the terms 'thought,' 'belief,' and
'opinion' from the more general notion of 'expression'.

The reasons for protecting such acts are, I believe, several and are
grounded in the interests of speakers, of their audiences, and of the
general public. Attempts to reduce these intersecting and sometimes
competing considerations to a monistic theory have not met with
great success,[3] for a cluster of different kinds of interests is at stake
here. Surely consequentialist considerations, such as J. S. Mill's claim
that free expression promotes knowledge of the truth, have weight

[2] The qualification is necessary because an act can try to get others to share a belief
in some other way. If A wants B to think it is cold in the room, A can achieve this
communicatively, e.g. by telling B that it is cold, or non-communicatively, e.g. by
opening a window and making B cold. The second does not require for its success that
B recognize A's intention in opening the window, and thus is not a communicative act
in the sense under discussion here.

[3] Alexander Meiklejohn, for instance, thought that speech should be protected only
when it can be reliably thought to promote self-government. Thus it excludes commercial radio broadcasts: 'The radio, as we now have it, is not cultivating those qualities of
taste, of reasoned judgment, of integrity, of loyalty, of mutual understanding upon
which the enterprise of self-government depends. On the contrary, it is a mighty force
for breaking them down' (Meiklejohn 1960: 87). What would he have thought of comic
books, pop music, or television?

(Mill 1962: ch. 2). At the same time, it fosters and expresses both collective and individual autonomy: it serves democratic decision making, artistic and cultural endeavor, the expression of individual identity, and so on. Interestingly, the Supreme Court of Canada has explicitly endorsed such a pluralistic account of the grounds of free expression (*Irwin Toy* at 976–7; *Ford* at 712) and that is the view I shall adopt here.

I do want to reiterate, however, that the interests at stake in free expression are not, on this view, just individual ones. They have an important social dimension, recognition of which is, contrary to the allegations of some theorists, deeply rooted in the liberal tradition. Mill, for example, held that: 'Were an opinion a personal possession of no value except to the owner; if to be obstructed in the enjoyment of it were simply a private injury, it would make some difference whether the injury was inflicted only on a few persons or on many' (Mill 1962: 142). But, he continued, the restriction of opinion harms not just the individual but the public interest, and it is not just for the sake of a single speaker that we protect expression. To prevent even one person from speaking is wrong, not mainly because of the value of this liberty to her or to him, but because of the contribution it makes to the common good.

Meiklejohn took the public interest justification even further, denying the speaker's interest any independent moral importance at all: 'What is essential is not that everyone should speak, but that everything worth saying shall be said' (Meiklejohn, 1960: 26). Of course, principles of free expression do not require that everyone should speak; at most they require that everyone has the opportunity to speak or remain silent. And the connection between what is worth saying and what is worth protecting is more complex than Meiklejohn allows. We do not want to claim that a speaker's interest in uttering a banal, commonplace ideal should count for little merely on the ground that, having been said before, its contribution to the public interest is slight. Indeed, a single-minded concern that, as Meiklejohn puts it, 'everything worth saying shall be said', could easily lead to the violation of what we normally think of as paradigm rights of free expression. We do not believe that only those things worth saying should be permitted to be said nor even that scarce resources should be apportioned among speakers according to how socially valuable their views are. Moreover, in some cases we do regard it as important that everyone has an opportunity to speak, even if that means that the amount of time devoted to the worthless and the worthwhile is about the same. Meiklejohn thought his argument a democratic one, but the notion that everyone should speak in fact has deep roots in democratic theory, beginning with the classical Greek notion of *isogoria*. While the public interest is essential to understanding the full importance of freedom of expression, there is also an individual interest that cannot be discounted.

2 MEDIUM AND MESSAGE

There is an objection, however, to thinking that choice of language should be protected by such principles. They protect expressive acts in virtue of their expressive character; but not all features of such acts *are* expressive. For example, it is commonly thought that free expression does not protect the time, manner, or place of expression. Thus the regulation of radio frequencies, or the quality and supply of paper during war time, or the chemical additives present in artists' paints and materials, may all have effects on the character and quality of expressive acts, and may at the margin even inhibit some forms of expression and promote others. But, according to the proposed distinction they would count as regulation of the media of communication only and not of the message itself. These normally bear, the argument goes, on the form rather than content of expression. Likewise, it may be said, whether the medium of expression is French, English, or Cree, the message remains invariant, so restrictions of medium need not offend principles of free expression.

That was how one Canadian court saw the issue. In *Irwin Toy*, a case testing the constitutionality of legislation restricting advertising directed at children, Hugessen, ACJ. introduced a distinction which was to prove pivotal. He said, 'The late Dr McLuhan notwithstanding, message and medium are, in law, two very different things' (*Irwin Toy* at 58). He held that a legislature which regulates or restricts the medium in which some message is communicated is not regulating or restricting the message itself and thus cannot be said to be regulating or restricting any expressive act.

This reasoning also dominates the trial judgment in *Devine* which, though overturned on appeal, nicely puts the objection we now consider. Dugas, J. applied the distinction between medium and message to the case of language: 'Language, after all, is nothing more than a code of written or oral signs, used by those who know it to communicate with each other' (*Devine* at 375). Prohibiting the use of a particular code, he stated, does not therefore interfere with the communicative intention, for any other code might be used to express the same propositions or attitudes. Hence 'Freedom of expression does not include the freedom to choose the language of expression' (*Devine* at 379).

There are many interesting and important aspects of these judgments that we need not consider here. What I do want to focus on is the central distinction between medium and message and the use to which it was put. The reasoning seems to have gone something like this:

1. Only expressive acts are candidates for the protection of freedom of expression;
2. A language is nothing more than a content-neutral code;
3. Thus, restricting the choice of language cannot restrict any expressive act.

Now I have already endorsed (1) and suggested some of the reasons one might have for protecting such acts, so let us turn to (2). The word 'code' which I draw from the judgment is unhappy, suggesting as it does an artificial medium used in place of a natural language. The fact that the same meaning may be borne by a sentence spoken in English and the same English sentence sent over the wire in Morse code would hardly suffice to establish the semantic equivalence of that sentence and its best French translation. There are codes and then there are 'codes'. We must take care not to become enchanted with the jargon of some fashionable linguistic theory. The sense in (2) just amounts to this: it is roughly true that anything that can be said in English can also be said in French. But, as we shall see below, the fact that this is only *roughly* true allowed the Supreme Court of Canada in *Ford* to reject (2) and the inference drawn from it. That result was not too surprising, for there were plenty of other clouds on the horizon for this distinction, at least as a matter of law.

First, medium of communication is expressly mentioned in the Charter as being included in the guarantees of section 2. It is true that, in that context, the central cases of such media are the press and airwaves, but neither the language of the constitution nor the decided cases inhibits its development by analogy. Even if medium is distinct from message, in at least some cases the Canadian constitution finds reasons for protecting both.

Second, the following words of an earlier Supreme Court judgment suggest a view of language as something more than a content-neutral code:

The importance of language rights is grounded in the essential role that language plays in human existence, development and dignity. It is through language that we are able to form concepts; to structure and order the world around us. Language bridges the gap between isolation and community, allowing human beings to delineate the rights and duties they hold in respect of one another, and thus to live in society. (*Reference re: Manitoba Language Rights* at 19)

Finally, and perhaps most important for present purposes, this view of language seemed inconsistent with the very statute the trial judge was attempting to interpret. For its preamble opens with the ringing declaration that 'the French language ... is the instrument by which that people [i.e. Quebeckers] has articulated its identity' (Charter of the French Language, 1977). As Boudreault J. shrewdly observed in the trial judgement in *Ford*, this makes it very difficult to suppose that the *legislators* conceived of language merely as a neutral code and thus that they intended that the Act should regulate its use only in that respect (*Ford* at 724).

So in deciding as it did, the Supreme Court certainly had a reasonable footing: nothing in Canadian law prohibited their finding that freedom of expression includes the freedom to choose one's language and there was enough directing them along that path. But was it, in the end, a wise decision? Can it be defended in principle? I turn now to examine three arguments to that conclusion.

3   A SEMANTIC ARGUMENT

One of the arguments the Supreme Court accepted, and one that has an obvious appeal, is to deny the premise of the objection. If it is wrong to think of a natural langauge as a content-neutral code, then it is wrong to think that regulating the code is not regulating content. Thus, in *Ford* the Court unanimously rejected (2) in the following words:

Language is so intimately related to the form and content of expression that there cannot be true freedom of expression by means of language if one is prohibited from using the language of one's choice. Language is not merely a means or medium of expression; it colors the content and meaning of expression[4] (*Ford* at 748).

The Court thus exploits the inevitable haziness of the boundary between medium and message. That what can be said in French can also be said in English is only *roughly* true because choice of language colours the content and meaning of expression. Language is not, therefore, a content-neutral code.

Was the Court right about that? It is true that the expressive power of language varies, and that exact synonymy may be unavailable in some cases. Considering cultural resonance and sonorities, it would be hard to say that there are no semantic differences between the roughly equivalent idioms, *'filer à l'anglais'* and 'to take French leave'. Language does in such cases colour the meaning of the expression.

But is this sufficiently important and pervasive to bring choice of language under the comprehensive protection of free expression? I do not think so. Valerie Ford's offence, after all, was to have displayed the word 'wool' alongside 'laine' in the window of her wool shop. It is surely not to secure against any possible semantic slippage that we would defend her right to freedom of expression. This is not to deny that such slippage can occur, even in the context of commercial signs. A *'dépanneur'* is not exactly a 'convenience store'. The differences in meaning are real; but they are occasional and do not matter much. If we are about to impose duties and disabilities on people as a matter of general policy, we must make sure that the stakes are high enough to warrant it. To show that language does in some cases flavour the meaning of expression will not warrant adopting a general policy of protecting choice of language just in order to catch such cases of heteronymy. The availability of circumlocutions, or the adoption of some foreign word and terms, would be a satisfactory alternative.

For this reason the tempting analogy with obscenity is misguided. One might initially be inclined to regard choice of natural language as being on a par with choice of tone or force and, reasoning along the lines of the US Supreme Court in *Cohen* v. *California*, argue that to

---

[4] There is in fact a complication in the judgment, for while the above passage suggests that choice of language is protected because regulation of language is regulation of content, the Court also says that the reference in s. 2 to freedom of 'thought', 'belief', and 'opinion' shows that the *Charter's* protections *go beyond* what it calls 'mere content', or at least 'content of expression in its narrow sense'.

restrict language is to restrict a whole mode of communication. But to exclude obscene or vulgar speech from the protections of free expression *is* to remove a distinctive tool, one which might prove useful or even necessary in circumstances that cannot easily be isolated in advance.[5] The potential heteronymy of French and English near-equivalents is neither as pervasive nor as undirectional as the power of vulgar speech, so the analogy is unhelpful. There just is not a general linguistic tone or pragmatic effect that accrues to speaking English in the way that one might be thought to accrue to speaking vulgarly. So while it is certainly true as a descriptive matter that semantic slippage occurs, it is hard to endorse the normative thesis that this is what ought to bring choice of language under the protective umbrella of free expression.

4 AN INSTRUMENTAL ARGUMENT

A better route to the protection of choice of language is surely the instrumental one. Restricting the use of certain languages simply cuts off potential audiences or makes it more difficult to reach them, and that harms one of the core interests underlying freedom of expression on any plausible account.

To take a clear example: suppose a government restricted the language in which political commentary might appear in the newspapers, requiring that all published criticism of its policies to be in Ojibway, while favourable comment could be in any language. What matters here is not the possible semantic slippage, but the closing down of channels of communication by restricting both speakers and their potential audiences.

Now this argument bears, one must concede, less heavily on requirements than on prohibitions. Canada's Official Languages Act of 1969, for example, requires various officials and Government agencies to use both French and English, and Quebec's Charter of the French Language makes wide use of such requirements in order to promote the use of French in the working world. And they do so

---

[5] Cf. *Kopyto* per Corry, JA, at 226: 'Hyperbole and colourful, perhaps even disrespectful language, may be the necessary touchstone to fire the interest and imagination of the public to the need for reform, and to suggest the manner in which that reform may be achieved'. Per Goodman, JA, at 259 'The expression of an opinion which may be lawfully expressed in mild, polite, temperate, or scholarly language does not become unlawful because it is expressed in crude, vulgar, impolite, or acerbic words'.

partly for instrumental reasons that are ultimately based on audience interests. The Charter of the French Language, for example, seeks to establish French as the normal working language of commerce and Government in Quebec thereby directly protecting the substantial interest that the francophone majority has in being able to understand communications of all sorts. It is important to note, moreover, that the audience interest is not exhausted by the immediate benefits of intelligible communication. It is well-known that patterns of language use will also have substantial secondary effects on people's life chances, including their opportunities for education, occupational advancement, and social and geographic mobility.

In the case of intended audiences, speakers will generally aim to communicate in a language that the audience understands. We should not, however, assume on that basis that everyone's interests can be best served without any regulation of language at all. The free market can fail in language as it can elsewhere. When the audience is linguistically fragmented there may be complex problems of coordination involved in finding a common language. When the minorities are bi- or multilingual there is the potential for collective action problems in sustaining the use of minority languages, and there is the risk of majorities oppressing linguistic minorities. None the less, it is easy to see why speakers have an interest in the freedom to use the language that they feel is best suited to their audiences. Unintended audiences also have an interest in the intelligibility of communication, however. It matters not only what others say to you, but what is being said generally. Since speakers have weaker, and in some cases no, incentives to serve the needs of unintended audiences, this may provide another reason for required use.

Might one argue that forcing someone to use a language other than the one he or she would otherwise use in that context limits the speaker's choice of medium and therefore must, at the very least, call for a persuasive justification? To assess this claim, one must investigate more closely the structure of speaker's interest. In part, it derives from the intended audience's interest in intelligible communication: the intention to reach them is frustrated if one cannot do so. But we are not now considering a case in which the speaker's audience is limited by prohibition, but only a case in which the potential audience is expanded. A requirement that commercial signs and publicity be in French as well as another language, for example, does not inhibit the speaker's capacity to communicate with the audience at which the signs are directed. Could a speaker wish that a certain audience *not* receive a particular communication? No doubt, although plausible cases will turn, not on freedom of expression, but on the right to privacy.

The instrumental argument for protection for choice of language is thus an important one, though it may fail in some circumstances. Widespread individual bilingualism, or even the availability of convenient translation, lessens its force. A more discriminating policy of protecting choice of language where it is necessary for effective communication might answer to the same concerns and have fewer costs. And over time languages can be learned, so the need to do so stimulates investment in language learning. Quebec's language regime weighs less heavily on the anglophone community now than it would have done twenty years ago. Such are the limitations on the instrumental argument, so it seems unlikely that general protection for choice of language could be completely defended on instrumental grounds alone.

5 AN EXPRESSIVE ARGUMENT

There is, however, a third and independent reply to the objection that language is merely a non-expressive medium of communication, one noticed though not much elaborated by Supreme Court. Choice of language should be protected because it is an expression of identity and individuality:

It is, as the preamble of the Charter of the French Language itself indicates, a means by which a people may express its cultural identity. It is also the means by which the individual may express his or her personal identity and sense of individuality (*Devine* at 375).

This is an aspect of the romantic, as opposed to rationalist, tradition in free expression. Its context is not the forum or market-place of ideas, but rather the organic relations between an individual and his or her community. I say this is an independent objection, for it may succeed even where the instrumental argument fails, and even when the thesis of content-neutrality holds.

Returning now to the argument set out in section 2, above, we can see a further mistake. The thesis of content-neutrality does not show that a natural language is 'nothing more than a code'. Compare the following inference:

4. A flag is a piece of cloth,
5. Therefore, a flag is nothing more than a piece of cloth.

The conclusion does not follow because a flag can be both a piece of cloth *and* something more than a piece of cloth. Likewise, a language can be a content-natural code *and* something more than a content-neutral code. If the something more makes it expressive, then the fact that it may also appropriately be described as a neutral code cannot change that.

To be still more precise, we do not even need to show that language is something more than a neutral code in order to justify the protection we want to accord it. Even if it were true that a natural language is nothing but a neutral code, and even if restrictions on language would not restrict the potential audience, the argument given above would still be invalid. For consider:

6. Choice of language is a candidate for protection of free expression only if it is an expressive act;
7. Language is nothing more than a neutral code;
8. So, freedom of expression does not include freedom to choose language of expression.

Even if (7) were true, (8) would still not follow, for (8) is about *choice* of language, and not about language itself. The error thus lies not just in the arguable falsehood of (7), but in an equivocation between 'language' as an abstract entity and 'choice of language' as an act. Invoking again our earlier analogy, we might compare:

9. Waving a flag is a candidate for protection of free expression only if it is an expressive act;
10. A flag is nothing more than a piece of cloth;
11. So, freedom of expression does not include freedom to wave a flag.

Here, the fallacy is patent, for the supposed truth of (10) plainly has nothing whatever to do with (11). A flag, like a language, is not an act of any kind, let alone an expressive one. But *speaking* a particular language, like *waving* a flag, is indeed an act and very possibly expressive. Thus, the purported distinction between medium and message is irrelevant. The fact, if it be one, that medium and message are two different things does not even begin to show that choice of medium cannot be intended to convey a message.

It is important to distinguish between the expressive argument defended here and the semantic argument that I rejected above.

Suppose it were permitted to say 'Long live a free Quebec!' but prohibited to say '*Vive le Québec libre!*' What is most significant: the fact that there are nuances of meaning, historical and cultural resonances, poetics of sound present in 'Vive' but absent from 'long live'? I doubt it. The significance of choice of language here lies not in what it says but in what it shows. Saying it in French is a doubly political act, for the propositional content is backed up by the fact that the utterance displays the legitimacy of the language and its relation to nationhood.

The argument we are pursuing is a normative one, but it does depend on certain social facts. It fails unless it actually is the case that language use has a social or individual meaning. This cannot be established *a priori*. But at least in Canada there is plenty of evidence that in many contexts it does. As I said earlier, the expressive function of language was not missed even by the legislators. The Charter of the French Language begins, 'Whereas the French language, the distinctive language of a people that is in the majority French-speaking, is the instrument by which that people has articulated its identity'. . . .[6] What is distinctively nationalistic here is merely the suggestion that a group of people who are only 'in the majority' francophone constitute '*a* people'. The reality in a pluralistic society is that language choice permits each people to express its identity. The way this is done is largely a social creation, governed by convention, context and history.[7] In Canada, choice of language bears a number of meanings, of which ethnic identification and political affirmation are the most important.

[6] The equally authoritative French version reads: 'Langue distinctive d'un peuple majoritairement francophone, la langue française permet au peuple québécois d'exprimer son identité'.

[7] The context-dependence of meaning provides an illustration of the limits of abstract argument in political philosophy. One cannot resolve these issues solely by appeal to our concepts of 'expression', 'language', etc. It is no thesis of mine that choice of language is always, universally, or necessarily, protected by principles of free expression. I am merely trying to identify cases in which it is. Does this need to attend to context suggest that language is ill-suited for protection by constitutionally entrenched rights? I make no claims about that here: the question turns on the nature of rights, and on moral and institutional arguments for putting certain matters beyond the reach of ordinary politics. The issues are well known. But I might note one general point. One might object that, in view of the social character of our interests in language, it *must* be an inappropriate matter for rights, for they only protect individuated interests. The objection is too hasty, for it elides a number of interestingly different ways in which interests may fail to be fully individuated. For example, individuals may have rights to certain collective goods. See, Green (1991) and cf. Réaume (1988).

Those who choose to use a particular language often thereby signal their sense of identification with an ethnic or cultural group. This is most commonly true of minority language speakers in circumstances where use of their language imposes some social or economic cost. The language establishes a link with an intended audience, a link which simultaneously invokes a boundary between those inside and those outside the group. This mark of distinction is often a source of value to minority language speakers, and legitimately so. Notice that ethnic identification may be expressed even by those who are monolingual minority-language speakers. The notion of 'choice' in play may well be an attenuated one. For language use to have the expressive character I have attributed to it, it is not necessary that a person deliberately use one language and avoid another in circumstances where options are available. The expressive act need not be, for example, speaking Italian instead of English, but simply speaking Italian instead of remaining silent or allowing others to speak on one's behalf.

Language may also be an expression of political identity. Quebec's policies of *francisation* express not only a boundary-defining sense of common feeling, but also a political position which celebrates the distinctiveness of Quebec society and its aspirations for autonomy. It is no accident that minority language use is often a political marker, and not surprising that suppression of such languages is often undertaken with political aims in mind. The various forms of compulsion to which Estonian, Croatian, or Welsh speakers have been subject by their governments was motivated by a desire to suppress social formations which embody and promote nationalist politics.'[8] That repression was unjust, but it was not ill-informed: use of those languages was indeed a political act.

Here again, the consequences of requiring the use of a certain language are likely to differ from those of prohibiting the use of others. The decision *not* to use a particular language may in some circumstances be expressive: it may be an act of resistance. In other cases, it may be understood that to use a particular language is not necessarily to identify with the ethnic group whose language it

---

[8] Political affirmation is often but not always coincident with ethnic identification. Some bilingual Canadians use their second official language in post offices or at border crossings in order to make a political statement without thereby intending to express any sense of ethnic identification with the other group.

characteristically is, nor to endorse any political view. A language may simply be, and be understood to be, a *lingua franca*. Moreover, the burden of required use may be partly alleviated by the division of labour. Organizations like companies and bureaucracies may have the power to arrange their affairs so that, for example, only those willing to use English must do so. And where the regulations apply directly to individuals, they often do so only for limited contexts and purposes. This is not to deny that required use is ever onerous. When language has become politically charged with the burden of nationality, use of language is almost inevitably an expressive act. Both prohibitions and requirements on use limit that expression, though generally in different degrees.

Unlike the semantic thesis, the expressive thesis is pervasive; the use of a language may have an expressive function without regard to subject matter. The sign in Valerie Ford's shop had a social and political significance quite apart from its semantic content. Indeed, Quebec nationalists have often correctly noticed that the use of English by merchants is not purely a matter of commercial expediency but is in part a collective *non placet*, sometimes even a political provocation. To denounce it in one breath and then in the next defend prohibitions on English on the ground that they merely regulate a neutral code is either blindness or hypocrisy.

Since this expressive character may break out at any point, even on a commercial sign, there seems to be no way one might adopt narrower protections to serve the same ends. Unlike the instrumental argument, the expressive argument is capable of supporting broader principles. The strongest objection to this argument is rather different. It is that the interests at stake are not sufficiently weighty or general to warrant holding others duty-bound to protect them or disabling them from infringing them. Is that a credible position? The power of ethnicity and nationality in organizing personal identity, the widely felt need for rootedness, and the structuring power of culture all suggest that identification with an ethnic group may be a substantial human good. Expressing such identification is good to the extent that it constitutes, reinforces and adapts it.

Perhaps one might object that these interests, though powerful, are purely private. A follower of Chafee, for example, might be tempted in that direction. He saw the underlying values of free expression to be these:

There is an individual interest, the need of men to express their opinions on matters vital to them if life is to be worth living, and a social interest in the attainment of truth, so that the country may not only adopt the wisest course of action but carry it out in the wisest way[9] (Chafee 1964: 33).

Ignoring the social interest, Chafee thought, leads people systematically to underestimate the importance of free speech. But his view of what the social interest actually comprises is an implausibly narrower one. The expressive need is not merely individual, nor is the social interest merely that of attaining the truth. Sound public policy is to be guided, not merely by the true, but by the good. There is a common interest in a regime which enables and supports the expression and exploration of ethnic identities, at least when these help structure valuable forms of life. Not only is this good in itself, but it indirectly contributes to a climate of ethnic tolerance and to the public good of linguistic security, so that each may speak his or her mother tongue without unfair pressure to conform. The expressive interest is thus of general value and not what Mill called a 'personal possession'; its violation is not merely a 'private injury' (Mill 1962).

It is here, I think, that one finds the deepest and most important roots of free expression and why, of the three arguments I have canvassed, the expressive one is so important in completing the case for protecting choice of language.

References

Chafee, Zechariah (1964), *Free Speech in the United States* (Harvard University Press, Cambridge, Mass.).

Green, Leslie (1991) 'Two Views of Collective Rights', *Canadian Journal of Law and Jurisprudence*, 4: 315–27.

Greenawalt, Kent (1989), *Speech, Crime, and the Uses of Language* (Oxford University Press, New York).

Meiklejohn, Alexander (1960), *Political Freedom: The Constitutional Powers of the People* (Oxford University Press, New York).

Mill, John Stuart (1962), *Utilitarianism, On Liberty, Essay on Bentham* ed. Mary Warnock (New American Library, New York).

Réaume, Denise (1988), 'Individuals, Groups, and Rights to Public Goods', *University of Toronto Law Journal*, 38: 1–28.

---

[9] The passage refers to the interests protected by the First Amendment to the American Constitution, but there is no evidence that Chafee thought that there were any important expressive interests not protected by that document.

Scanlon, Thomas (1972), 'A Theory of Freedom of Expression', *Philosophy and Public Affairs*, 1: 204–26.

Cases Cited

Cohen *v.* California (1971) 403 US 15.
Devine *c.* PG Québec et PG du Canada mis en cause (1982) CS 355 (Can.)
Ford *v.* AG Quebec (1984) 18 DLR (4th) 711 (Can.)
Ford *v.* AG Quebec (1988) 2 SCR 712 (Can.)
Irwin Toy Ltd. *c.* PG du Québec et Gilles Moreau (1982) CS 96 (Can.)
Reference re: Manitoba Language Rights (1985) 19 DLR (4th) 1 (Can.)
R. *v.* Kopyto (1988) 47 DLR (4th) 213 (Ont CA) (Can.)

Statutes Cited

Canadian Charter of Rights and Freedoms s. 2(b), Part I of the Constitution Act of 1982 being Schedule B of the Canada Act of 1982 (UK), 1982, chap. 11.
Charter of the French Language RSQ 1977 c.C-11 (Can.).
Official Languages Act of 1969.

6. Hate Propaganda and Charter Rights

L. W. SUMNER

Hate literature is deeply problematic for liberal societies because it exposes an awkward conflict between two of their most cherished values. On the one hand, the dissemination of racist propaganda, however odious it might be, seems to fit easily within the definition of political speech. Racists typically have a political agenda, and the public circulation of their views is an indispensable means of carrying out that agenda. The freedom to advocate deeply held political convictions is one of the cornerstones of a liberal democracy. Classically, the vigorous protection of this freedom has been claimed to yield a number of important pay-offs, both individual and social. For the holders of such convictions this freedom provides an essential means of self-expression or self-fulfilment and ensures their opportunity to participate effectively in the democratic process, while for the public at large it plays the crucial role of exposing comfortable orthodoxies to productive challenge and criticism. While the individual benefits derived from freedom of expression may not vary with the content of the ideas being expressed, the social benefits may actually be greatest when the convictions in question are unpopular, unsettling, irritating, or even offensive. In any polity what gets labelled as propaganda is by definition controversial or heterodox. Liberals will therefore assign a high value to political propaganda, and will take special pains to protect the right of citizens to circulate it freely.

On the other hand, the public expression of hatred or contempt for minorities can cause those groups demonstrable harm. No society is free of racism, and the unhindered circulation of propaganda which portrays visible minorities as inferior or despicable is likely to encourage the spread of this poison. The immediate result for the target groups will be diminished self-esteem and a questioning of the extent to which they are valued members of the social order. This may in turn encourage a response of quietism or passivity—a reluctance to compete too vigorously for conspicuous social positions, or to press claims of social justice, lest success breed a backlash of resentment and hostility. Those who are not so easily intimidated may none the less find their progress impeded by discrimination which is reinforced by derogatory racial stereotypes. Nor do the indignities stop there: enmity or contempt are likely also to be expressed in racial taunts or slurs, social ostracism, the desecration of sacred places, and personal violence.

Hate propaganda therefore forces liberals to choose between protecting individual liberty and promoting social equality. The stakes are high, since any choice they make will necessarily circumscribe or curtail some important basic rights. For Canadians this conflict takes an especially acute form. In common with a number of European jurisdictions, but in sharp contrast to the United States, Canada has a criminal statute governing the dissemination of hate propaganda. Recent judicial challenges to this statute have highlighted its seeming inconsistency with the constitutional guarantee of freedom of expression. In examining these challenges, and their ultimate resolution by the courts, my principal aim is to draw some conclusions concerning the nature and grounding of basic legal rights. But I have a further purpose as well. For years I accepted the civil libertarian case against the criminalization of hate propaganda, not on grounds of abstract right but out of the purely pragmatic conviction that the social costs of attempting to control the circulation of this kind of material were likely to be higher than the costs of leaving it unhindered. Now I am no longer quite so sure, and I want to try to explain (and also understand) why I have come to change my mind.

1   THE CRIMINAL CODE AND THE CHARTER

Under s. 319(2) of the Canadian Criminal Code 'every one who, by communicating statements, other than in private conversation, wilfully promotes hatred against any identifiable group' is guilty of an offence carrying a maximum penalty of imprisonment for two years.[1] For the purpose of this section an 'identifiable group' is defined as 'any section of the public distinguished by colour, race, religion or ethnic origin'. Section 319(3) then adds the following schedule of defences:

---

[1] RSC 1985, c. C-46. After the cases discussed below had reached the appeal stage, the previous s. 281.2 (RSC 1970, c. C-34) was renumbered as s. 319. For uniformity of reference, I have converted all citations to the new numbering.

No person shall be convicted of an offence under subsection (2)

    (*a*) if he establishes that the statements communicated were true;

    (*b*) if, in good faith, he expressed or attempted to establish by argument an opinion upon a religious subject;

    (*c*) if the statements were relevant to any subject of public interest, the discussion of which was for the public benefit, and if on reasonable grounds he believed them to be true; or

    (*d*) if, in good faith, he intended to point out, for the purpose of removal, matters producing or tending to produce feelings of hatred towards an identifiable group in Canada.

Meanwhile, s. 2 of the Canadian Charter of Rights and Freedoms states that 'everyone has the following fundamental freedoms: ... (*b*) freedom of thought, belief, opinion and expression, including freedom of the press and other media of communication'.[2] Under s. 1 of the Charter these freedoms are 'subject only to such reasonable limits prescribed by law as can be demonstrably justified in a free and democratic society'.

The materials for a Charter challenge to the hate propaganda statute are therefore ready to hand. So far this challenge has been raised in two cases: *Keegstra* and *Andrews*.[3] James Keegstra was convicted under s. 319(2) of making anti-Semitic comments to his high school students, while Donald Andrews was convicted under the same section of publishing and distributing a white supremacist periodical known as the Nationalist Reporter. Both convictions were appealed, and both appeals turned in part on the claim that s. 319(2) is an unjustifiable infringement of s. 2(b) of the Charter. At this second stage, the paths followed by the two cases diverged. In *Keegstra* the Alberta Court of Appeal accepted this argument (among others) and quashed Keegstra's conviction, while in *Andrews* the Ontario Court of Appeal rejected the argument and upheld Andrews's conviction. Both cases were appealed to the Supreme Court, where s. 319(2) was upheld by a majority of 4–3.[4] Andrews's conviction was confirmed,

---

[2] Part I of the Constitution Act 1982, being Schedule B of the Canada Act 1982 (UK) 1982, c. 11.

[3] *R.* v. *Keegstra* (1988) 43 CCC (3d) 150, reversing (1984) 19 CCC (3d) 254 (referred to hereafter as *Keegstra* (1988) and (1984) respectively); *R.* v. *Andrews* (1988) 43 CCC (3d) 193 (hereafter *Andrews* (1988)). *R.* v. *Zundel* (1987) 31 CCC (3d) 97 raised a similar challenge to the then s. 177 (now s. 181) of the Criminal Code; it will here be disregarded.

[4] *R.* v. *Keegstra* (1990) 3 SCR 697; *R.* v. *Andrews* (1990) 3 SCR 870 (hereafter *Keegstra* (1990) and *Andrews* (1990) respectively).

while Keegstra was eventually committed to trial a second time on the original charges. He was convicted once again.

It would be tiresome to rehearse all of the Charter issues which have surfaced, both at trial and on appeal, in the two cases. Fortunately, there is general agreement among all the courts involved that two questions are paramount:

The section 2 issue: Does s. 319(2) infringe the right of freedom of expression protected by s. 2(b) of the Charter?

The section 1 issue: If so, does this infringement fall within the 'reasonable limits' of s. 1 of the Charter?

These two questions yield three possible decision paths, all of which have been pursued during the various stages of adjudication of the two cases. As the flow chart on p. 157 shows, there are two paths which result in upholding s. 319(2) but only one which leads to striking it down. There are also two different ways of sorting the various opinions in *Keegstra* and *Andrews*. One looks only to their ultimate conclusion: do they hold the hate propaganda statute to be an unjustifiable infringement of the Charter right of freedom of expression? This line of division separates the various supporters of the statute (those on the two outside paths) from its opponents (those on the middle path). The other way looks strictly to their handling of the s. 2 issue: do they hold the hate propaganda statute to be any infringement of the Charter right at all? On this question some of the statute's supporters (those on the left-hand path) agree with its opponents (still the middle path). Both lines of division raise interesting issues concerning the nature and grounding of fundamental rights. These issues will be explored in the next two sections.

2   THE BALANCING ACT

All parties to the judicial debate agree on some fundamental points. The purpose of s. 319(2) of the Criminal Code is to protect racial, ethnic, and religious minorities against the harms which are likely to result from the spread of contempt or enmity directed toward them. Equal respect for minorities is an important value in a liberal society. The purpose of s. 2(b) of the Charter is to protect freedom of expression, especially where the ideas or opinions being expressed are unpopular or offensive. Freedom of expression is also an important

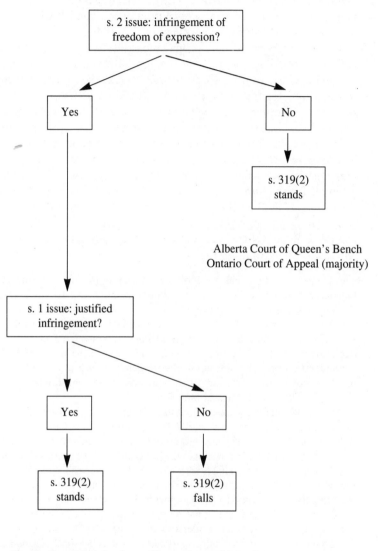

value in a liberal society. Where hate propaganda is concerned, these values appear to conflict. Any resolution of this conflict will necessarily favour one value at the expense of the other.

The defenders of the hate propaganda statute declare themselves willing, in this instance, to limit freedom of expression in order to safeguard equal respect. Contrariwise, its attackers declare themselves willing, in this instance, to put the latter at risk in order to protect the former. Although the two sides to the debate reach opposed conclusions, they both get there by engaging in the same exercise of balancing the two values in question against one another. The lower-court judgments in *Keegstra* and *Andrews* are full of this language of balancing,[5] as are both the majority and minority opinions for the Supreme Court. Writing for the majority, Dickson CJ speaks of 'finding the correct balance between prohibiting hate propaganda and ensuring freedom of expression'.[6] But the most elaborate and developed account of the balancing act is provided by McLachlin J., writing for the minority:

The Court's function under s. 1 of the *Charter* is that of weighing and balancing. Before reaching s. 1, the Court must already have determined that the law in question infringes a right or freedom guaranteed by the *Charter*. The infringement alone, however, does not mandate that the law must fall. If the limit the law imposes on the right infringed is 'reasonable' and 'can be demonstrably justified in a free and democratic society', the law is valid. The demonstration of this justification, the burden of which lies on the state, involves proving that there are other rights or interests which outweigh the right infringed in the context of that case.

The task which judges are required to perform under s. 1 is essentially one of balancing. On the one hand lies a violation or limitation of a fundamental right or freedom. On the other lies a conflicting objective which the state asserts is of greater importance than the full exercise of the right or freedom, of sufficient importance that it is reasonable and 'demonstrably justified' that the limitation should be imposed. The exercise is one of great difficulty, requiring the judge to make value judgments. In this task logic and precedent are but of limited assistance. What must be determinative in the end is the court's judgment, based on an understanding of the values our society is built on and the interests at stake in the particular case. As Wilson J. has pointed out in *Edmonton Journal*, this judgment cannot be made in the abstract. Rather than speak of values as though they were Platonic ideals, the judge must situate the analysis in the facts of the particular case, weighing the

---

[5] See e.g. *Keegstra* (1984), 274–5, and *Keegstra* (1988), 171, 176.
[6] *Keegstra* (1990), 754; cf. 734, 735.

different values represented in that context. Thus it cannot be said that freedom of expression will always prevail over the objective of individual dignity and social harmony, or vice versa. The result in a particular case will depend on weighing the significance of the infringement on freedom of expression represented by the law in question, against the importance of the countervailing objectives, the likelihood the law will achieve those objectives, and the proportionality of the scope of the law to those objectives.[7]

Although Dickson CJ and McLachlin J. eventually come to contrary conclusions about s. 319(2) (he is on the left-hand path, she on the middle), they agree on the nature, and the necessity, of the balancing exercise. Implicitly or explicitly, this agreement runs through all of the various judgments, at every level, in *Keegstra* and *Andrews*. In each instance, the ultimate conclusion reached concerning the status of s. 319(2) reflects an opinion about the balance which it strikes between protecting minorities, on the one hand, and safeguarding freedom of expression, on the other. There is also general agreement concerning the questions to be raised in the course of the balancing exercise:[8]

1. Is the objective of s. 319(s) an important one?
2. Does the statute employ measures reasonably likely to achieve this objective?
3. Do these measures impair freedom of expression as little as possible in order for them to achieve the statute's objective?
4. Are the resulting costs to freedom of expression proportional to the expected gains from achieving this objective?

Since all parties agree on the importance of safeguarding equal respect for minorities, the main points of contention are questions (2)–(4). The judicial opponents of s. 319(2) advance two main arguments. The first is that the criminal prosecution of hatemongers may actually be self-defeating, since it provides them with a public platform for the advocacy of their opinions.[9] In reply, the defenders of the statute point primarily to the symbolic effect of prosecution as a means of expressing social condemnation of hate propaganda.[10]

The opponents' second argument is that, in its present form, s. 319(2) is too broadly drawn and thus trenches too much on freedom

---

[7] Ibid. 844–5; cf. 846, 848, 863–5.
[8] Following *R.* v. *Oakes* (1986) 1 SCR 103.
[9] *Keegstra* (1988), 174; (1990), 852–3.
[10] *Keegstra* (1990), 769.

L. W. Sumner

of expression.[11] Its defenders deny this, citing the various restrictions and defences incorporated into the law:[12]

1. The communication must be public; s. 319(2) does not apply to private conversation.

2. The 'identifiable groups' protected are limited to sections of the public distinguished by colour, race, religion, or ethnic origin.

3. The promotion of hatred must be 'wilful', i.e. intentional. The offence is therefore one of specific intent, requiring at the very least some awareness on the part of the agent of the likely effects of the expression. Mere recklessness with respect to those effects will not suffice.

4. Establishing the truth of the statements communicated constitutes an absolute defence.

5. Opinions expressed in good faith on religious subjects are excluded from prosecution.

6. A 'public benefit' defence is available.

7. Publicizing hate propaganda for the purpose of combatting it is not an offence.

8. The consent of the Attorney-General is required for a prosecution under s. 319(2).

Thus are the terms of the debate set. It should be obvious by now that, at bottom, this is an argument about public policy. Where two important social values conflict we are forced to seek an acceptable trade-off between them. This is precisely what the courts are doing in all their talk of 'balancing'. The optimal trade-off, or balance, is that at which any further gains in one of the values would be outweighed by greater losses in the other. Freedom of expression would be better protected were there no legal constraints whatever on the circulation of hate propaganda, while the security of minority groups would be more effectively safeguarded by legislation a good deal more restrictive than 2. 319(2). Somewhere between these extremes we seek a balance point at which the greater protection for minorities afforded by stronger legislation would be outweighed by the chilling effect on political speech, while the greater protection for expression afforded by weaker legislation would be outweighed by the increase in racial hatred. Whether s. 319(2) properly locates that balance point is, of

[11] *Keegstra* (1988), 175–8; (1990), 844–65.
[12] The following list is adapted from *Keegstra* (1984), 274. See also *Keegstra* (1990), 772–83; *Andrews* (1988), 216–19; and Law Reform Commission of Canada, *Hate Propaganda* (Working Paper 50, 1986), 30–8.

course, open to legitimate doubt. That is what the judicial debate concerning the constitutionality of the statute is all about.

That legislation regulating hate propaganda should aim to strike such a balance has been understood from the beginning. The Special Committee on Hate Propaganda in Canada (hereafter referred to as the Cohen Committee), whose 1966 report led to the enactment of the Canadian legislation, formulated the issue in the following terms:

> The prevailing view in Canada is that freedom of expression is a qualified right, representing the balance that must be struck between the social interest in the full and frank discussion necessary to a free society on the one hand, and the social interests in public order and individual and group reputation on the other.[13]

In striking this balance, the Committee's view was that the higher priority should be assigned to freedom of expression:

> as among conflicting values, preference must always be given to freedom of expression rather than to legal prohibitions directed at abuses of it. This is not to say that freedom of expression is regarded as an absolute, but only to insist that it will be esteemed more highly and weighted more significantly in the legislative scales, so that legal markings of the borderline areas [between 'legitimate' and 'illegitimate' public discussion] will always be such as to permit liberty even at the cost of occasional license . . . legislation should be so drafted as to permit the maximum freedom of expression consistent with its purpose and the needs of a free society.[14]

What the Cohen Committee recommended, in effect, is that we begin with an initial presumption in favour of unfettered freedom of expression, and then impose the least extensive restrictions necessary in order to safeguard social values of equal importance. The question to be asked for every proposed restriction, therefore, is whether the marginal gain in the rival value is worth purchasing at the marginal cost to freedom of expression. Section 319 followed the Committee's recommendations in all essential respects, especially in the relatively high threshold which it established for successful prosecution.

If this is the correct way to understand the exercise of balancing (and what else could it be?), then it falls into an argumentative pattern familiar to moral or political philosophers. We have located the

---

[13] House of Commons, *Report of the Special Committee on Hate Propaganda in Canada* (1966), 61 (referred to hereafter as the Cohen Committee Report). See also Law Reform Commission, *Hate Propaganda*, ch. 2, s. I, 'Freedom of Expression versus Freedom from Hate: The Search for a Balance'.

[14] Cohen Committee Report, 61.

optimal balance between conflicting values when the costs of a departure in either direction exceed its benefits. But in that case the optimal balance is that point any departure from which will result in a net loss of value, i.e., the point at which the sum total of the values in question is maximized. Philosophers have a name—consequentialism—for the kind of moral/political theory which tells us always to prefer the outcome which maximizes value on the whole. It is an interesting feature of the judicial debate about s. 319(2) that all of its parties appear to agree on this consequentialist methodology.

This may seem a surprising result. After all, on the surface of it the Charter does not have the look of a consequentialist document. How then does it happen that in Charter adjudication judges come to behave as consequentialists? A full answer to this question would take us much too far afield, but it is easy to see in very rough outline how such an answer would go. The political function of the Charter is to confer a special degree of legal protection on a set of selected social values by entrenching them as constitutionally guaranteed rights. Which values are to be protected in this way is itself a policy question, the best mix presumably being that which best safeguards the flourishing of a liberal democratic society. Whatever the favoured values may be, however, they will be capable of conflicting both with one another and with other values which do not enjoy the same degree of constitutional protection. These conflicts will require interpretation of the abstract and perfunctory formulae enshrined in the Charter, interpretation which will perforce be carried out not by politicians but by judges. When judges are confronted by legislation which protects some significant social value but appears to trench on a Charter right, and when they have no unambiguous precedent to guide them, then it is difficult to see how they might proceed other than by seeking a reasonable balance between the values in conflict. But in that case their objective will be the resolution of the conflict which promises to yield the best outcome on the whole.

There is in this an important lesson about the nature and role of rights.[15] Legal rights are best regarded as instruments whose function is to safeguard important individual and social values. They are morally justified when they perform this function well—that is, when they strike an optimal, or at least an acceptable, balance among the values in question. It follows from this that rights cannot be the

---

[15] A lesson which I have urged in *The Moral Foundation of Rights* (Clarendon Press, Oxford, 1987).

ultimate premisses of moral/political argument; rather, they follow as conclusions from premisses specifying the values which they are to protect, plus some understanding of how these values are to be weighed against one another. What may on the surface appear to be appeals to abstract right, therefore, are to be understood on a deeper level as consequentialist arguments concerning matters of public policy. In this respect constitutional adjudication conforms to the general pattern of moral/political argument, in which the good is prior to, and foundational for, the right.

What may be disquieting in all this is not that conflicting values need to be commensurated, nor that the optimal balance is the maximizing option, but that it is judges who are carrying out this entire exercise. Unlike politicians they are not answerable to the electorate, and unlike special committees or commissions they have little opportunity to collect empirical data. How can they be expected to reach informed judgments on large questions of social policy, such as the trade-off between freedom of expression and racial toleration, and how can they be held responsible for the judgments they do reach? The worry about information may be somewhat alleviated by reflecting that, while judges have little opportunity to engage in primary research themselves, they can and do avail themselves of the findings of others. Doubtless their conclusions remain to a large degree intuitive; these are, as we say, judgment calls. However this may be, the role of judges as practising consequentialists seems to come with the territory. The abstract rights of the Charter cry out for interpretation, and much of this interpretation will necessarily take the form of defining them in socially optimal ways. If we do not give this job to judges, then to whom might we entrust it?

3   INTERNAL *v.* EXTERNAL LIMITS

Earlier, I distinguished two different ways in which the judicial opinions on s. 319(2) could be classified. The first of these we can now identify as the outcome of the consequentialist cost/benefit balancing, which settles the constitutionality issue. This line of division, as I said then, separates the friends of the hate propaganda statute from its foes, the former taking the view that the marginal loss in freedom of expression is outweighed by the marginal gain in protection for minorities, the latter being of contrary mind. The second line of division concerns the different routes by which the friends of the statute reach their common destination. Here the crucial question is *not* whether s. 319(2) is an unjustifiable infringement of the s. 2(b) right of freedom of expression—for all its friends agree that it is not—but whether it is any infringement of that right at all. This is the issue which divided the Ontario Court of Appeal in *Andrews*. The majority, consisting of Grange and Krever JJA, agree with Quigley J. of the Alberta Court of Queen's Bench in *Keegstra* that s. 319(2) does not infringe s. 2(b). Cory JA, delivering the minority opinion in *Andrews*, agrees with the Alberta Court of Appeal in *Keegstra* that it does (unlike the Alberta Court, he then finds that the infringement is justified under the terms of s. 1).

As Grange JA observes, 'Everything depends on the interpretation of "freedom of expression" in the Charter.'[16] On the face of it, the various rights guaranteed by s. 2 are unqualified: 'Everyone has the following fundamental freedoms: ... (b) freedom of thought, belief, opinion and expression'. Not 'freedom of expression, except in the following circumstances' but just 'freedom of expression', full stop. Notwithstanding this absolutist language, however, Grange JA and the others of like mind take the view that the right delineated by s. 2(b) is not absolute. Leaving the hate propaganda issue to one side, they claim that the right does not protect expression which is obscene, seditious, or libellous. Grange JA includes group defamation among the forms of unprotected expression: 'In my view [s. 2(b)] never was intended to and does not give constitutional protection to hate-mongering such as that of the appellants ... I simply do not believe [s. 319(2)] offends the traditional protection of the freedom of speech or s. 2(b) of the Charter.'[17] Quigley J. takes the same view: 'In my opinion, the words "freedom of expression" as used in s. 2(b) of the Charter does [*sic*] not mean an absolute freedom permitting an un-bridged [*sic*] right of speech or expression. In particular, I hold that [s. 319(2)] of the *Criminal Code* does not infringe upon the freedom of expression granted by s. 2(b) of the Charter.'[18]

After his discussion of the same issue, Cory JA comes to exactly the opposite conclusion: 'Offensive as it may seem, the expressions used in the case at bar do come within the purview of s. 2(b) of the Charter.'[19] In their treatment of the hate propaganda cases, there-fore, the lower courts offered two quite different interpretations of

---

16 *Andrews* (1988), 221.   17 Ibid.
18 *Keegstra* (1984), 268.   19 *Andrews* (1988), 210.

s. 2(b). On the wide interpretation it simply means what it appears to say: the right to freedom of expression is unqualified. Since s. 319(2) clearly qualifies that right, it clearly infringes s. 2(b); the issue of its validity must then be referred to s. 1.[20] On the narrow interpretation, by contrast, s. 2(b) already includes a number of implicit qualifications, so that obscenity, sedition, and defamation (including group defamation) are excluded from its scope. On this reading s. 319(2) does not trench on the s. 2(b) right and so need not be justified by reference to s. 1.

The legal issues raised by these competing interpretations are interesting and important. One of them is whether the various specific sections of the Charter are to be read as incorporating rights extant in pre-existing jurisprudence, or whether the Charter starts with a clean slate. If the former view is taken, then, since freedom of expression was clearly not absolute in the pre-Charter era, s. 2(b) will be read as implicitly qualified. If the latter view is preferred then these internal limits are not dictated, and the right may be read as having a much broader scope. A related issue concerns the structural difference between the Charter and the American Bill of Rights. Because the latter contains no analogue to s. 1, the limits which are judicially imposed on the scope of its abstract rights must often be treated as internal and implicit. If similar limits are then read into the various rights enumerated by the Charter, the function of s. 1 may thereby be pre-empted. The wide interpretation of s. 2 may therefore be thought to be more congruent with the unique character of the Charter, since it reserves to s. 1 the inevitable task of balancing conflicting values.

Such, in any case, was the view ultimately taken by the Supreme Court, where both the majority and minority agreed on the wide interpretation, and on the balancing role of s. 1. Following the line of analysis it had laid out in commercial expression cases,[21] the Court favoured 'a large and liberal interpretation' of s. 2(b), under which any activity will qualify as expression as long as it 'conveys or attempts to convey a meaning', regardless of the content of that

---

[20] The Alberta Court of Appeal, of course, also uses the wide interpretation, but then parts company with the friends of the hate propaganda statute by holding its infringement of s. 2(b) to be unjustified under the terms of s. 1. See *Keegstra* (1988), 162 ff.

[21] *Ford* v. *Quebec (Attorney General)* (1988) 2 SCR 712; *Irwin Toy Ltd.* v. *Quebec (Attorney General)* (1989) 1 SCR 927.

meaning.[22] All expression in turn falls under the protection of s. 2(b), unless it takes a physically violent form. Since hate propaganda is not normally communicated in a violent manner, s. 2(b) guarantees a right to disseminate it.[23] The question whether that right is over-ridden by a competing consideration of equal or greater importance is then referred to s. 1. On that question the Court, of course, divided, the majority agreeing with Cory JA of the Ontario Court of Appeal, the minority siding with the Alberta Court.

To a philosopher's eyes, it can be a little difficult to make out just what is at stake in this judicial debate concerning the scope of the right guaranteed by s. 2(b) of the Charter. After all, when they get down to cases all the friends of the hate propaganda statute defend it on the same substantive ground, namely that it strikes a reasonable balance between freedom of expression and the protection of minorities. They are therefore united on the important moral/political conclusion, and seemingly divided only on the legal gloss to be placed on it. One party takes its cost/benefit balancing to show that s. 319(2) does not infringe s. 2(b) in the first place, while the other uses precisely the same calculation to establish that the infringement of s. 2(b) falls within the 'reasonable limits' of s. 1. Since both parties agree that s. 319(2) is consistent with the Charter, why does it matter which construction of the constitutional issues they choose?

I can imagine a legal reason for thinking that it matters: assigning a robust balancing role to s. 1 might be thought to provide a more coherent interpretation of the Charter as a whole. However, I can also see a philosophical reason for favouring the narrower read-ing of s. 2(b). The question is whether we should regard the right to freedom of expression as internally limited or as overridden by a competing right. On the former view the right to circulate hate propaganda has no Charter protection; on the latter view it does have such protection but it is trumped by a right of greater weight, namely the right of minorities to be protected against racial hatred. Now in many contexts this distinction can make a normative difference. I have the right to walk along a public footpath but no right to insist that you get out of my way if you happen to be using the same path. Because you infringe no right on my part, you owe me no compen-sation for forcing me to detour around you. By contrast, I have ownership rights over my land but the municipal government may have the right to expropriate that land for a public project. Because

---

[22] *Keegstra* (1990), 728–9.   [23] Ibid. 730–3, 829–31.

the expropriation infringes my property right, I am owed compensation for my loss. The philosophical point is that where a genuine right is justifiably infringed it does not simply vanish, as though it had never existed in the first place. Rather, something of normative significance has occurred, which may entitle the rightholder to remedial action. No remedy of any kind would be owed, however, where there was no right in the first place.

The Supreme Court now seems irreversibly committed to a 'broad, inclusive approach to the protected sphere of free expression',[24] leaving the strength of the protection in a particular instance to be determined by reference to s. 1.[25] It has therefore determined that racists have a constitutionally protected right to circulate hate propaganda, but that this right may be justifiably infringed in order to protect their intended victims. Is the Court then prepared to acknowledge that Keegstra and Andrews are owed compensation for their normative loss? Apparently not, since the Court is willing to see them convicted of a criminal offence. But then how does this resolution of their cases differ substantively from finding that hate propaganda is a form of expression no one has a right to engage in, so that its restriction is no infringement of right in the first place?

We have already seen that strictly juridical considerations might incline us toward the wide interpretation of s. 2(b), and the corresponding activist role for s. 1, as ingredients in the best interpretation of the Charter as a distinctive constitutional document. However, there is another way of thinking about the interpretive issue. Suppose we ask the same question all the courts are asking in deciding whether to uphold s. 319(2) or to strike it down, namely which alternative will make for the better public policy. Suppose further, for a moment, that there is a good consequentialist case for legislation like s. 319(2). In that case, which interpretive approach is more likely to enhance the objective of the legislation, which is to discourage the circulation of hate propaganda? Will it be more effective to concede hatemongers a legal right to disseminate their views, which the State is justified in infringing, or to deny them that right in the first place? Put in these terms, the narrow interpretation of s. 2(b), with its internal limits on freedom of expression, may

[24] *Irwin Toy* (1989), 970.
[25] Since deciding *Keegstra* and *Andrews*, the Court has reconfirmed this commitment in *R.* v. *Butler*, where the form of expression at stake is pornography.

be found morally and politically preferable to the wide interpretation, which relies on the external controls of s. 1.

To say no more about the interpretive question would leave a misleading impression of the degree of constitutional protection which the Supreme Court is actually prepared to accord to hate propaganda. On the one hand, the entire Court shares the official view that all (non-violent) expression falls under the protection of s. 2(b), regardless of its content. On the other hand, the majority also holds that hate propaganda merits only relatively weak protection, because of its content.[26] Writing for the majority, Dickson CJ argues that the expression prohibited by s. 319(2) is only 'tenuously connected to the values underlying s. 2(b)'—namely, the collective search for truth, individual self-development, and the effective participation of all citizens in the political process. Now this conclusion is certainly open to dispute (it is disputed by the minority).[27] But its quite explicit effect is to weaken the s. 2(b) protection of hate propaganda; as Dickson CJ puts it, this material 'should not be accorded the greatest of weight in the s. 1 analysis'.[28] While hate propaganda falls within the scope of constitutionally protected expression, it is located on the periphery of this domain rather than at its core. The threshold is therefore lowered for a successful s. 1 argument in favour of limiting the s. 2(b) right: competing values deemed to be sufficiently weighty to override the right in this case might be too slight to limit a form of expression which has been accorded a higher initial degree of protection.

The Court majority is therefore somewhat at odds with itself over the issue of content restrictions on political expression. Why the particular content of hate propaganda should suffice to diminish its constitutional protection, but not to remove it altogether, remains unexplained. However, it seems obvious that the line taken by the majority foreordains the outcome of its s. 1 analysis of the hate propaganda statute; if the threshold has already been lowered then it is scarcely surprising that the majority is able to find an argument which surmounts it. As McLachlin J. points out on behalf of the minority, the entire argument appears to be circular: 'If one starts from the premise that the speech covered by s. 319(2) is dangerous and without value, then it is simple to conclude that none of the commonly-offered justifications for protecting freedom of expression are served by it.'[29] Certainly the majority's approach does rather

---

[26] *Keegstra* (1990), 759–67.   [27] Ibid. 840–2.   [28] Ibid. 765.   [29] Ibid. 841.

compromise its commitment to the wide interpretation of s. 2(b). It now appears that the broader the domain of the Charter right the thinner the protection it affords, at least around the edges.[30]

4 HATE PROPAGANDA AND CIVIL LIBERTIES

Whether the limits on freedom of expression are already implicit in s. 2(b) or are imposed by s. 1, it is clear that there are such limits. It also seems clear from the adjudication of *Keegstra* and *Andrews* that the proper location of these limits is ultimately a question of public policy. The hate propaganda statute is consistent with the Charter if and only if it strikes a reasonable balance between the two important social values in conflict. We are therefore left with the substantive issue: does the statute protect minorities from vilification at too high a cost to freedom of expression?

Like the Supreme Court minority and the Alberta Court of Appeal, civil libertarians answer this question in the affirmative. They are able to marshal some very powerful considerations in favour of their position.[31] They claim that during the twenty years of its life s. 319(2) has had no discernible effect on the level of racial intolerance in Canada, or even on the circulation of hate propaganda. Indeed, by providing priceless publicity for their odious views, court proceedings against hatemongers may well have worsened the position of the very groups which the legislation purports to protect. However this may be, the law has certainly had a chilling effect on political speech, all the more so because it has tended to be applied not against the racist bigots which the Cohen Committee had in mind but against innocent or even progressive parties. If there were some way of deleting hate propaganda without thereby endangering other forms of political expression then, the civil libertarians say, they might have no objection to criminal legislation. But it is Utopian to think that a law, however carefully drafted, will not be abused and misapplied in practice. In that case, even if it does succeed in protecting minorities against discrimination, this success will come at an unacceptably high cost.

---

[30] The Court has located at least two other forms of expression at the periphery of the Charter right: communication for the purpose of prostitution (in *Reference re ss. 193 and 195.1(1)(c) of the Criminal Code (Man.)* (1990) 1 SCR 1123), and pornography (in *Butler*).
[31] See e.g. A. Alan Borovoy, *When Freedoms Collide: The Case for Our Civil Liberties* (Lester & Orpen Dennys, Toronto, 1988), 40–53.

These are very forceful arguments, the selfsame arguments which I used to accept. Now I find myself no longer able to do so, at least with my former level of confidence. What has led me to part company on this issue with my usual civil libertarian allies? For one thing, with the prosecution of Keegstra and Andrews the hate propaganda statute is now being used against its rightful targets, namely the tireless merchants of racial enmity. Since the statute has now survived constitutional challenge, it might well begin to have just the sort of chilling effect on hate propaganda itself which the Cohen Committee had in mind.

More importantly, I have latterly come to be more impressed by the depth and tenacity of the intolerance towards racial and ethnic minorities which is both felt and openly expressed by a great many otherwise perfectly ordinary Canadians. While I do not believe that most of these people are as obsessive in their bigotry as Keegstra or Andrews, I fear that they provide a very fertile ground indeed for the seeds of enmity sown by the dedicated hatemongers. There is no shortage of opportunists aiming to cultivate this potential audience. In Vancouver a telephone hotline provides interested callers with a variety of recorded messages claiming that the Holocaust is a Jewish hoax, that a Jewish conspiracy controls the media, and that non-white 'aliens' are importing crime and social problems as they immigrate to Canada. In Toronto a similar service dishes out racist slurs against native people. Furthermore, there is some evidence that racial intolerance is on the increase in Canada. For the past eight years the League for Human Rights of B'nai Brith Canada has polled attitudes toward minority groups. Much to their dismay, the researchers have discovered 'an increased willingness on the part of the population to express prejudicial opinions about all minorities'.[32]

I have also been struck by what I perceive to be a shift of target for Canadian racial hatred. While the old guard, like Keegstra and Andrews, still rant on about the Jews, most bigots now seem at least equally concerned with francophones, or native peoples, or blacks, or Asians. It is arguable, indeed is often argued, that Canadian Jews are now secure enough not to need special protection against anti-Semitic propaganda.[33] Be this as it may, the same cannot be claimed for blacks or Métis or Sikhs. These socially marginalized and relatively

[32] *Toronto Star*, 22 Feb. 1992.
[33] It is worth noting, however, that in 1991 reported incidents of anti-Semitism in Canada were 42% higher than two years earlier (see ibid.).

powerless groups, it seems to me, are at genuine risk of harm from the racist attitudes of employers, landlords, police, bureaucrats, and thugs. Early in 1992 police arrested a group of neo-Nazi skinheads minutes before they were going to fire-bomb an apartment occupied by a black family in Montreal, where there have been a number of clashes between gangs of blacks and white neo-Nazis. Since 1988 white police officers in Toronto have shot eight black civilians, some fatally. In Manitoba an inquiry into the justice system found it riddled with prejudice against native peoples, while a Quebec coroner's report found a 'totally unacceptable' level of racism in the Montreal police force. It does not seem far-fetched to think that the racial attitudes which have been manifested in these and other ways are capable of being reinforced and legitimized by the negative portrayal of visible minorities in hate propaganda.

Canadian racism is not an isolated phenomenon. Stimulated by a deepening economic recession, expressions of racial intolerance, and perhaps also the level of intolerance itself, are on the increase in most industrialized societies. In the United States the incidence of hate crimes rose to a record level in 1991, while the number of active hate groups showed a similar surge.[34] According to a European Parliament report, as many as 70,000 racial attacks occur annually in the United Kingdom, which is plagued by an especially 'high level of racial harassment and violence'.[35] In western Europe similar violence against racial and ethnic minorities is on the upswing in Germany, and in such models of decency and social justice as Belgium and Sweden, while in the East the collapse of communism has allowed the resurgence of old nationalist rivalries often marked by intolerance and xenophobia. Furthermore, racist platforms are finding their way more and more into the political mainstream, led by the electoral successes of right-wing parties in France and Germany which have openly targeted immigrant populations. Everywhere, it seems, blaming visible minorities for our social and economic ills is becoming politically respectable.

When we keep before us a vivid sense of the corrosive effects of racism on those who are its actual or potential victims, then it seems to me that there is no convincing case against some form of criminal legislation governing hate propaganda. In order to minimize the impact of such legislation on freedom of expression, it will need to establish a very high threshold for successful prosecution. However,

[34] *The Globe and Mail*, 25 Feb. 1992.   [35] Ibid. 12 Oct. 1990.

when we bear in mind the safeguards built into s. 319(2), it also seems to me that there is no convincing case against the statute in its present form. It is already a well-established fact that the right to express one's opinions is not absolute. In Canada defamatory libel against individuals is a criminal offence.[36] Section 319(2) seeks to extend the same protection to certain specified groups. That racial, religious, and ethnic groups are in need of such protection was accepted by the Cohen Committee in 1966. Following a survey of some materials being circulated in the years 1963–5, the Committee came to the following conclusion:

It is evident from the foregoing that there exists in Canada a small number of persons and a somewhat larger number of organizations, extremist in method and dedicated to the preaching and spreading of hatred and contempt against certain identifiable minority groups in Canada.[37]

And again:

The amount of hate propaganda presently being disseminated and its measurable effects probably are not sufficient to justify a description of the problem as one of crisis or near crisis proportions. Nevertheless the problem is a serious one. We believe that, given a certain set of socio-economic circumstances, such as a deepening of the emotional tensions or the setting in of a severe business recession, public susceptibility might well increase significantly. Moreover, the potential psychological and social damage of hate propaganda, both to a desensitized majority and to sensitive minority groups, is incalculable.[38]

Sadly, the Committee's fears have been borne out during these recessionary times a quarter of a century later. During the intervening years neither the incidence nor the intensity of Canadian racism seems to have diminished. There still appear to be a distressingly large number of Canadians whose dislike for one or more minority groups is sufficiently deep and persistent to be capable of being fanned into open enmity by demagogues and hatemongers, should they be permitted a platform from which to spread their message. It is true that the prosecution of racists may have the unintended effect of providing them with just such a platform. However, their conviction will also send a clear signal that the fomenting of hatred through the circulation of racist literature will not be tolerated in a liberal society. To tolerate it in the interest of freedom of expression would

---

[36] Criminal Code, ss. 297–317.
[37] Cohen Committee Report, 25.   [38] Ibid. 59.

inevitably be to confer upon it a certain degree of legitimacy. This is something no society can afford to do, if it wishes to safeguard the status of minorities as equal citizens.[39]

Doubtless, s. 319(2) is not perfect as it stands.[40] The very small number of prosecutions under the section tends to show that its safeguards for freedom of expression have been quite effective. If anything, the hate propaganda law might be drawn somewhat more broadly than at present. One change worth consideration is expansion of the range of protected groups, at least far enough to include all those embraced by s. 15 of the Charter, which would add the further distinguishing features of sex, age, and disability, but perhaps farther still, so as to encompass groups identified by sexual orientation. If the scope of the statute were widened in this way then the circulation of hate propaganda against women would become a criminal matter. In that case, the expanded version of s. 319(2) might better accomplish the only legitimate work to be done by an obscenity statute. Since not all material promoting hatred against women has sexual content, and since not all sexually explicit material portrays women in a degrading way, hate propaganda legislation could provide a more focused instrument against the objectionable forms of pornography.[41]

I advance these proposals with diffidence; indeed, I defend the present version of s. 319(2) with equal diffidence. I am not at all certain of the case in favour of hate propaganda legislation, not nearly as certain as I once was of the case against it. But my earlier diagnosis of the nature of the debate goes some way toward both explaining and justifying my present state of mind. If at bottom this is a public policy issue, and if the best policy is the one which strikes the best balance between competing social values, then a view on either side of the issue reflects a highly speculative consequentialist calculation. Since none of the parties to the debate has a secure command over the relevant empirical data, it would seem to behove all of us to hold our views with considerable modesty and circumspection. I am

[39] The expressive purpose of hate propaganda legislation was well understood by the Cohen Committee. In their opinion, such legislation 'sets out as a solemn public judgment that the holding up of identifiable groups to hatred or contempt is inherently likely to dispose the rest of the public to violence against the members of these groups and inherently likely to expose them to loss of respect among their fellow men' (Report, 64–5).

[40] It is, however, noteworthy that the Law Reform Commission recommended only minor changes in it; see *Hate Propaganda*, 39–41.

[41] This is, however, less likely to happen now that the Supreme Court has upheld the obscenity statute in *Butler*.

acutely conscious of having provided very little evidence to support the various factual claims I made above: that minority groups in Canada today are vulnerable to racist propaganda, that the criminal law can provide some of the protection they need, that effective legislation need not trench too deeply on freedom of expression, and so on. But then the civil libertarians on the other side of the question have provided equally scanty support for their claims: that the existing law has been ineffective or counter-productive, that the abuses to which any such law is subject will more than cancel out any benefits it might yield, and so on. The difference between us is that their confidence in their view of the matter seems unassailable. It is this tone of absolute conviction which I find hardest to understand. Like everyone else who addresses this issue, their arguments are empirical and pragmatic. How then can they be so sure they are right?

7. An American's View of the Canadian Hate Speech Decisions

JAMES WEINSTEIN

INTRODUCTION

Comparative constitutional law is fraught with what may be an insuperable difficulty: cultural differences. If law depends on culture, then fundamental law depends fundamentally on culture. Constitutions will often reflect a nation's defining moments—revolutions that brought the country into being, civil wars that tore it apart, as well as more subtle traditions and mores known only to everyday participants in that nation's culture. I have thus been dubious as to whether American constitutional scholars invited to advise far flung nations in the writing of new constitutions really have much of value to offer without first obtaining a thorough understanding of the culture of the countries in question. In this paper I have been asked to comment on the Canadian Supreme Court's recent decisions upholding the prohibition of hate propaganda. It is with some diffidence that I do so, for despite obvious similarities, there are substantial differences between US and Canadian culture.

To minimize the difficulties inherent in discussing another society's constitutional law, I will limit my critique to two topics which by their very nature reduce the significance of any cultural differences. First, I will critique the Supreme Court of Canada's discussion of US law. Admittedly, the Canadian Court's view of US precedent may contain a purely Canadian contribution in the same way that a US rendition of an English folksong contains something essentially American. Thus what I might characterize as a 'misunderstanding' of US law might instead be seen as a culturally-driven variation of US law.

I am grateful to Professors David Kaye, Gerald Gunther and W. J. Waluchow for their helpful comments and suggestions and to Lisa Duran and Glenn Hamer for their valuable research assistance.

While acknowledging this possibility, I will nevertheless point out what seem to be inaccurate statements of US law without attempting to discover possible cultural explanations for the disparity. Next, I will suggest that there is an irreconcilable conflict between the various rationales offered by the Supreme Court of Canada for upholding the prohibition of hate propaganda, on the one hand, and the overarching vision of freedom of expression depicted in these decisions, on the other. Once again, however, the inherent problem of cross-cultural critique will have been minimized rather than eliminated, for an assessment of the consistency of a given rationale for limiting expression consistent with a meaningful free speech principle cannot be totally divorced from the cultural context.

On 13 December 1990, the Canadian Supreme Court decided three hate propaganda cases. In each case the Court held 4–3 that the hate propaganda law at issue was constitutional. In each case Chief Justice Dickson (as he then was) wrote for the majority.[1] In each case the Court found that the law in question infringed the guarantee of freedom of expression found in section 2(b) of the *Canadian Charter of Rights and Freedoms*,[2] but was justifiable under section 1 of the *Charter*[3] and therefore constitutional. *R.* v. *Keegstra*[4] upheld a conviction under a statute that prohibits, on pain of imprisonment for up to two years, 'communicating statements, other than in private conversation, [that] wilfully promote hatred against any identifiable group'.[5] 'Identifiable group', in turn is defined as 'any section of the public distinguished by color, race, religion or ethnic origin'.[6] Keegstra, a high school teacher in Alberta, was convicted under this statute for making various anti-Semitic statements to his class, including the description of Jews as 'treacherous', 'subversive', 'sadistic', 'money-loving', 'power hungry', and 'childkillers'.[7] In addition, Keegstra

[1] In each case Dickson's opinion was jointed by Justices Wilson, L'Heureux-Dubé, and Gonthier, and in each case Justices La Forest, Sopinka, and McLachlin dissented.

[2] S. 2 of the *Charter* provides: 'Everyone has the following fundamental freedoms: ... (b) freedom of thought, belief, opinion and expression, including freedom of the press and other media communication.'

[3] S. 1 of the *Charter* provides: 'The *Canadian Charter of Rights and Freedoms* guarantees the rights and freedoms set out in it subject only to such reasonable limits prescribed by law as can be demonstrably justified in a free and democratic society.'

[4] [1990] 3 SCR 697.

[5] S. 319(2) of the *Criminal Code*.

[6] S. 319(7), incorporating by reference the definition set forth in s. 318(4).

[7] 3 SCR at 714.

taught that the Jews 'created the Holocaust to gain sympathy'.[8] In *R.
v. Andrews*,[9] the Court upheld the convictions of two leaders of the
Nationalist Party, a white supremacist political organization. The
defendants were convicted under the same hate propaganda statute
on the basis of material found in their homes, including sticker cards
containing such messages as 'Nigger go home', 'Hoax on the Holocaust', 'Israel stinks', and 'Hitler was right. Communism is Jewish'.[10]
The third case in this trilogy, *Canada (Human Rights Commission)* v.
Taylor,[11] upheld a contempt citation incurred by Taylor for continuing to run a recorded anti-Semitic telephone message after being
ordered to cease and desist by the Human Rights Tribunal. The
Tribunal had found that these messages, which alleged that Canada
was controlled by a Jewish conspiracy responsible for 'unemployment and inflation' as well as 'perversion, laziness, drug use and
race-mixing',[12] constituted a 'discriminatory practice' in violation of
the Canadian Human Rights Act. Since the rationale of *Andrews* and
Taylor is more or less a rehash of the Court's reasoning in *Keegstra*,
most of my critique will focus on the Court's *Keegstra* analysis.

1   THE COURT'S USE AND MISUSE OF US LAW

In a section of his opinion entitled, 'The Use of American Constitutional Jurisprudence', Chief Justice Dickson writes:

Though I have found the American experience tremendously helpful in
coming to my own conclusions regarding this appeal, and by no means reject
the whole of the First Amendment doctrine, in a number of respects I am ...
dubious as to the applicability of this doctrine in the context of a challenge to
hate propaganda legislation. First, it is not entirely clear that *Beauharnais* [a
1951 decision of the United States Supreme Court upholding a criminal
conviction for group libel] must conflict with existing First Amendment
doctrine. Credible arguments have been made that later Supreme Court cases
do not necessarily erode its legitimacy.

Second, the aspect of First Amendment doctrine most incompatible with [the
hate propaganda law], at least as that doctrine is described by those who
would strike down the legislation, is its strong aversion to content-based
regulation of expression. I am somewhat skeptical, however, as to whether
this view of free speech in the United States is entirely accurate. Rather, in

---

[8] Ibid.   [9] [1990] 3SCR 870.   [10] Ibid., at 874.
[11] [1990] 3 SCR 892.   [12] Ibid., at 902–3.

rejecting the extreme position that would provide an absolute guarantee of free speech ... the [United States] Supreme Court [has often upheld content regulation, including laws forbidding] obscenity ... (see, e.g., Roth v. United States, 354 U.S. 476 (1957)) ... laws proscribing child pornography ... (see New York v. Ferber, 458 U.S. 747 (1982)), [laws regulating] commercial expression ... (see, e.g., Posadas de Puerto Rico Associates v. Tourism Co. of Puerto Rico, 478 U.S. 328 (1986)) ... and ... restrict[ing] government employees in their exercise of the right to engage in political activity (Cornelius v. NAACP Legal Defense Fund, 473 U.S. 788 (1985)).[13]

1.1 Is *Beauharnais* Still 'Good Law'?

In January of 1950, Joseph Beauharnais, the President of the White Circle League, circulated a leaflet containing a petition to the mayor and city council of Chicago calling for racial segregation.[14] The leaflet stated that if 'persuasion and the need to prevent the white race from becoming mongrelized by the negro will not unite us, then the aggressions ... rapes, robberies, knives, guns and marijuana of the negro, surely will'.[15] Beauharnais was convicted under an Illinois statute prohibiting the publication of any matter which 'portrays depravity, criminality, unchastity, or lack of virtue of a class of citizens, of any race, color, creed or religion which ... exposes [such] citizens to contempt, derision or obloquy'.[16] The United States Supreme Court, in a 5–4 decision, affirmed the conviction, finding that libellous utterances, whether directed at individuals or 'designated collectivities',[17] was not 'within the area of constitutionally protected speech'.[18] In addition, the Court rejected the argument that it was constitutionally required that truth alone be an absolute defence to a charge of group libel, holding that it was not unconstitutional to require a defendant charged with criminal libel to show not only the truth of the statement but also that it was made 'with good motives and for justifiable ends'.[19]

Justice Dickson acknowledges that '*Beauharnais* appears to have been weakened by later pronouncements of the Supreme Court'.[20] This is an understatement. Rather, as the vast majority of courts and

---

[13] *Keegstra*, at 741–2.
[14] *Beauharnais* v. *Illinois*, 343 US 250, 252 (1952).
[15] Ibid.   [16] Ibid., at 250.   [17] Ibid., at 257–58.
[18] Ibid., at 266.   [19] Ibid., at 265.   [20] *Keegstra*, at 739.

commentators who have discussed the issue have concluded,[21] including commentators who are proponents of hate speech prohibition,[22] these 'later pronouncements' have knocked the legs out from under *Beauharnais* to the extent that it is a virtual certainty that the Supreme Court would overrule that precedent if presented with a proper case in which to do so. There are both global and specific reasons why *Beauharnais* is no longer good law. To begin with the global, the sea change in first amendment methodology that has taken place in the last three decades shows that *Beauharnais* would not be decided the same way today. *Beauharnais* is a product of the categorical exclusion approach to free speech introduced into the law in 1942 by *Chaplinsky* v. *New Hampshire*.[23] In the key passage upholding the conviction of a Jehovah's Witness for calling a city official 'a God damned racketeer' and 'a damned fascist',[24] the United States Supreme Court stated:

There are certain well-defined and narrowly limited classes of speech, the prevention and punishment of which have never been thought to raise any Constitutional problem. These include the lewd and obscene, the profane, *the libelous*, and the insulting or 'fighting' words—those which by their very utterance inflict injury or tend to incite an immediate breach of the peace. It has been well observed that such utterances are no essential part of any exposition of ideas, and are of such slight social value as a step to truth that any benefit that may be derived from them is clearly outweighed by the social interest in order and morality.[25]

In that same year, the Supreme Court added commercial speech as a category of expression that is totally excluded from first amendment protection.[26]

---

[21] See, e.g., *Collin* v. *Smith*, 578 F. 2d 1197, 1205 (7th Cir.), cert. denied, 439 US 988 (1978); L. Tribe, *American Constitutional Law* (1988), 926–7; Strossen, *Regulating Racist Speech on Campus: A Modest Proposal?*, Duke L.J. (1990) 484, 518; Karst, *Boundaries and Reason: Freedom of Expression and The Subordination of Groups*, Ill. L Rev. (1990) 95, 134–35 n. 160; Post, *Cultural Heterogeneity and Law: Pornography, Blasphemy, and the First Amendment*, Cal. L. Rev. 76, (1988), 297, 330. But see *Smith* v. *Collin*, 436 US 953 (1978) (Blackmun, J., joined by Rehnquist J., dissenting from denial of a stay) (*'Beauharnais* has never been overruled or formally limited in any way.').

[22] See Kretzmer, *Freedom of Speech and Racism*, Cardozo L. Rev. 8 (1987), 445, 449–50 & n. 27; Lawrence, *If He Hollers Let Him Go: Regulating Racist Speech On Campus*, Duke L.J. (1990), 431, 464.

[23] 315 US 568 (1942).   [24] Ibid., at 569.   [25] Ibid., at 571–2 (emphasis added).
[26] *Valentine* v. *Chrestensen*, 316 US 52 (1942).

Ten years after *Chaplinsky* was decided, the Supreme Court issued its opinion in *Beauharnais*. Beauharnais argued that the statements in his petition to city officials could not be punished without proof that they presented a 'clear and present' danger of violence or law violation.[27] Finding the statements libellous, the Court invoked the *Chaplinsky* categorical exclusion methodology and rejected the need for a finding of 'clear and present danger':

Libelous utterances not being within the area of constitutionally protected speech, it is unnecessary ... to consider the issues behind the phrase 'clear and present danger'. Certainly no one would contend that obscene speech, for example, may be punished only upon a showing of such circumstances. Libel, as we have seen, is in the same class.[28]

By the 1960s, however, it became apparent that the *Chaplinsky* methodology posed severe dangers to free speech in the United States. For instance, the categorical exclusion of libel from the first amendment was a powerful weapon in the hands of Southern officials as they tried to suppress protest against racial segregation. Thus an Alabama jury awarded a police commissioner $500,000 in damages against the *New York Times* and several civil rights activists, finding that an advertisement carried by the paper in support of the activities of Dr Martin Luther King, Jr., was libellous.[29] The finding was based on several false statements contained in the advertisement, such as the charge that King had been arrested seven times when, in fact, he had been arrested only four times.[30] Similarly, the exclusion of 'fighting words' from first amendment protection was used by government officials to squelch protest against the Vietnam war.[31] Fortunately, the Supreme Court was alert to the repressive potential of the *Chaplinsky* approach and in *New York Times* v. *Sullivan* and *Gooding* v. *Wilson* afforded libel and 'fighting words', respectively, substantial first amendment protection.[32] More

[27] 343 US, at 253.   [28] Ibid., at 266.

[29] See *New York Times* v. *Sullivan*, 376 US 254, 256 (1964).

[30] Ibid., at 259.

[31] See e.g. *Gooding* v. *Wilson*, 405 US 518 (1972) (antiwar protestor arrested and convicted for calling a policeman a 'son of a bitch').

[32] In *Sullivan* the Court held that public officials could recover for a defamatory statement only if the statement was made with knowledge that it was false or with reckless disregard for whether it was true or not. 376 US at 278–80. In *Gooding*, the Court did not expressly discard the fighting words doctrine, but instead found a state statute that proscribed 'opprobrious words or abusive language, tending to cause a breach of the peace' to be overbroad. 405 US at 519–20. In light of *Gooding* and other

recently, commercial speech has been brought into the ambit of the first amendment,[33] leaving only obscenity (and its close relative, child pornography[34]) completely outside of its protective scope. Thus the definite trend of American free speech methodology during the last thirty years has been to eschew the categorical exclusion approach of *Chaplinsky* in favour of a methodology that focuses on the harm caused or likely to be caused by the particular speech at issue.[35] And recent cases have insisted that this harm be both serious and palpable.[36]

Given these developments, the prohibition of group libel is no longer talismanically immune from first amendment scrutiny. Still, it could be argued that such a prohibition would survive modern first amendment analysis, for the case law makes clear that *some* libellous statements may, under certain circumstances, be actionable. For instance, a government official can recover for defamatory remarks made with knowledge of their falsity or with reckless disregard for

---

cases in which the Court has refused to sustain convictions based on face-to-face insults, (see *Rosenfeld* v. *New Jersey*, 408 US 901 (1972); *Lewis* v. *City of New Orleans*, 408 US 913 (1972); *Brown* v. *Oklahoma*, 408 US 914 (1972); *Houston* v. *Hill*, 482 US 451 (1987)) the continued validity of the 'fighting words' doctrine is in doubt. Indeed, since announcing the fighting words doctrine fifty years ago in *Chaplinsky*, the Court has not sustained a single conviction under that rationale, and recently, in *R.A.V.* v. *City of St. Paul*, (discussed at text accompanying n. 62–72, below) the Court once again reversed such a conviction. See also n. 65, below. In a recent symposium on campus hate speech I suggested that the Court would do well to formally limit the doctrine as applying only to face-to-face insults that are not part of public discourse and not to personal insults in debates in a public forum or to epithets directed to public officials by angry citizens. See Weinstein, *A Constitutional Roadmap to the Regulation of Campus Hate Speech*, *Wayne L. Rev.* 38 (1991), 163, 186–7, n. 87.

[33] *Virginia Pharmacy Board* v. *Virginia Consumer Council*, 425 US 748 (1976).

[34] *New York* v. *Ferber*, 458 US 747 (1982) (photographs and films depicting explicit sexual conduct involving children not protected by the first amendment (ibid., at 764–65); Court relies on the harm to the child so photographed exacerbated by the circulation of the photographs (ibid., at 759–60), as well as the economic motive for further child abuse in the production of child pornography provided by the advertising and selling of such pornography (ibid., at 761–2)).

[35] See e.g. *Gertz* v. *Robert Welch, Inc.*, 418 US 323, 349 (1974) (damage awards in libel suits brought by private plaintiffs ordinarily limited to 'compensation for actual injury').

[36] See e.g. *Brandenburg* v. *Ohio*, 395 US 444, 447 (1969) (advocacy of force or law violation may not be forbidden unless such advocacy is directed to inciting imminent lawless action and is likely to incite or produce such action); *Texas* v. *Johnson*, 491 US 397, 407–9 (1989) (generalized assumption that flag burning will lead to breach of the peace by those offended by such expression is an insufficient showing of likely harm to warrant prohibition of flag burning).

whether the statements were false.[37] And a private defendant can recover for injury actually caused by defamatory remarks so long as strict liability is not imposed on the defendant (e.g. a negligence standard is applied).[38] Accordingly, one could argue that knowingly (or perhaps even negligently) false statements about racial or ethnic groups remain punishable, and thus *Beauharnais* survives despite the radical change in methodology.

Once again, it is a global view of modern first amendment doctrine that most strongly refutes any such argument. In bringing libel within the sphere of first amendment protection in *New York Times* v. *Sullivan*, the Court emphasized that the first amendment demands 'that debate on public issues should be uninhibited, robust, and wide-open'.[39] And in subsequent cases the Court continued to put significant limitations on libel laws to ensure that such laws did not encroach upon the free exchange of ideas on issues of public concern.[40] Indeed, if there is a leitmotif in the free speech cases since *Sullivan* it is that restrictions of any type that are likely to interfere with robustness of public discourse are unconstitutional. It was thus to ensure a safe haven for public discourse that the Court recently struck down as a violation of free speech a statute barring a criminal from receiving the proceeds from a book about his crimes;[41] laws prohibiting the desecration of the American flag;[42] and a civil judgment against a pornographer for publishing a vicious parody stating that Jerry Falwell, a nationally known minister, had his first sexual experience in a drunken tryst with his own mother in an outhouse.[43]

One need only imagine the conviction of an angry black nationalist for writing that caucasians are 'white devils' or prosecutions for the stereotypes expressed in the televised dialogues between African-Americans and Korean-Americans in the aftermath of the recent Los Angeles riots, to appreciate that a racial libel law such as at issue in

[37] *New York Times* v. *Sullivan*, 376 US 254, 279–80 (1964). See *Harte-Hanks Communication* v. *Connaughton*, 491 US 657 (1989) (affirming libel judgment obtained by public figure).

[38] *Gertz* v. *Robert Welch, Inc.*, 418 US 323, 349 (1974).

[39] 376 US at 270.

[40] See e.g. *Philadelphia Newspapers, Inc.* v. *Hepps*, 475 US 767 (1986) (plaintiff in libel action governed by *Gertz* standard bears burden of showing falsity).

[41] *Simon & Schuster, Inc.* v. *New York Crime Victims Bd.*, 112 S. Ct. 501 (1991).

[42] *United States* v. *Eichman*, 110 S. Ct. 2404 (1990); *Texas* v. *Johnson*, 491 US 397 (1989).

[43] *Hustler Magazine* v. *Falwell*, 485 US 46 (1988).

Beauharnais would chill public discourse far more than any of the recent speech restrictions voided by the Court. It is thus inconceivable that the Court would reaffirm the validity of *Beauharnais*.

I mentioned above that there are specific as well as global reasons that belie Dickson's position that *Beauharnais* may still be good law. For one, the Court would likely hold that the harm said to flow from racial defamation—be it psychic injury to individual members of the group[44] or the risk of increased discrimination against these individuals[45]—is neither severe enough nor certain enough to justify the inhibition of public discourse that enforcement of group libel laws would cause. Relatedly, the Court might find that racial defamation, particularly such statements as, 'The Jews created the Holocaust to gain sympathy',[46] is not sufficiently 'of and concerning' any individual to constitute actionable defamation consistent with the first amendment.[47] But more significantly, the Court would almost certainly hold that almost all of what proponents of hate speech regulation want to punish as group defamation cannot constitutionally be punished as such. This is because the first amendment requires that 'a statement on matters of public concern must be provable as false before there can be liability' for defamation.[48]

Consider Beauharnais's statement about 'aggressions ... rapes, robberies, knives, guns and marijuana of the negro'. If it means that *all* African-Americans are aggressors, rapists, robbers, knife- and gun-toting pot-smokers, the statement is demonstrably false, but so demonstrably false as not to be believable by anyone, let alone the reasonable person, and is therefore not libellous. If it means that *some* blacks are rapists, robbers, etc., then this statement is demonstrably true, as it would be about some members of any racial or ethnic group

---

[44] Cf. *Hustler Magazine, Inc.* v. *Falwell*, 485 US 46, 55 (1988) (damage award against publisher of vicious parody that caused emotional injury to nationally known minister violates the first amendment; Court refers to the 'longstanding refusal to allow damages because the speech in question may have an adverse emotional impact on the audience'). For a further discussion of the inherent difficulties of prohibiting public discourse based on the psychic injury it may cause, see text accompanying nn. 168–176, below. See also Weinstein, above n. 32, at 176–80.

[45] See text accompanying nn. 75–100, below.

[46] *Keegstra*, at 714.

[47] See *New York Times* v. *Sullivan*, 376 US at 288 (false statements not sufficiently 'of and concerning' the plaintiff); *Rosenblatt* v. *Baer*, 383 US 75, 82–3 (1966) (same).

[48] *Milkovich* v. *Lorain Journal Co.*, 110 S. Ct. 2695, 2706 (1990). Moreover, the first amendment imposes upon the plaintiff the burden of proving falsity in defamation cases involving matters of public concern. See *Philadelphia Newspapers* v. *Hepps*, 475 US 767 (1986).

in the USA, and is, again, not libellous. Another possible interpretation of Beauharnais's statement is that, per capita, more blacks in Chicago engage in these activities than do whites in Chicago. Under such an interpretation, this statement is of the type that is arguably falsifiable by reference to empirical data. Unfortunately, statements about any subordinated group ghettoized in large US cities to the effect that they disproportionately engage in crime and drug use may well be true, or at least be based on enough data to privilege the statement, even if it is ultimately proved false. But surely Beauharnais did not intend to make merely a dry, descriptive statement about the condition of inner-city blacks, and just as surely that was not the gravamen of the offence for which he was convicted. If an African-American minister had petitioned the Mayor of Chicago for more aid for the black community and cited the high and growing incidence of rapes, robberies and marijuana use among blacks in support of his plea, it is inconceivable that he would have been punished for these statements, even if they turned out to be false according to the best data available, and even if the minister was reckless in not consulting these data.

What Beauharnais most probably meant to say, and what the prosecution plainly assumed he meant, is that blacks are *inherently* prone to violent criminal activity and drug use. Thus our disagreement with Beauharnais and his ilk is not so much about the existence or non-existence of particular data, but rather about the meaning to be attached to the data. Beauharnais and his kind believe that blacks commit crimes because that is their inherent nature; we believe that grinding poverty with no hope of escaping it, together with a long and continuing history of discrimination and injustice, will cause crime in any community. He believes the solution is State-decreed segregation; we believe that the solution is inclusion rather than exclusion. I am confident that our inferences are more logical and better supported by the data than are Beauharnais's hate-driven conclusions. But the real evil of Beauharnais's beliefs is not so much that they are false in any empirical sense, although I believe that they are, but that they are a product of hateful, racist ideology.[49] As such, however, his statement about the inherent nature of blacks is not the stuff that the

[49] That the primary concern of racial defamation laws is not with the falsity of the statement but with the *beliefs* that motivate the statement is revealed by the Illinois statute at issue in *Beauharnais*. Under that statute proof by the defendant that his statements were in fact true was not a sufficient defence. Rather, in addition to proving truth, the defendant had to show that the statements were made 'with good motives and for justifiable ends'. See 343 US at 254. Similarly, the majority in *Keegstra* expressed

Supreme Court would characterize as a factual statement 'provable as false'.

For one, even if Beauharnais's empirical claims could be isolated from the expression of his political beliefs, the courtroom is not an appropriate forum to assess the empirical accuracy of theories asserting that traits of particular groups are biological rather than a product of the environment. Even on the dubious assumption that such theories are presently susceptible to conclusive empirical testing in some forum, the judicial system is simply not designed to deal with questions this complex and imponderable. But more significantly, biological theories of race are often inextricably bound up with value judgments, often ugly and pernicious value judgments, but value judgments none the less.[50] Thus I believe that the present Court would find such statements to be 'ideas' rather than statements of fact. And under first amendment jurisprudence 'there is no such thing as a false idea'.[51]

Much of what proponents of hate propaganda laws seek to punish as group defamation would similarly be considered 'ideas' rather than falsifiable factual assertions. Such would plainly be the case, for instance, with regard to most of the hateful comments at issue in the Canadian hate speech cases: e.g., Jews are 'treacherous'[52] and 'money-loving';[53] 'Israel stinks';[54] 'Communism is Jewish';[55] and that a Jewish conspiracy is responsible for 'unemployment and inflation'.[56]

---

doubt 'as to whether the *Charter* [as opposed to the statute at issue in that case] mandates that truthful statements communicated *with an intention to promote hatred* need be excepted from criminal condemnation'. [1990] 3 SCR at 781 (emphasis on the original). Today in the United States the first amendment forbids recovery for defamation about matters of public concern unless the plaintiff proves the allegedly defamatory statement to be false. See *Philadelphia*, 475 US 767 (1986).

[50] See Post, *Racist Speech, Democracy, and the First Amendment*, William & Mary *L.Rev.* 32 (1991), 267, 298, ('The fundamental issue [raised by statements such as Beauharnais'] is the nature of the group's identity, an issue that almost certainly ought to be characterized as one of evaluative opinion.'); D. Richards, *Toleration and the Constitution*, 191 (1986) ('[T]he communications, restricted by group libel, express general conscientious views of speakers and audiences, whose nature and effect both depend on evaluative conceptions.').

[51] *Gertz* v. *Robert Welch, Inc.*, 418 US 323, 339 (1974).

[52] *Keegstra*, at 714.   [53] Ibid.

[54] *Andrews*, at 874.   [55] Ibid.

[56] *Taylor*, at 903. Moreover, even on the dubious assumption that false stereotypes about racial or ethnic groups could constitutionally be characterized as statements of fact rather than opinion, a recent Supreme Court opinion might preclude government from singling out racial defamation for criminal punishment, while leaving most other types of defamation subject only to civil actions. See *R.A.V.* v. *City of St. Paul*, 112 S. Ct. 2538 (1992), discussed at text accompanying n. 62–72, below.

1.2 Banning Hate Speech under a Theory Other than Group Defamation

Just because a racist statement is not constitutionally actionable in the USA as defamation does not mean that it cannot be constitutionally punished under some other rationale. It could be argued, for instance, that racist speech, like obscenity, child pornography, knowingly or recklessly false statements of fact, and 'fighting words' is 'no essential part of any exposition of ideas, and ... of such slight social value as a step to truth'[57] that it is categorically unworthy of first amendment protection.[58] Additionally, it could be argued that the harm caused by racist speech warrants its suppression. Neither of these theories, however, either separately or in combination, supports a general prohibition of racist speech under current doctrine.

1.2.1 Categorical Exclusion of Racist Speech from First Amendment Protection and the Lesson of R. A. V.

As documented above,[59] a strong trend in US free speech jurisprudence in the last thirty years has been away from *per se* exclusions of large categories of speech and towards a more particularized, harm-based methodology. This trend alone should have been sufficient to prove that the Supreme Court would not consign racist speech to that small realm of unprotected expression reserved for obscenity and a few increasingly narrow categories of other expression. Further proof was provided several years ago in dicta in *Texas* v. *Johnson*,[60] the landmark case in which the Court upheld the right of a protestor to burn the US flag.[61] And in *R. A. V.* v. *City of St. Paul*,[62] the Court finally confirmed that there is no general first amendment exception permitting the suppression of hateful racist expression.

In *R. A. V.* a juvenile who had burned a cross on a black family's lawn was prosecuted under a statute that provided:

Whoever places on public or private property a symbol, object, appellation, characterization or graffiti, including, but not limited to, a burning cross or

---

[57] *Chaplinsky* v. *New Hampshire*, 315 US 568, 572 (1942).
[58] See text accompanying nn. 23–6, above.
[59] See text accompanying nn. 32–6, above.
[60] 491 US 397 (1989).
[61] The First Amendment does not guarantee that other concepts virtually sacred to our Nation as a whole—*such as the principle that discrimination on the basis of race [is] odious and destructive*—will go unquestioned in the market-place of ideas. Ibid., at 41.
[62] 112 S. Ct. at 2538 (1992).

Nazi swastika, which one knows or has reasonable grounds to know arouses anger, alarm or resentment in others on the basis of race, color, creed, religion or gender commits disorderly conduct and shall be guilty of a misdemeanor.[63]

Recognizing that as drafted the statute was unconstitutionally over-broad, the Minnesota Supreme Court construed it to reach only such symbolic expressions of hate that also constituted fighting words.[64] Despite this limiting construction, the United States Supreme Court unanimously found the statute still violated the first amendment. The opinion of the Court, written by Justice Scalia, held that even though St. Paul might have been able to proscribe the entire class of fighting words,[65] by singling out only certain fighting words for proscription the city was engaging in viewpoint discrimination.[66] The Court reached this conclusion because the Minnesota Supreme Court repeatedly acknowledged that the statute was aimed at 'messages "based on virulent notions of racial supremacy"', and because both the Minnesota court and St Paul stated that the ordinance was 'directed at expression[s] of group hatred'.[67] Having found that the statute 'regulate[d] expression based on hostility towards its *protected* ideological content',[68] the Court subjected the regulation to the strict scrutiny reserved for content-based prohibitions of political speech in the public forum.[69]

The Court acknowledged that 'ensur[ing] the basic human rights of members of groups that have historically been subject to discrimination, including the right of such groups to live in peace where they wish', was a compelling State interest.[70] The Court found, however, that the 'existence of adequate content-neutral alternatives' to achieve this end made this restriction on speech not strictly *necessary*, and thus unconstitutional.[71]

---

[63] Ibid., at 2541.   [64] Ibid., at 2541–2.

[65] The Court noted that the petitioner and *amici* had urged the Court to modify *Chaplinksy's* formulation of the fighting words doctrine and thereby invalidate the St Paul ordinance as overbroad. Cf. n. 32, above. The Court, however, found it unnecessary to consider the continued validity of the fighting words doctrine. 112 S.Ct. at 2542. The concurring Justices, although not expressly calling for the modification of the fighting words doctrine, found the St Paul statute substantially overbroad. Ibid., at 2558–60 (White J., concurring in the judgment); 2561 (Blackmun J., concurring in the judgment); 2561 (Stevens J., concurring).

[66] 112 S. Ct. at 2547–8.   [67] Ibid., at 2548.

[68] Ibid., at 2549 (emphasis added).

[69] See text accompanying nn. 103–116, below.

[70] 112 S. Ct. at 2549.   [71] Ibid., at 2550.

The Court continued:

In fact the only interest distinctively served by the content limitation is that of displaying the city council's special hostility towards the particular biases thus singled out. That is precisely what the First Amendment forbids. The politicians of St. Paul are entitled to express that hostility—but not through the means of imposing unique limitations upon speakers who (however benightedly) disagree.[72]

There can thus no longer be any doubt that the expression of even virulent racist ideas is entitled to full first amendment protection.

1.2.2 Suppression of Racist Speech Because of its Tendency to Cause Harm

Just because a category of speech has not been cast outside the protection of the first amendment does not mean that individual incidents of speech within a generally protected category can never be suppressed regardless of the circumstances. For better or worse (and as we shall see, mainly for worse) it has always been a tenet of US free speech jurisprudence that the right even to express ideas is not absolute, but may be curtailed if the expression of an idea presents an unacceptable risk of grave and imminent harm.

In upholding Keegstra's conviction Chief Justice Dickson noted 'the possibility that prejudiced messages will gain some credence, with the attendant result of discrimination, and perhaps even violence against minority groups in Canada'.[73] Or, as Professor Mari Matsuda explains:

[A]t some level, no matter how much both victims and well-meaning dominant-group members resist it, racial inferiority is planted in our minds as an idea that may hold some truth ... We reject the idea, but the next time we sit next to one of 'those people' the [message of inferiority] is triggered. We stifle it, reject it as wrong but it is there, interfering with our perception and interaction with the person next to us.[74]

Dickson and Matsuda are surely correct that negative stereotypes of minority groups can shape people's images of members of those

[72] Ibid., cf. *Keegstra*, at 764–5 (justifying prohibition of hate propaganda on the ground that such a prohibition is itself 'expression by democratic government ... on behalf of the vast majority of citizens').

[73] *Keegstra*, at 748.

[74] Matsuda, *Public Response to Racist Speech: Considering the Victim's Story*, *Mich. L. Rev.* 87 (1989), 2320, 2339–40.

groups, and we may assume that, in least in some instances, these images can lead to discrimination and perhaps even violence. But this harm would not, under current first amendment doctrine, support the prohibition of racial defamation. Such harm results from an 'idea' that is 'planted in ... [the] minds' of others, so as to affect their 'perceptions' of the group in question and thus their behaviour towards individual members of the group. But it is precisely because the harm flows from the expression of *ideas* persuading others to perceive social phenomena in a way that is likely to have harmful consequences, that the theory would fail under present first amendment methodology.

The very first US free speech case of any significance held that dangerous ideas may be punished only upon a specific judicial finding that the ideas were expressed 'in such circumstances ... as to create a clear and present danger that they will bring about the substantive evils that [government] has a right to prevent'.[75] It could be argued that racist statements do create 'a clear and present danger' of racial discrimination, or even perhaps racial violence, both of which are evils that government has a right to prevent. If the 'clear and present danger test' were still the same as formulated in the World War I cases, the criminal syndicalism cases of the 1920s and 1930s, or perhaps even the McCarthy era cases of the 1950s, then there would be a chance that the prohibition of racist speech might be constitutional.[76] Under the current version of that test, however, formulated by the Supreme Court in *Brandenburg* v. *Ohio*,[77] the expression of racist ideas would ordinarily be immune from prosecution. In *Brandenburg*, a Ku Klux Klan leader was convicted under an Ohio criminal syndicalism statute for stating that 'some revengeance' might have to be taken if the government 'continues to suppress the white, Caucasian race'.[78] The Supreme Court reversed the conviction, holding that 'the constitutional guarantee of free speech and free press do not permit a State to forbid or proscribe advocacy of the use of force or of law violation except where such advocacy is directed to inciting or producing imminent lawless action and is likely to incite or produce such action'.[79]

Imagine (it is not very hard to do) a US version of Keegstra who

---

[75] *Schenck* v. *United States*, 249 US 47, 52 (1919).
[76] See text accompanying nn. 147–56, below.
[77] 395 US 444 (1969) (*per curiam*).
[78] Ibid., at 446.   [79] Ibid., at 447.

publishes a pamphlet stating that Jews are 'treacherous', 'subversive', etc. If he were prosecuted for expressing these ideas, could a conviction constitutionally be supported under a 'clear and present danger' rationale? For two reasons, it could not. First, except in some extraordinary circumstances that *are* hard to imagine (e.g. the anti-Semitic speech is given as the keynote address of a job fair where offers are being made on the spot) the discriminatory harm that might result from the statements is far from imminent. The imminence standard of *Brandenburg* derives from Holmes's classic *Abrams* dissent[80] and from Brandeis's influential *Whitney* concurrence,[81] and was applied with teeth by the Court in *Hess* v. *Indiana*.[82] During an anti-Vietnam war protest over 100 demonstrators blocked the street, until after several arrests, the police succeeded in clearing the street by moving the protestors to the kerb.[83] Hess was arrested for yelling: 'We'll take the fucking street later [or again]'.[84] Purporting to apply *Brandenburg* the state court found that this statement 'intended to incite further lawless action on the part of the crowd . . . and was likely to produce such action'.[85] The United States Supreme Court reversed, finding that Hess had not intended to produce imminent lawless action:

At best, [the] statement could be taken as counsel for present moderation; at worst, it amounted to nothing more than advocacy of illegal action at some indefinite future time.

[S]ince there was no evidence, or rational inference from the import of the language, that his words were intended to produce, and likely to produce, *imminent* disorder, those words could not be punished by the State on the ground that they had 'a tendency to lead to violence'.[86]

If a call to a mob to take the street again, or even later, does not present an imminent enough danger of lawless conduct to justify

---

[80] '[W]e should be eternally vigilant against attempts to check the expression of opinions that we loathe and believe to be fraught with death, unless they so imminently threaten immediate interference with the lawful and pressing purposes of the law that an immediate check is required to save the country.' *Abrams* v. *United States*, 250 US 616, 630 (1919) (Holmes J., dissenting).

[81] '[N]o danger flowing from speech can be deemed clear and present, unless the incidence of the evil apprehended is so imminent that it may befall before there is opportunity for full discussion. If there be time to expose through discussion the falsehood and fallacies, to avert the evil by the processes of education, the remedy to be applied is more speech, not enforced silence. Only an emergency can justify repression.' *Whitney* v. *California* 274 US 357, 377 (1927) (Brandeis J., concurring).

[82] 414 US 105 (1973) (*per curiam*).

[83] Ibid., at 106.   [84] Ibid., at 107.

[85] Ibid., at 108.   [86] Ibid., at 107–8.

speech suppression under *Brandenburg*, then certainly the possibility of discrimination resulting from anti-Semitic statements such as Keegstra's is not imminent enough to warrant suppression. Far from presenting an evil 'so imminent that it may befall before there is opportunity for full discussion',[87] the untruth and unfairness of such stereotypes can be and have been exposed by 'full discussion'.[88] Indeed, a danger of imminent discrimination or violence would ordinarily be lacking even if the speaker not only charged that Jews were inherently treacherous and subversive but expressly advocated that for this reason businesses should not hire Jews.

Keegstra and his compatriots, however, did not directly advocate violence or other law violation. This brings us to the second reason why they could not have been constitutionally punished in the USA for their racist statements. Perhaps the most important innovation of *Brandenburg* is that it rejects the 'bad tendency' approach of earlier 'clear and present danger' cases and adopts the requirement, long ago suggested by Judge Learned Hand, [89] that the speaker must explicitly,

---

[87] *Whitney* v. *California*, 274 US 357, 377 (1927) (Brandeis J., concurring).

[88] In addition, it is not at all certain that the Court would find risk of job discrimination (or most any other type of discrimination for that matter) a sufficiently grave harm to justify a speech prohibition. See ibid., at 378 ('The fact that speech is likely to result in some violence or in destruction of property is not enough to justify its suppression. There must be the probability of serious injury to the State.') The Court might well point to the civil remedies available to anyone discriminated against in employment on the basis of race or ethnicity, (see, e.g., Title VII of the Civil Rights Act of 1964, 42 USC §2000e *et seq.*), and conclude that in light of these remedies, the inhibition on public discourse that would result from punishing advocacy of such discrimination is not justified. See *Whitney*, 274 US at 378 (Brandeis J., concurring) ('Among free men, the deterrents ordinarily to be applied to prevent crime are education and punishment for violations of the law, not abridgment of the rights of free speech and assembly.') The availability of means other than speech suppression to combat racial discrimination was expressly invoked by the Court in *R.A.V.* in support of its holding that, although insuring the basic human rights of minorities is surely a compelling state interest, suppression of racist ideology is not necessary to achieve that goal. See nn. 70–72, above.
  In contrast, racist speech posing an imminent risk of violence against minorities might pose a sufficiently grave harm to warrant suppression of such speech. (But see the first quotation from Brandeis's *Whitney* concurrence, above.)

[89] See *Masses Publishing* v. *Patten*, 244 F. 535, 540 (SDNY), *rev'd* 246 F. 24 (2d Cir. 1917) ('Political agitation, by the passions it arouses or the convictions it engenders, may in fact stimulate men to the violation of the law ... [But if] one stops short of urging upon others that it is their duty or their interest to resist the law, it seems to me one should not be held to have attempted to cause its violation'). See also Gunther, *Learned Hand and the Origins of Modern First Amendment Doctrine: some Fragments of History*, *Stan. L. Rev.* 27 (1975), 719, 755. ('The inciting language of the speaker—the Hand focus on "objective" words—is the major consideration [under *Brandenburg*].) Several

not just inferentially, call for others to engage in lawless activity before he can be punished for the expression of a dangerous idea.[90] Thus the first amendment protects a speaker in discussing the moral necessity of discriminating against or even killing Jews, so long as he does not call for others to immediately put these ideas into action. *A fortiori*, a speaker who does not even go so far as abstractly discussing the desirability of illegal discrimination or violence but merely makes hateful statements about the traits of certain groups is protected by the first amendment, even if the speaker both hopes and expects that his ideas will stir his listeners to imminent lawless action, and even if such illegal conduct is in fact likely to occur.

Indeed, a case decided several years before *Brandenburg* suggests that so long as direct advocacy of conduct is lacking, there is an absolute right to advocate any idea, even if it might lead to illegal conduct. In *Kingsley International Picture Corp.* v. *Regents*,[91] the state of New York had denied a theatre a licence to show the film *Lady Chatterly's Lover* because it presented adultery as a practice that might be right and desirable under certain circumstances.[92] Just as the Canadian Supreme Court reasonably assumed that the depiction of racial or ethnic groups in an unfair, stereotypical manner can lead to acts of discrimination, so New York could have fairly assumed that the depiction of adultery as morally justified could lead to acts of adultery, then illegal under New York law.[93] None the less, the Supreme Court found the denial of the license unconstitutional, stating:

[New York has denied the licence] because the picture advocates an idea— that adultery under certain circumstances may be proper behavior. Yet the First Amendment's basic guarantee is of freedom to advocate ideas. The

---

years before *Brandenburg* the Supreme Court, animated by constitutional concerns, adopted Hand's approach as a matter of statutory construction of the Smith Act. See e.g. *Yates* v. *United States*, 354 US 298, 318–20 (1957) (distinguishing between 'advocacy of forcible overthrow as an abstract doctrine', and 'advocacy of action to that end', and reversing Smith Act convictions for lack of evidence of the latter type of advocacy); *Noto* v. *United States*, 367 US 290, 291 (1961) (reversing Smith Act convictions because evidence of 'advocacy of action' was 'sparse indeed').

[90] Thus *Brandenburg* permits a speaker to be punished for causing an imminent risk of violence or law violation only if he directly incites such conduct, not merely for the 'abstract teaching ... of the moral propriety or even the moral necessity for a resort to force and violence' 395 US at 448 (quoting *Noto* v. *United States*, 367 US 290, 298 (1961)).

[91] 360 US 684 (1959).   [92] Ibid., at 687–8.   [93] Ibid., at 688.

State, quite simply, has struck at the very heart of constitutionally protected liberty.

Advocacy of conduct proscribed by law is not ... 'a justification for denying free speech where the advocacy falls short of incitement'.[94]

A more recent decision by a federal appellate court, *American Booksellers Ass'n.* v. *Hudnut*,[95] makes the same point. That case involved a city ordinance that allowed civil sanctions for the distribution of 'pornography', defined as 'the graphic sexually explicit subordination of women'.[96] The city justified the ordinance on the ground that 'pornography affects thoughts [and] [m]en who see women as depicted as subordinate are more likely to treat them so'.[97] The court agreed that '[p]eople often act in accordance with the images and patterns they find around them', and that therefore '[d]epictions of subordination tend to perpetuate subordination [of women, including] lower pay at work, insult and injury at home [and] battery and rape on the streets'.[98] None the less, the court held that under current first amendment doctrine the ordinance was unconstitutional:

All of these unhappy effects depend on mental intermediation. ... The Alien and Sedition Acts [rested] on a sincerely held belief that disrespect for the government leads to social collapse and revolution—a belief with support in the history of many nations. Most governments of the world act on this empirical regularity, suppressing critical speech. In the United States, however, the strength of the support for this belief is irrelevant. Seditious libel is protected speech unless the danger is not only grave but also imminent. [Similarly], [r]acial bigotry, anti-semitism, violence on television, reporters' biases—these and many more influence the culture and shape our socialization. ... Yet all is protected speech, however insidious. Any other answer leaves the government in control of all the institutions of culture, the great censor and director of which thoughts are good for us.[99]

Finally, it should be noted that even if the suppression of hate speech on the theory that it persuades others to discriminate against minorities could overcome all of the difficult hurdles imposed by the clear and present danger test, such a prohibition might still be invalid under

---

[94] Ibid., at 688–9, quoting *Whitney*, 274 US at 376 (Brandeis J., concurring).
[95] 771 F.2d. 323, 328 (7th Cir. 1985), aff'd 475 US 1001 (1986).
[96] Ibid., at 324. [97] Ibid., at 328. [98] Ibid., at 328–9.
[99] Ibid., at 329–30. The United States Supreme Court summarily affirmed this decision. 475 US 1001 (1986).

R.A.V. for singling out only one type of speech likely to cause illegal discrimination or violence.[100]

1.3 Room for One More?: Precedent Upholding Certain Types of Content Regulation of Speech as an Argument for the Constitutionality of the Prohibition of Hate Propaganda

In a recent decision the United States Supreme Court said this about laws that regulate speech based upon its content:

> [Our] cases indicate that ... a *content-based* restriction on *political speech* in a *public forum* ... must be subjected to the most exacting scrutiny. Thus, we have required the State to show that the 'regulation is necessary to serve a compelling state interest and that it is narrowly drawn to achieve that end'.[101]

Brandenburg's incitement of violence standard, and perhaps even the *New York Times* v. *Sullivan's* standard for defamation recovery, can be seen as specific instantiations of a more general 'strict scrutiny' standard for content regulation of public discourse in the public forum.

Chief Justice Dickson, however, suggests that the Court's professed hostility to content regulation might be more talk than action. He points to several areas in which the Court has applied something less than strict scrutiny in upholding content-oriented speech restrictions, in areas such as obscenity, child pornography, commercial

---

[100] The Court in *R.A.V.* sent mixed signals about both the scope and rigour of the presumption of invalidity for under-inclusive regulation of unprotected categories of speech. Despite some strong language condemning the singling out of only certain types of unprotected speech, the Court explained that laws singling out sexual harassment in the work-place are not unconstitutional because such restrictions are 'incidental' to the regulation of discriminatory conduct. 112 S. Ct. at 2546.

[101] *Boos* v. *Barry*, 485 US 312, 321 (1988) (emphasis in the original). In that case the Court struck down a District of Columbia ordinance law that prohibited, within 500 feet of any foreign embassy, 'the display of any signing [tending] to bring the foreign government into "public odium" or "public disrepute".' Ibid., at 316. The Court held that the interest in protecting the dignity of foreign diplomatic personnel, although an interest recognized by international law, was not 'compelling', and even if it were there were less restrictive alternatives available to accomplish this objective. Ibid., at 329. See also *Texas* v. *Johnson*, 491 US 397, 412 (1989) (content based restrictions on speech must be subjected to 'the most exacting scrutiny'). For even a stronger statement of judicial hostility to content regulation, see *Simon & Schuster* v. *New York Crimes Victim Brd.*, 112 S. Ct. 501, 508 (1991) ('Regulations which permit the Government to discriminate on the basis of the content of the message cannot be tolerated under the First Amendment.'), quoting *Regan* v. *Time, Inc.* 468 US 641, 648–9 (1984).

speech, and limitations on the expressive rights of government employees.[102] With all due respect, the Chief Justice has missed two crucial distinctions: (1) the distinction between public discourse and private speech; and (2) the distinction between speech in the public forum and speech in the non-public forum. In the quotation above, the Court emphasizes that the strict scrutiny standard applies only to content-oriented restrictions on *political speech* (which I take to be synonymous with 'public discourse' or 'speech on matters of public concern'[103]) *in the public forum.*

Chief Justice Dickson cannot be faulted too much for missing the distinction between speech on matters of public concern and private speech, for he was doubtless led down the garden path by US proponents of hate speech legislation who should know better.[104] And to some extent he was also misled by the Supreme Court itself, which has neither often nor clearly enough elucidated this crucial distinction that has driven much of its first amendment jurisprudence. A good example of the distinction is revealed when we compare two landmark decisions in the area of free speech and libel. In *Gertz* v. *Robert Welch, Inc.*,[105] the Court, although rejecting the application of the *New York Times* v. *Sullivan* 'malice' standard for libel suits brought by private defendants, none the less imposed substantial first

---

[102] See text accompanying n. 13, above.

[103] Thus the Court's use of strict scrutiny for content oriented restrictions is not limited to speech that is overtly political but extends generally to matters of public concern. See e.g. *Simon & Schuster* v. *New York Crimes Victims Board*, 112 S. Ct. 501, 508 (1991) (subjecting to strict scrutiny and holding unconstitutional New York's 'Son of Sam' law requiring an accused or convicted criminal's income from works describing his crime be deposited in an escrow account for the benefit of the crime victim). See also *Burson* v. *Freeman*, 112 S. Ct. 1846, 1850 (opinion of Blackmun J., joined by Rehnquist CJ, White and Kennedy JJ.) (term 'political speech' used interchangeably with term 'speech concerning public affairs'). In any event, as recognized by the Canadian Supreme Court, the racist speech at issue in the cases before them qualified as 'political speech' (*Keegstra*, at 764), as would most of what the American proponents of hate speech legislation wish to prohibit. Similarly, the expression at issue in the most prominent American cases involving racist speech—*Beauharnais* v. *Illinois*, 343 US 250 (1952); *Brandenburg* v. *Ohio*, 395 US 444 (1969) (*per curiam*); and *Collin* v. *Smith*, 578 F.2d 1197, 1205 (7th Cir.), cert. denied, 439 US 916 (1978)—all involved overtly political speech.

[104] See Matsuda, above n. 74 at 2354–5; Delgado, *Campus Antiracism Rules: Constitutional Narratives in Collision, Nw.* U. L. Rev. 85 (1991), 343, 377–8. In support of their argument for the constitutionality of hate speech legislation both authors give a litany of speech restrictions, but fail to note that much of the speech on their list, unlike the speech they want suppressed, is not public discourse.

[105] 418 US 323 (1974).

amendment barriers to such suits.[106] Several years later, however, in
Dun & Bradstreet v. *Greenmoss Builders*,[107] Justice Powell explained
that this heightened first amendment protection applies only to
speech 'on matters of public concern', such as was involved in *Gertz*,
and not to speech 'on matters of purely private concern', as was
involved in the case at hand.[108] It is precisely this distinction that
explains why the first amendment protects an advocate in the
speakers' corner of the park in peppering his address with the vilest
profanities,[109] but might not privilege a person to use the same words
in addressing another during an argument about a parking space on
the perimeter of this same park.[110] It explains why a man has a first
amendment right to send a letter to the editor saying that a woman's
place is in the home, preferably as a sex object for her husband,[111] but
constitutionally may be prevented from repeatedly announcing this
position to his female employees in the work place;[112] and why
commercial speech (speech that does no more than propose a commercial transaction) is afforded far less protection than what the
Court sometimes calls 'political speech', and at others refers to as
'speech on matters of public concern' or 'public discourse'.[113]

---

[106] Ibid., at 343, 347–50 (states may not impose liability based on strict liability, nor
may damages be presumed or punitive damages recovered in the absence of a showing
of malice).

[107] 472 US 749 (1985).

[108] Ibid., at 758–9 (plurality opinion). See also *Connick* v. *Myers*, 461 US 138, 146
(1983). ('When employee expression cannot be fairly considered as relating to any
matter of political, social, or other concern to the community, government officials
should enjoy wide latitude in managing their offices, without intrusive oversight by the
judiciary in the name of the First Amendment.')

[109] See *Cohen* v. *California*, 403 US 15 (1971) (first amendment protects wearing a
jacket that says 'Fuck the Draft'); *Papish* v. *Board of Curators*, 410 US 667 (1973) (first
amendment right to publish a campus newspaper containing the term 'motherfucker').

[110] See n. 25, above. See also Post, above n. 50 at 315 n. 216 ('*Chaplinsky*...attempts
to distinguish private fracases from political debate'). But cf. n. 32, above.

[111] See *American Booksellers Ass'n* v. *Hudnut*, 771 F.2d 323, 328–30 (7th Cir. 1985),
aff'd 475 US 1001 (1986).

[112] See *Robinson* v. *Jacksonville Shipyards*, 760 F.Supp. 1486 (MD Fla. 1991) (sexist
statements and displays of pornography causing 'hostile environment' in the work-
place not protected by the first amendment); B. Lindemann and D. Kadue, *Sexual
Harassment in Employment Law* (1992), 592–600. See generally, *Meritor Savings Bank*
v. *Vinson*, 477 US 57 (1986) (holding that verbal harassment in the work-place can
constitute employment discrimination in violation of federal law).

[113] Compare e.g. the rather lax scrutiny of the prohibition of commercial speech in
Posadas De Puerto Rico Assocs. v. *Company of Puerto Rico*, 478 US 328 (1986), with
the strict scrutiny given the regulation of political speech at issue in *Boos* v. *Barry*, 485
US 312 (1988), discussed at n. 101 and accompanying text, above.

As I have explained in more detail in a previous article,[114] there are good reasons for the disparate protection afforded public discourse, such as the expression involved in the Canadian hate speech cases, and other types of expression, such as commercial speech.[115] For one, the harm caused by speech such as false or misleading advertising is far more objectively demonstrable and measurable than is the psychic injury caused by hate speech, or even the discrimination resulting from perceptions of minorities changed by such expression. But even more significantly, regulation of expression such as commercial speech does not present the same dangers of governmental abuse as does the regulation of public discourse. When government officials seek to suppress speech criticizing social or political conditions because the speech contains dangerous ideas, we should be suspicious that the motivation for the suppression might be that the officials are offended by the message, or more sinisterly, that they are trying to maintain the *status quo* so as to preserve their own power. In contrast, when government punishes a business for false or misleading advertising, it is far less likely that the government officials are offended by the speech, or that they are afraid that it will persuade others to turn them out of power.[116]

The US Supreme Court may not have often enough explained the

---

[114] See Weinstein, above n. 32 at 184–5.

[115] Of course, the line between public discourse and private speech will not always be an easy one to draw. See Post, 'The Constitutional Concept of Public Discourse: Outrageous Opinion, Democratic Deliberation, and *Hustler Magazine* v. *Falwell*', *Harv. L. Rev.* 103 (1990), 601, 667. Indeed, in certain unusual cases commercial speech should perhaps be considered to fall on the public discourse side of the line. See *Bigelow* v. *Virginia*, 421 US 809 (1975) (striking down prohibition on advertising for abortion services).

[116] In contrast to American free speech doctrine, under which the test for assessing the validity of restrictions on public discourse is far more rigorous than the test applicable to restrictions of commercial speech, (see n. 113, above), Canadian jurisprudence draws no such sharp contrast between commercial speech and other types of expression. See e.g. *R.* v. *Butler*, 70 CCC (3d) 129, 163 (1992) (in deferring to legislative finding that certain types of pornography alters people's attitudes so as to cause sexual violence, Court invokes standard developed in a commercial speech case). If I am correct that a vital free speech principle should more sedulously protect speech on matters of public concern than it does commercial speech, then the Canadian approach will tend to under-protect public discourse while overprotecting commercial speech. But the problem may be more general. In measuring the validity of restrictions of fundamental freedoms the Canadian Court has adopted a detailed test that applies to everything from restrictions on political speech to where the burden of proof should lie in drug cases. See *Keegstra*, at 734–5. But just as some types of speech are more imperiled by the political process than others, so too are some rights and thus require more judicial protection than others.

distinction between public discourse and other types of expression that obviously animates modern first amendment doctrine. In contrast, it has often drawn the distinction between speech in the public forum and speech on government owned property dedicated to purposes other than free expression.[117] As explained by the Court in the quotation above, governmental regulation of the content of 'political speech' in the public forum is subject to the 'most exacting scrutiny'. In contrast, government is held to a far less exacting standard for content-based restrictions in a non-public forum, where the government need only show that such restrictions are 'reasonable in light of the purpose served by the forum and are viewpoint neutral'.[118] For instance, public universities have undoubted power to set reasonable regulations on the content of speech in the classroom. Thus it would be perfectly constitutional for a dean to insist that a mathematics professor talk about number theory rather than about Shakespeare's sonnets when teaching his class. Such a restriction is constitutional because a classroom at a state university is not a public forum, but a forum dedicated to a specific purpose, in this case the learning of mathematics.[119] But if after class the same professor walked over to the mall in the middle of campus, where by tradition people gather to watch artistic performances or listen to speakers talk about the issues

[117] The Court's most recent opinions on the subject are *Int'l Soc. For Krishna Consc.* v. *Lee*, 112 S. Ct. 2701 (1992) (finding airport to be a non-public forum and upholding ban on solicitations of monetary contributions) and *Lee* v. *Int'l Soc. For Krishna Consc.*, 112 S. Ct. 2709 (1992) (striking down ban on leafleting in airport).

[118] *Cornelius* v. *NAACP Legal Defense and Educ. Fund, Inc.*, 473 US 788, 806 (1985). See also *Perry Ed. Assn* v. *Perry Local Educators' Assn*, 460 US 37 (1983); *United States* v. *Kokinda*, 110 S. Ct. 3115 (1990). For two excellent discussions of the public forum doctrine and the greater power government has to regulate the content of speech on public property that is not a public forum, see Stone, *Fora American: Speech in Public Places*, Sup. Ct. Rev. (1974), 233; Post, *Between Governance and Management: The History and Theory of the Public Forum*, UCLA L. Rev. 34 (1987), 1713.

[119] Thus, under American constitutional doctrine, school administrators could have prohibited a public school teacher from making the anti-Semitic remarks to his class made by Keegstra, if these remarks were not germane to the subject matter of the class. (Since the first amendment applies only to governmental restriction of speech, and not to purely private restrictions (see n. 204, below), the administration of a private school would have *carte blanche* so far as the first amendment is concerned to regulate the content of classroom speech. In contrast, a state law preventing a teacher in a private school from regaling his students with anti-Semitic propaganda would raise difficult constitutional questions, as would restrictions at a public school that prevented a teacher expressing anti-Semitic views that were germane to the subject matter he was assigned to teach). For a detailed first amendment analysis of the state's ability to limit racist speech in classrooms at public universities, see Weinstein, above n. 32 at 192–226.

of the day, he could not be prohibited from reciting the sonnets, or even from spewing racist or anti-Semitic venom.

With the distinction between the public and non-public forums in mind, it becomes clear that Chief Justice Dickson's description of *Cornelius* v. *NAACP Legal Defense and Education Fund, Inc.*,[120] which he says stands for the proposition that 'it is permissible to restrict government employees in their exercise of the right to engage in political activity',[121] tells but half the story, and not the important half at that. *Cornelius* involved a federal regulation that excluded legal defence and political advocacy organizations from participating in the Combined Federal Campaign, a charity drive aimed at federal employees.[122] The Court found that the Campaign was a non-public forum and thus judged the content restriction according to whether it reasonably furthered the purpose of the forum, rather than applying the strict scrutiny applicable to content-oriented restrictions on expression in the public forum.[123] The merits of the Court's decision that the work-place Campaign was not a public forum are certainly open to criticism, as are many of the Court's recent attempts to draw the line between public and non-public forums.[124] But the basic dichotomy is none the less a useful one. In any event, the dichotomy reveals that neither *Cornelius*, nor any of the other Supreme Court decisions allowing government leeway to regulate the content of speech in a non-public forum, belies the Court's stated hostility to content regulation of *political* speech in the *public forum*.[125]

---

[120] 473 US 788 (1985).
[122] Ibid., *Cornelius* 473 US at 792–9.
[121] *Keegstra*, at 742.
[123] Ibid., at 806, 808–11.
[124] e.g. *United States* v. *Kokinda*, 110 S. Ct. 3115 (1990) (sidewalk in front of post office not a public forum).
[125] Perhaps instead of *Cornelius* Dickson meant to cite *United States CSC* v. *National Ass'n of Letter Carriers*, 413 US 548 (1973), which does in fact uphold the federal government's power to 'restrict government employees in their right to engage in political activities'. In that case the Court noted the strong governmental interest in limiting partisan political activities of employees to assure that government operated 'effectively and fairly' and that employees remained 'free from improper influences': 413 US at 564. But more significantly for purposes of assessing whether *Letter Carriers* would support the constitutionality of the prohibition of hate speech, the Court emphasized that the restrictions 'were not aimed at particular parties, groups or points of view ... [nor] do they seek to control political opinions or beliefs' (ibid.), something that cannot be said of hate speech laws. *Letter Carriers* does show, however, that not all content-oriented restrictions on public discourse in the public forum are subjected to the most rigorous scrutiny, and thus perhaps it would be more accurate to say that the most searching judicial scrutiny is reserved for *viewpoint* restrictions. Accord, *Burson* v. *Freeman*, 112 S. Ct. 1846 (1992) (upholding statute prohibiting solicitation of votes and displays or distributions of campaign materials within 100 feet of entrance to polling place).

Chief Justice Dickson makes a more valid point with respect to the Court's obscenity opinions. Whereas every other category of speech cast outside the realm of the first amendment by *Chaplinsky* has either expressly or implicitly been brought within the scope of that amendment in the last thirty years, obscenity remains categorically excluded from such protection.[126] With respect to almost every other type of expression that it proposes to regulate because of its content, the government must show that the expression would be palpably harmful if left unregulated, and with respect to public discourse in the public forum, that devastating harm will result. Obscenity, on the other hand, can be regulated because of its content without a showing of demonstrable harm.[127]

A surface level explanation for the lack of judicial scrutiny of obscenity regulations is that, as *Chaplinsky* held, obscenity is not speech within the meaning of the first amendment and thus may be treated like any other type of conduct not protected by the constitution. This explanation does not advance the inquiry, however, for the question remains, *why* should extremely graphic depictions of sex not count as expression for purposes of the first amendment? The Court has relied exclusively on 'history' in jettisoning obscenity from constitutional protection, finding that those who framed and ratified the first amendment considered obscenity 'outside the protection intended for speech'.[128] But whatever might be said in support of a historical exception for obscenity, a similar argument would be ludicrous with regard to racist speech in light of the prevalent racist attitudes of even the most progressive of the founding fathers,[129] and the protection of the pre-eminent racist institution—slavery—in the body of the Constitution itself.[130]

Recently, Professor Frederick Schauer has advanced another theory supporting the exclusion of obscenity from first amendment

[126] See *Paris Adult Theater I* v. *Slaton*, 413 US 49, 54 (1973).

[127] Contrast, for instance, the harm based rationale for excluding child pornography from first amendment protection. See *New York* v. *Ferber*, 458 US 747 (1989), discussed n. 34, above.

[128] See *Roth* v. *United States*, 354 US 476, 483 (1957).

[129] See e.g. T. Jefferson, *Notes on the State of Virginia* (1787), 138–43 (reprinted 1955, ed. W. Pedden) (arguing that blacks are inherently intellectually inferior to whites).

[130] See US Art. I, §9 (prohibiting Congress from outlawing importation of slaves until 1808); Art. IV., §2 (requiring states to return fugitive slaves); Art. V. (exempting from the amendment process ART. I, §9 limitation on Congress' power to abolish the slave trade).

protection. Schauer maintains that because such material lacks any 'intended intellectual appeal',[131] but is designed merely to sexually stimulate the viewer, obscenity 'is more accurately treated as a physical rather than a mental experience'.[132] Like the historical justification, Schauer's explanation is problematic.[133] But more significantly for the purposes of the inquiry here, like the historical argument it offers no support for the exclusion of hate speech, for vicious hate propaganda is no more a purely physical experience than any other type of highly inflammatory political rhetoric.

1.4 Other Relevant American Precedent

In May 1977 the village of Skokie, an Illinois community where many Holocaust survivors lived, tried to prevent the American Nazi Party from marching there by enacting an ordinance that, among other restrictions, prohibited 'dissemination of any material within [Skokie] which [intentionally] promotes and incites hatred against persons by reason of their race, national origin, or religion'.[134] Both the United States District Court[135] and Court of Appeals[136] found this provision unconstitutional, and the United States Supreme Court denied Skokie's motion for a stay of the Court of Appeals decision, thereby allowing the march to take place.[137]

In the last few years a number of universities in the United States have enacted 'campus codes' prohibiting hate speech on campus.[138] Even though these codes prohibit a much narrower class of speech than does the general prohibition of hate propaganda found in Canadian law, the two cases in which campus codes have been tested

[131] F. Schauer, *Free Speech: A Philosophical Enquiry* (1982), 183.

[132] Ibid., at 182.

[133] Music can arouse deep emotions without directly appealing to the intellect in much the same way that obscenity arouses sexual desire. Yet I take it that the government could not constitutionally prohibit the performance of Mahler's 9th symphony.

[134] See *Collin* v. *Smith*, 578 F.2d 1197, 1199 (7th Cir. 1978).

[135] *Collin* v. *Smith* 447 F. Supp. 676 (ND Ill. 1978).

[136] *Collin*, 578 F.2d 1197.

[137] *Smith* v. *Collin*, 436 US 953 (1978). Contrast this refusal to stay a decision *allowing* the Nazi march with the Supreme court's earlier stay of an injunction *preventing* the march. See *Nationalist Socialist Party* v. *Skokie*, 432 US 43 (1977).

[138] See Post, above, n. 50 at 268–77; Weinstein, above n. 32 at 239, n. 214.

found the regulations to violate the first amendment.[139] And just recently, a federal appeals court upheld the first amendment right of a university professor to publish racist statements.[140]

1.5   An Incomplete Assessment of the American Experience

As we have seen, *New York Times* v. *Sullivan* and *Brandenburg* v. *Ohio* stand as twin bulwarks providing strong protection against content regulation of public discourse in the United States. These decisions are not the product of abstract theories of free speech, but rather reflect difficult lessons learned through many wrong turns and false starts. In *Keegstra*, Chief Justice Dickson acknowledges that 'there is much to be learned from First Amendment jurisprudence with regard to freedom of expression and hate propaganda'.[141] But not only does he fail to appreciate the intense hostility of modern doctrine to content regulation of political speech, more significantly Dickson seems unaware of the unfortunate experiences that gave rise to the vigilance with which public discourse is protected in the USA.

As an abstract matter, the protection *Sullivan* affords defamatory statements and *Brandenburg* affords extremist speech might seem unjustified. Why, after all, should false factual statements or advocacy of unlawful violence be protected? Are there not certain types of highly offensive and arguably dangerous speech that, like the people on the Lord High Executioner's little list, never will be missed? As a matter of abstract theory one could make a strong argument positing that the excision of false statements or antidemocratic ideas from public discourse will damage neither the truth seeking[142] nor the democracy protecting function of free speech.[143] Indeed, it would seem logical that banishing such expression from the realm of public

[139] See *Doe* v. *University of Michigan*, 721 F. Supp. 852 (ED Mich. 1989); *UWM Post, Inc.* v. *Board of Regents of the Univ. of Wisc. Sys.*, 774 F. Supp. 1163 (ED Wis. 1991). For a criticism of *UWM Post*, see Weinstein, above n. 32 at 236 n. 209.

[140] See *Levin* v. *Harleston*, 966 F.2d 85 (2d Cir. 1992) (finding unconstitutional college administrative sanctions and threat of sanctions against professor who expressed in letter to the *New York Times*, a scholarly journal, and a book review, the opinion that 'on average, blacks are significantly less intelligent than whites').

[141] [1990] 3 SCR at 744.

[142] But see J. Mill, *On Liberty* (Blackwell, Oxford, 1947), 15 ('the clearer perception and livelier impression of truth [is] produced by its collision with error').

[143] Such prohibitions would, however, implicate an autonomy-based right to free expression.

discourse would promote truth and protect democracy.[144] But as Holmes said, 'the life of the law has not been logic; it has been experience'.[145] And the American experience has shown that any attempt to microsurgically remove even small categories of 'worthless' speech from public discourse can seriously damage the vitality of the free expression crucial to a democracy.

I have already mentioned how the categorical exclusion of false statements from first amendment protection was used by government officials to try to squelch the civil rights movement of the 1960s, and how the 'fighting words' exception was similarly used to silence Vietnam war protestors.[146] Unfortunately, these are far from the only examples in US history that show how seemingly narrow exceptions permitting the punishment of particularly pernicious speech have led to the punishment of citizens agitating for peaceful social change. During World War I there were German sympathizers who attempted to disrupt the war effort by urging conscripts to refuse service. In order to eliminate this danger Congress passed a carefully crafted law[147] aimed specifically at this limited category of expression, and the Supreme Court, using the famous 'clear and present danger' test,[148] upheld the law. No doubt much speech of German sympathizers calculated to disrupt the war effort was eliminated by this law. But the same law was also used to punish communists who opposed US troops being sent to Russia in an attempt to put down the Bolshevik revolution,[149] and even to jail Eugene Debs, the Socialist presidential candidate, for criticizing the war as motivated by capitalistic interests.[150]

If there was ever a category of expression that, as a matter of abstract theory, should not be protected by a free speech principle primarily in service of democracy, it is expression that advocates the

---

[144] Thus in *Keegstra* Chief Justice Dickson states that 'limitations upon hate propaganda are directed at a special category of expression which strays some distance from the spirit of [the guarantee of freedom of expression found in the *Charter*]'. [1990] 3 SCR at 766.

[145] O. W. Holmes, Jr., *The Common Law* (1881), 1.

[146] See text accompanying n. 31, above.

[147] Espionage Act, c.30, § 3, 40 stat. 217, 219 (1917), which made it a crime, among other things, to 'wilfully cause or attempt to cause insubordination, disloyalty, mutiny, or refusal of duty, in the military or naval forces of the United States'.

[148] *Schenck* v. *United States*, 249 US 47 (1919).

[149] *Abrams* v. *United States*, 250 US 616 (1919).

[150] Professor Gerald Gunther reports that there were over 2,000 convictions under the 1917 Espionage Act, and a similar law passed in 1918. See G. Gunther, *Constitutional Law*, 12th edn. (1991), 1018 n. 3.

violent overthrow of democratic institutions. But experience has shown that not even such virulently antidemocratic expression can be put off limits without, ironically, endangering democracy. After President McKinley was assassinated by an anarchist, and later as part of the 'red scare' following the Russian Revolution, several states enacted criminal syndicalism statutes that outlawed advocacy of the overthrow of government by force or violence.[151] Applying a watered-down version of the 'clear and present danger test' the Court in the 1920s affirmed the application of such statutes against members of the communist party.[152] In the 1930s, however, Georgia used such a law to convict a black man for agitating against segregation.[153]

Taking its cue from the state legislation affirmed by the Supreme Court, Congress in 1940 passed the Smith Act,[154] making it a federal crime to advocate the violent overthrow of the United States Government. This law, which was upheld by the Supreme Court in 1951 as applied to high-ranking members of the American Communist party,[155] became a terrifying weapon in the hands of those who suppressed loyal dissent during the McCarthy era.[156] It was this background that led to the Court's gradual tightening of the 'clear and present danger' test in the late 1950s and early 1960s[157], and ultimately to the highly speech protective version of that test announced in *Brandenburg*.

The lesson from the abuses leading up to *Brandenburg* and *Sullivan* is that what in the abstract seems like a sensible and narrowly confined limitation can in practice be used to thwart legitimate social protest.[158] Whether the Canadian Supreme Court was able in *Keegstra* and its companion cases to carve out a hate propaganda excep-

---

[151] Ibid., at 1026, n. 1.

[152] See *Gitlow* v. *New York*, 268 US 652 (1925); *Whitney* v. *California*, 274 US 357 (1927).

[153] See *Herndon* v. *Lowry*, 301 US 242 (1937) (reversing the conviction).

[154] Ch. 439, 54 Stat. 671, 18 US C §§ 2385 (1940).

[155] *Dennis* v. *United States*, 341 US 494 (1951).

[156] See T. Emerson, *The System of Free Expression* (1971), 159–60.

[157] See *Yates* v. *United States*, 354 US 298 (1957); *Noto* v. *United States*, 367 US 290 (1961), discussed above, n. 89.

[158] Indeed, despite the speech protective safeguards erected in the last thirty years by the United States Supreme Court this phenomenon continues today as a result of the Court's continued position that extremely graphic depictions of sexual conduct are not protected by the first amendment. Thus obscenity laws have recently been used to prosecute a museum for showing homoerotic art by the prominent photographer, Robert Mapplethorpe, and to convict an African-American record dealer for selling a recording by the black rap group '2 Live Crew'. See Weinstein, above n. 32, at 189.

tion without damaging public discourse in Canada remains to be seen. Perhaps there are political and cultural differences that make such excisions less dangerous to free speech in Canada. But what can be said with certainty is that despite the Canadian Court's expressed willingness to learn from the US experience, there was precious little in any of Chief Justice Dickson's opinions that showed awareness of the devastating results of US attempts to perform microsurgery on the content of public discourse.

2 THE CANADIAN HATE SPEECH OPINIONS: DECISIONS IN SEARCH OF A CABINABLE RATIONALE

In the preceding section I demonstrated that in the USA seemingly narrow content-based restrictions on public discourse have, as a practical matter, proved difficult to confine. Too often these restrictions were used to punish speech that clearly should not be forbidden in a democracy. Having discussed the practical difficulties in confining content-based restrictions on public discourse, I will now examine the theoretical side of the coin. In doing so I will suggest that the rationales proffered in the Canadian Supreme Court hate speech decisions are inconsistent with the larger vision of robust public discourse envisioned in these opinions.

Dickson's opinions in *Keegstra* and the companion cases leave no doubt that as a general matter he is committed to an open society in which public discourse is vibrant and uninhibited. According to the Chief Justice, even before the Charter was ratified freedom of expression was thought so crucial to the functioning of a democracy that it was judicially protected from governmental infringement in Canada, despite the absence of positive law empowering the courts to do so;[159] now that freedom of expression has been explicitly entrenched as a fundamental liberty the judiciary should even more sedulously guard it;[160] freedom of expression is 'a crucial aspect of the democratic commitment, not merely because it permits the best policies to be chosen from among a wide array of proffered options, but additionally because it helps ensure that participation in the political process is open to all persons';[161] majoritarianism is not synonymous with democracy and thus 'the Charter will not permit even the democratically elected legislature to restrict the rights and

---

[159] *Keegstra*, at 726.   [160] Ibid., at 727.   [161] Ibid., at 764.

freedoms crucial to a free and democratic society';[162] and thus content-neutrality must be an important part of free speech doctrine,[163] so that 'unpopular or discredited positions are not ... accorded reduced constitutional protection as a matter of routine'.[164]

The Court's reasons for nevertheless finding the hate propaganda laws consistent with the Charter's guarantee of freedom of expression are these: (1) hate propaganda may be harmful both to the individual members of the group attacked by the speech[165] and to 'society at large'[166] and (2) hate speech is less worthy of constitutional protection than other political speech because it is inimical to other provisions of the Charter.[167] Analysis reveals, however, that these rationales, whether considered separately or together, are inconsistent with the Court's more global view of freedom of expression as outlined in the preceding paragraph.

2.1 The Harmful Tendency of Hate Speech

2.1.1 *Psychic Injury to Members of the Attacked Group*

There can be no doubt that vicious hate speech can, as the Chief Justice noted, make its targets feel 'humiliated and degraded',[168] and otherwise inflict psychic injury. But occasional psychic injury is an unavoidable side effect of vigorous public discourse in an open society, for when matters of great importance and intense emotion are under discussion people sometimes say things that may have a devastating emotional impact on others. For instance, while the Vietnam war raged, some antiwar protestors in the USA marched through the streets waving Vietcong flags. One can imagine the emotional distress that such a display caused parents whose sons had been recently killed by the Vietcong. More recently, some Harvard law students wrote a parody of a feminist article that had been posthumously published in the *Harvard Law Review* soon after the author was brutally murdered. The parody, which contained several highly disrespectful references to the author, such as calling her the 'Rigor-Mortis Professor of law,' was distributed at the annual

---

162 Ibid., at 765.   163 *Taylor*, at 922.   164 Ibid.
165 *Keegstra*, at 746–7.   166 Ibid., at 747.   167 Ibid., at 755–8.
168 Ibid., at 746, citing the Report of the Cohen Committee.

Harvard Law Review banquet.[169] I am saddened to think of how much emotional distress this parody caused the late author's husband, a member of the Harvard law faculty. And as noted above,[170] Jerry Falwell, a nationally prominent minister in the United States, suffered severe emotional distress as a result of a parody published in *Hustler* magazine suggesting that he had sexual intercourse with his mother in an outhouse.

The world would certainly be a nicer place if the antiwar protestors, the Harvard students, and the publishers of *Hustler* magazine had made their points in a more civil and less hurtful way. But there is no practicable way that government can cleanse public discourse of expression that is likely to cause emotional harm without also severely inhibiting the vitality of that discourse. Emotional distress caused by public discourse will vary greatly from individual to individual and is inherently difficult to document and quantify. As such it is far too uncertain a standard to serve as a ground for limiting expression on matters of public concern. For instance, is the infliction of the message 'Fuck the Draft' upon unwilling recipients[171] sufficient to cause emotional distress, or is it merely offensive—a ground which the Canadian Court seems to acknowledge is insufficient to punish speech?[172] What about the adorning of an Israeli flag with a Swastika by a Palestinian protesting against Israeli policy on the West Bank?[173] Permitting the prohibition of public discourse on such a subjective standard as the likelihood that the speech might cause emotional injury is, for two reasons, inconsistent with a vigorous free speech principle. First, it gives government a tremendous amount of discretion to pick and choose the expression it will punish—discretion that can be used to stifle ideas that offensively critique the *status quo*.[174] Additionally, there is the 'chilling effect' that would result from such an inherently uncertain standard. Not sure just where the line between offensiveness and emotional injury lies, many people will

---

[169] See 'Two Controversial Incidents Said to Spotlight Harvard Woes', *The National Journal*, 25 May 1992, 4.

[170] See n. 44, above.

[171] See *Cohen* v. *California*, 403 US 15 (1971) (upholding first amendment right of antiwar protestor to wear in public a jacket bearing that message).

[172] See *Keegstra*, at 746.

[173] An actual incident that occurred at the University at which I teach.

[174] I am here relying upon the US experience (e.g. the selective use of the fighting words doctrine against antiwar protestors, discussed at n. 31, above and accompanying text) and acknowledge that there may be reasons to be less suspicious of such abuse by the Canadian authorities.

'make only statements which steer far wider of the unlawful zone',[175] thereby forgoing their constitutional right to make inflammatory political statements that in fact do not inflict emotional injury. The emotional distress rationale is thus far too encompassing to serve as an adequate standard for prohibiting expression about matters of public concern in a society dedicated to robust public discourse.[176]

The following objection could be raised against what I have just said: Canada has not enacted a general law criminalizing all public discourse that inflicts emotional distress, or even a number of more particular laws aimed at various types of expression. Rather it has enacted only a single prohibition to prevent the emotional distress likely to be caused by a narrow and carefully defined class of political speech. Thus any argument that the Canadian Government will now outlaw a wide variety of speech based on that rationale is a 'slippery slope' argument, which is not a very powerful indictment of a law.[177] But the argument that I have just made against the emotional injury rationale, and the argument that I will soon make against the competing constitutional values rationale, are not 'slippery slope' arguments. A 'slippery slope' argument invokes the fear that once government infringes a right ever so slightly it will keep on infringing until there is nothing left of the right.[178] The National Rifle Association is fond of making such arguments, as in their position that prohibiting the ownership of automatic assault weapons or armor-piercing bullets will lead to the banning of all guns, including hunting rifles.[179] An example of a 'slippery slope' argument in the freedom of expression arena is this: government prohibition of any expression,

---

[175] *New York Times* v. *Sullivan*, 376 US at 279.

[176] Expression likely to cause psychic injury that is *not* part of public discourse, such as much of the expression constituting sexual harassment in the work-place (e.g. threats by the boss to fire an employee if she does not have sex with him, or even persistent gender-demeaning remarks directed by men to a female employee) can be regulated without jeopardizing the democracy-protecting purposes of free speech to nearly the same extent. See B. Lindemann and D. Kadue, above n. 112, at 599–600. Thus the Chief Justice's analogy of the prohibition of verbal sexual harassment in the workplace as support for the prohibition of hate speech (*Keegstra*, at 746) as part of public discourse in a public forum is inapposite.

[177] See e.g. *Keegstra*, at 766, where Dickson briefly considers the 'slippery slope' argument against the hate speech law involved in that case, and rejects it as a reason for holding the law unconstitutional.

[178] See Schauer, 'Slippery Slopes', *Harv. L. Rev.* 99 (1985) 361, 361–2. ('[T]he phenomenon referred to [by the term "slippery slope"] is that a particular act, seemingly innocuous when taken in isolation, may yet lead to a future host of similar but increasingly pernicious events'.)

[179] See Anderson, 'Extraordinary People', *New Yorker*, 12 Nov. 1984, at 159–60.

such as misleading advertising, will lead the government to punish core political speech, such as loyal disagreement with government policies. In contrast, I am *not* arguing that the upholding of the hate propaganda laws on an emotional injury rationale will prompt the Canadian parliament to prohibit all parodies that cause emotional injury or to prohibit waving an enemy flag. I *am* saying that, if such legislation were enacted, the rationale of *Keegstra* and its companion cases would require the Court to uphold those laws.[180]

Perhaps, however, there is a way to narrow the emotional harm rationale in such a way as to encompass hate speech but exclude other types of inflammatory public discourse. I am not aware of any such limiting principle expressed by the Court in *Keegstra* or its companion cases, but have heard proponents of hate speech legislation argue as follows: Racist speech is particularly harmful because it attacks a person for an immutable characteristic. This argument cannot be lightly dismissed, for there is something particularly unfair about humiliating a person for a characteristic over which he or she has no control. Still, I take it that the gravamen of the psychic injury rationale is that expression can be prohibited not because it is unfair but because of the *injury* that it causes. Perhaps the unfairness of hate speech makes it more injurious, or perhaps there are other reasons why hateful comments about one's race or ethnicity are more injurious than the other types of psychic injury that occur in the rough and tumble of public discourse. But I have my doubts. I would be far more injured by reading a parody making light of the brutal murder of someone I loved than I would by reading a tract addressed to the public at large[181] filled with even the most vicious anti-Semitic slurs,

---

[180] See Schauer, above n. 178, at 366 ('[A]n argument directed against the excess breadth of a principle ... is prompted by the worry that the linguistic or doctrinal boundaries of the principle or rule under discussion embrace the danger case ... An objection to the excess breadth of the proposed principle ... [thus] differs markedly from a slippery slope claim'.)

[181] Face-to-face racial or ethnic insults, or other hate messages directed to a particular recipient are another matter. Thus it seems to me that Justice Scalia, in writing the majority opinion in *R.A.V.* v. *City of St. Paul*, 112 S. Ct 2538 (1992) (discussed at text accompanying n. 62–72, above) much too facilely dismissed the possibility that face-to-face racial insults might often cause more harm, both in the psychic injury they cause and the likelihood of violence it might provoke, then do garden-variety 'fighting words'. In any event, most face-to-face use of racial epithets will occur as part of 'private fracases' (see Post, above n. 50 at 315 n. 216) rather than public discourse. Thus allowing government leeway to regulate such expression on a psychic harm rationale does not involve a broad, uncabinable principle inconsistent with a vigorous free speech principle.

and it is my distinct impression that most other Jews would react the same way.[182] However, the degree of psychic injury caused by hate speech as compared to other forms of expression is a question about which there is not yet any conclusive data. It is therefore possible that proponents of hate speech legislation might someday provide such data, or devise some other limiting principle that will make the psychic harm rationale compatible with a vigorous free speech principle. But they have not yet done so.[183]

2.1.2 Harm to Society at Large

Chief Justice Dickson starts with the premiss, for which there is unfortunately plenty of evidence, that 'individuals can be persuaded to believe "almost anything" if information or ideas are communicated using the right technique and in the proper circumstances'.[184] From this premiss it follows that it is 'thus not inconceivable that the active dissemination of hate propaganda can attract individuals to its cause'.[185] Moreover, this 'alteration of views' can 'occur subtly'[186] so that even if the outward message of hate propaganda is rejected the message 'of racial or religious inferiority may persist in a recipient's mind as an idea that holds some truth'.[187] The harm to society from this 'alteration of views' is twofold: (1) it might create 'serious discord between various cultural groups';[188] and (2) it may lead to 'discrimination, and perhaps even violence, against minority groups in Canadian society'.[189]

Dickson is surely correct that the expression of ideas can shape the way we see the world, including members of cultural groups. He may also be correct that the *net effect* of hate speech is to cause discord

---

[182] Part of the reason that reading an anti-Semitic tract addressed to the public at large would not be psychologically devastating for most Jews is, sadly, that it comes as no great surprise to us that such views exist, as it is no startling revelation to African-Americans that there are some who hold virulently racist views about blacks.

[183] Which is not to say that even a much more cabinable rationale would be an adequate justification for limiting public discourse. One could still believe that the humiliation that racist speech causes is less of a cost than the inhibition on public discourse that would result from criminalizing even a small category of such discourse.

[184] *Keegstra*, at 747, quoting the Cohen Committee Report.

[185] *Keegstra*, at 747.   [186] Ibid.

[187] Ibid., at 747–8.   [188] Ibid., at 747.   [189] Ibid., at 748.

among cultural groups, discrimination against minorities, and, perhaps, even racial violence.[190] But one need only carefully consider his explanation of how this harm occurs to appreciate why this rationale for excluding hate speech from constitutional protection is inconsistent with a meaningful free speech principle. According to Dickson the harm is caused by the 'alteration of views', and by 'ideas' that may persist 'in a recipient's mind'. As a US judge recently said about a similar argument in support of an antipornography ordinance, restricting speech under such a theory is 'thought control'.[191] As such, it is an expansive rationale that includes expression that should not be prohibited in a democratic society.

This is particularly true of the prohibition of speech because it might cause 'serious discord between various cultural groups'. In the USA, for instance, the vocal opposition to affirmative action by several prominent Jewish organizations has caused 'serious discord' between blacks and Jews, and I am sure that there are issues of public concern in Canada that might lead to similar discord between cultural groups. But certainly no one would seriously contend that forbidding the B'nai B'rith from opposing affirmative action would be consistent with a vital free speech principle, no matter how much 'discord' this position caused. If psychic injury is inevitable in vigorous public debate, discord among cultural groups is even more inevitable, and unlike psychic injury, may sometimes even be beneficial to producing needed social change.

---

[190] There is, however, considerably more doubt as to whether the *net* effect of hate speech is negative. The most powerful indictment of a position is sometimes the wretched personality of the person spouting it. Some may be persuaded by the rantings of these unbalanced bigots, but how many more people who otherwise might incline towards bigotry, might reject racist ideas when they hear them espoused by such gruesome people? Similarly, hate speech by fringe elements may persuade some, but such speech begets refutation by much more reputable people that may more than offset the influence of the bigots. Finally, hate speech undoubtedly can cause 'discord between various cultural groups', but it can also be a unifying force between minority groups, such as when Jewish groups condemn racist statements against blacks and vice versa. This is not to say that I believe that the net effect of hard core racist statements is not harmful. I simply do not know, but neither does Chief Justice Dickson or anyone else. Far more certain is the harm caused by more subtle forms of racist speech that the Canadian Government either has not regulated (e.g. the subtle stereotyping of minorities on television and in movies) or could not hope to regulate (the prejudice passed on from parent to child).

[191] See *American Booksellers Assoc.* v. *Hudnut*, 771 F.2d 323, 328 (7th Cir. 1985), aff'd 475 US 1001 (1986), discussed at text accompanying n. 95–9, above.

Discrimination against minorities, however, is both a graver and more palpable harm than psychic injury, and violence against minorities is an even more serious and verifiable harm than discrimination. But there are many ideas capable of causing concrete and serious harm that could not be prohibited in accordance with a vigorous free speech principle. Presently in the USA[192] and Canada[193] abortion is a constitutionally protected activity, but it is not inconceivable that some day a woman's choice to terminate her pregnancy will again be criminalized in both countries[194]. If this happens then books and films favorable to abortion rights could be banned if the government were to show that such expression was likely to lead women to have illegal abortions.[195] Similarly, if homosexual activity were ever again criminalized in Canada,[196] as it is today in many parts of the USA,[197] books and films portraying homosexual couples as having loving, healthy relationships could be banned on the theory that the 'alteration of views' caused by such depictions might lead to illegal sexual conduct. What these examples show is that a rationale permitting government to outlaw expression just because it might lead to antisocial or even illegal conduct, but without a showing that the speaker has directly called for others to engage in such conduct, can easily encompass speech that attempts to persuade others peacefully and legally to change the law. As such,

[192] See *Roe* v. *Wade*, 410 US 113 (1973).

[193] *R.* v. *Morgenthaler*, [1988] 1 SCR 30.

[194] In *Planned Parenthood* v. *Casey*, 112 S. Ct. 2791 (1992) the core holding of *Roe* was reaffirmed, but by the narrowest of margins.

[195] In fact, in the early part of this century feminists were sent to jail in the United States for advocating birth control. See Gale and Strossen, 'The Real ACLU', *Yale J. of Law and Feminism*, 2 (1989), 161, 163, n. 16.

[196] Under the 1953–4 Statutes of Canada, Criminal Code s. 147, buggery was an offence punishable by imprisonment for fourteen years. Presently, anal intercourse, whether heterosexual or homosexual, is not a criminal act in Canada so long as it takes place in private by not more than two persons, both of whom are 18 years of age or older and consent to the act. See s. 159 of the Criminal Code. Cf. *Bowers* v. *Hardwick*, 478 US 186, 188, n. 2 (1986) (in rejecting constitutional challenge to sodomy law as applied to homosexual sodomy, the Court reserves the question as to whether the law would be constitutional as applied to heterosexual sodomy).

[197] In *Bowers*, in which the United States Supreme Court rejected a constitutional challenge to a state sodomy law brought by a man arrested for engaging in oral sex in the privacy of his own home with another man, the Court notes that twenty-five states and the District of Columbia have laws criminalizing sodomy. Ibid., at 193–94. See also ibid., n. 1 (Powell J., concurring) (listing statutes).

this rationale is at war with the very essence of free expression in a democracy.[198]

2.2 Restricting Speech by Reference to Other Values in the Charter

Perhaps recognizing that justifying suppression of public discourse because of the psychic injury that it might cause, or because of the tendency of the ideas to persuade others to engage in antisocial acts, are not sufficiently cabinable rationales, Chief Justice Dickson invokes another justification more specific to hate speech. Unlike the textually absolute command of the first amendment to the United States Constitution, section 1 of the Canadian Charter permits fundamental freedoms to be limited if the restriction 'can be demonstrably justified in a free and democratic society'. Relying on this language, Dickson reasons that the Court should conduct the inquiry as to the constitutionality of forbidding hate propaganda 'in light of a commitment to uphold the rights and freedoms set out in the other sections of the Charter'.[199] The Court then finds that the other Charter

---

[198] Recently, the Canadian Supreme Court used *Keegstra*'s 'alteration of views' rationale to uphold the constitutionality of Canada's obscenity law to the extent that it applied to sexually explicit material that is either violent or degrading or dehumanizing, *R.* v. *Butler*, [1992] 70 CCC (3d) 129, 151, 159. Conceding that 'a direct link between obscenity and harm to society may be difficult, if not impossible, to establish', the Court, per Justice Sopinka, nevertheless concluded that 'it is reasonable to presume that exposure to images bears a causal relationship to changes in attitudes and beliefs', and that these changes in attitudes, in turn, might lead to 'antisocial acts of sexual violence'. Ibid., at 163, quoting The Meese Commission Report. However, as to depictions of explicit sex 'that is not violent and neither degrading nor dehumanizing', the Court found in absence of such harm, unless children were employed in the production, and thus construed the obscenity law as not proscribing such expression. Ibid., at 151. The malleability and uncertainty of this 'alteration of views' rationale is demonstrated by the concurring opinion of Justice Gonthier, joined by Justice L'Heureux-Dubé. Gonthier disagreed with the majority's conclusion that graphic depictions of sex without violence that are neither degrading nor dehumanizing are not harmful. Thus Gonthier would hold that in certain circumstances even 'an explicit portrayal of "plain" sexual intercourse, where two individuals are making love' may create 'a likelihood of harm' because it 'distorts human sexuality by taking it out of any context whatsoever and projecting it to the public'. Ibid., at 174 (Gonthier J., concurring). '[T]he harm sought to be avoided is the same [as with violent or degrading or dehumanizing pornography] that is, attitudinal changes'. Ibid., at 176.

[199] *Keegstra*, at 755, quoting *Singh* v. *Minister of Employment and Immigration*, [1985] 1 SCR 177, 218. Perhaps there is something in the legislative history of the *Charter* that supports this position, but if not, then it seems to me that the Court is here engaging here in some sleight-of-hand. Section 1 says that the *restriction* on the fundamental freedom be demonstrably justified in a free and democratic society, not that a particular *exercise of the fundamental freedom* be so justified.

provisions pertinent to the question before it are sections 15[200] and 27[201] which 'represent a strong commitment to the values of equality and multiculturalism, and hence underline the great importance of Parliament's objective in prohibiting hate propaganda'.[202] The Court continues:

The message of the expressive activity covered by [the hate propaganda law] is that members of identifiable groups are not to be given equal standing in society, and are not human beings equally deserving of concern, respect and consideration. The harms caused by this message run directly counter to the values central to a free and democratic society, and in restricting the promotion of hatred Parliament is therefore seeking to bolster the notion of mutual respect necessary in a nation which venerates the equality of all persons.[203]

On the surface it may seem that the Court has constructed a rationale that, at least theoretically, is not so broad as to encompass expression that should not be prohibited in a democracy. Viewed charitably, the Court may be saying that neither psychic injury nor the harmful tendency of ideas is in itself sufficient harm to warrant the prohibition of expression, but may become so when this harm interferes with another right or freedom protected by the Charter. Analysis quickly reveals, however, that the Canadian Supreme Court's hate propaganda decisions are not explainable by reference to any such limited principle.

I take it that in relying on other constitutional provisions in *Keegstra*, Chief Justice Dickson did not mean to imply that a private person spewing racist venom in the speakers' corner of the park would literally be violating the equality, the multiculturalism, or any other provision of the Charter.[204] Rather, as he explains with respect

---

[200] S. 15(1) provides: 'Every individual is equal before and under the law and has the right to the equal protection and equal benefit of the law without discrimination and, in particular, without discrimination based on race, national or ethnic origin, colour, religion, sex, age or mental or physical disability.'

[201] S. 27 states as follows: 'This Charter shall be interpreted in a manner consistent with preservation and the enhancement of the multicultural heritage of Canadians.'

[202] *Keegstra*, at 755.　　　[203] Ibid., at 756.

[204] In *RWDSU* v. *Dolphin Delivery Ltd.*, [1986] 2 SCR 573 the Supreme Court of Canada (including Chief Justice Dickson) unanimously decided that the freedoms guaranteed in the *Charter* do not restrict purely private conduct. Accord, *Keegstra*, at 833 (McLachlin J., dissenting) 'This is not a case of the collision of two rights ... There is no violation of s. 15 ... since there is no law or state action which puts the guarantee of equality into issue'.) Similarly, most restrictions in the United States Constitution are addressed to government, not private individuals. For instance, it has been long

to his reliance on Section 15 of the *Charter*, the significance of this provision for purposes of assessing the hate speech statute's consistency with the free speech right found in Section 2(b) is as evidence of Canadian's 'society's dedication to promoting equality'.[205] Thus what is at issue in these cases is not a conflict between two constitutional *rights*, but between the constitutional right to free speech (for here the government is trying to prohibit the exercise of a liberty) and a *value* so fundamental that it finds expression in the Charter.[206] Because a great many values can either expressly or implicitly be found in a nation's fundamental charter,[207]

---

established that the equality provision of the fourteenth amendment can be violated only by 'state action', and 'erects no shield against merely private conduct, however discriminatory or wrongful'. *Shelley* v. *Kraemer*, 334 US 1, 13 (1948).

[205] *Keegstra*, at 755.

[206] An actual conflict between an equality right and a free speech right would occur if, for instance, a government worker in the course of his duties subjected a member of the public to racist rhetoric. Thus if Keegstra was a public school teacher and continued to make anti-Semitic diatribes then the s. 15 rights of any Jewish students in his class might well be at issue and in conflict with Keegstra's free speech rights under s. 2(b) (and given the lack of a public forum one would hope that the students' equality rights would prevail).

In reviewing a draft of this article, Professor Waluchow perceptively enquired what difference it makes whether the conflict is cast as one between a free speech right and equality *right*, on the one hand, or as between a free speech right and an equality *value*, on the other. On a theoretical level at least, the major difference that I see is this: the existence of a meaningful fundamental constitutional right entails a presumption in favour of any particular exercise of that right, unless government can demonstrably justify its curtailment. See e.g. s. 1 of the *Charter*. But if by exercising his constitutional right, Jones will necessarily infringe Smith's fundamental constitutional right, there can be a presumption in favour of neither person's right (unless some hierarchy of fundamental rights has been established). A countervailing constitutional value, on the other hand, is just another type of State interest, which, if pressing enough, can justify the curtailment of a fundamental right, but unlike an actual right belonging to a specific individual, carries with it no presumption in its favour. In addition, if constitutional rights are confined by a fairly restrictive State action doctrine, such as exists in the USA, justifying the suppression of speech in order to protect such rights is a narrow and cabinable rationale. By the same token, however, such a State action doctrine would, as a practical matter, usually make any such countervailing constitutional rights analysis otiose. In any case in which a State actor will be in a position to actually violate a constitutional right of another person, such expression will almost inevitably be in a nonpublic forum. Thus, under US doctrine at least, such expression would be proscribable as inconsistent with the nature of the forum, whether or not it actually violated another's constitutional rights. Such would be the case, for instance, in the case of a government employee who made racist statements in the course of his duties.

[207] In the USA, for instance, not only have equality, democracy, and freedom of expression been found to be core constitutional values, but so have capitalism (*Lochner* v. *New York*, 198 US 45 (1905)), federalism (*Younger* v. *Harris*, 401 US 37 (1971)), the power to wage war (*Woods* v. *Miller*, 333 US 138 (1948)); see also *Schenck* v. *United*

Dickson's rationale for suppressing hate speech is a broad one indeed.[208]

But the breadth of this rationale is not the only way in which it is inconsistent with a vigorous free speech principle. To be included in a nation's fundamental charter a value must be widely shared and deeply held. But it is precisely speech that offensively challenges the basic values of society that is most imperilled by the political process and hence most in need of constitutional protection.[209] When the government suppresses speech that denounces basic societal norms the risk is great that it is trying to control expression not because of any real danger that the expression will persuade people to violate the law or breach fundamental norms, but because government fears that the expression will persuade the people to legally *change* these laws or norms.

Indeed, although, he usually characterizes the harm in more concrete ways, Chief Justice Dickson gives away the game when he says, 'Hate propaganda seriously threatens ... the *enthusiasm* with which the value of equality is accepted and acted upon by society'.[210] Justifying the suppression of speech because it makes people less enthusiastic about a fundamental norm of society is antithetical to a meaningful free speech principle. It is also a formula for a conservative society, for the boundaries of permissible public discourse would then be set by the values expressed in the constitution. But a nation's constitution is in some important sense the *status quo* writ large. Thus it is particularly norms so fundamental that they find expression in

---

States, 249 US 47, 52 (1919) ('When a nation is at war many things that might be said in time of peace ... will not be endured so long as men fight')); the condemnation of affirmative action as racism (*City of Richmond* v. *Crosson, Co.* 488 US 469, 493 (1989) (opinion of O'Connor, J.) (finding affirmative action plan unconstitutional, in part, because such programmes may promote racism;) see also *Johnson* v. *Transportation Agency*, 480 US 616, 677 (1987) (Scalia J., dissenting) (Race- and gender-based affirmative action programmes are a 'powerful engine of racism and sexism')).

[208] Thus in *R.* v. *Butler*, discussed at n. 198 above, the Court, in addition to relying on *Keegstra's* 'alteration of views rationale', invoked 'the fundamental conception of morality' inherent in the *Charter* as a justification for suppressing certain types of explicit sexual materials, 70 CCC (3d) at 156.

[209] As Justice Holmes eloquently put it: '[I]f there is any principle of the Constitution that more imperatively calls for attachment than any other it is the principle of free thought—not free thought for those who agree with us but freedom for the thought we hate.' *United States* v. *Schwimmer*, 279 US 644, 654–5 (dissenting opinion).

[210] *Keegstra*, at 758.

the constitution that must be open to challenge if a society is not to stagnate.

For many years slavery was a norm that found expression and even protection in the United States Constitution,[211] and until relatively recently racial segregation remained a deeply valued norm in many parts of the USA. Even more recently there have been serious attempts in the USA to amend the constitution to protect foetal life.[212] It is not inconceivable that someday the Canadian Charter could be amended to protect foetuses, or that an existing provision of the Charter might be so interpreted.[213] Such an occurrence would be a bleak day for procreative rights in Canada, but it would be an even bleaker one if expression advocating abortion rights were thereafter presumptively proscribable, or even considered of 'limited importance',[214] because contrary to a value expressed in the Charter.

We do not, however, need to posit an amendment to the *Charter*, or even a novel interpretation of a present provision, to recognize that suppressing speech because its message is contrary to other constitutional values is inimical to a vibrant free speech principle. In *Keegstra*, Chief Justice Dickson invokes the core constitutional value of democracy as grounds for suppressing hate speech:

[E]xpression can work to undermine our commitment to democracy where employed to propagate ideas anathemic to democratic values. Hate propaganda works in just such a way, arguing as it does for a society in which the democratic process is subverted... [215]

But if hate speech is 'anathemic to democratic values' and hence presumptively proscribable, so is communist propaganda that 'argu[es] for a society in which democratic process is subverted'. It was upon not too dissimilar a rationale that the United States Supreme Court allowed the imprisonment of those who preached communism during the 1950s.[216] But if the jury of legal history has

---

[211] See n. 130, above.

[212] See SJ Res. 37, 102d Cong., 1st Sess., 137 Cong. Rec. S574 (proposed amendment to Constitution for the protection of unborn children).

[213] Indeed, in *Borowski* v. *A.-G. Canada* (1983) DLR (4th) 112 (Sask. QB), it was argued that section 7 of the *Charter* protected foetal life. And in 1975 what was then the West German constitutional court struck down a law liberalizing access to abortion on the ground that foetal life was constitutionally protected. Judgment of 25 Feb. 1975, 39 BVerfGE 1.

[214] See *Keegstra*, at 762.   [215] Ibid., at 764.

[216] See *Dennis* v. *United States*, 341 US 494, 545 (1951) (Frankfurter J. concurring) ('On any scale of values which we have hitherto recognized, speech of this sort ranks low').

delivered one clear verdict it is that these convictions did far more damage to democracy in America than the unmolested expression of communist propaganda could ever have done.[217]

Conclusion

The instinct of an individual or a society when first thinking about free speech problems is that certain ideas should not be allowed to be expressed because they are simply wrong, not so much in a factual sense, but in a moral sense. You and I know that racism is wrong, as do all decent, right thinking people. We passionately believe in our vision of equality and want desperately to bring it about. By the same token we also know that the bigot's vision of a society in which minorities are oppressed and excluded is an evil one, and thus we want to do everything in our power to make sure that this vision is not realized. There must, therefore, be some narrow principle that will exclude the expression of this evil vision from the realm of discourse that does not also apply to equally unpopular but arguably legitimate visions of the world. It was with this frame of mind, I believe, that Chief Justice Dickson and the majority of the Canadian Supreme Court, in the first major political speech cases decided under the *Charter*, faced the problem before them.

Intuitively, it would seem that the expression of such evil ideas must be harmful, so the Court invokes a utilitarian analysis to explain how the expression of racist ideas is harmful, but is unable to distinguish this harm from the harm flowing from many other inflammatory ideas. To narrow this far too encompassing rationale, the Court then makes a deontological argument: the racist's vision of the world is wrong and thus should be excluded from the realm of public discourse. The problem is that the racist, like every other citizen in a democracy, has a very strong presumptive right to try to persuade others of his view of the way society should be. Thus the Court owes Keegstra and his compatriots an explanation of why their vision of the world is out of bounds. But there's the rub, for there is no set of values that transcends the political process, and is therefore immune from the dialectics of public discourse, that the Court could consult to exclude an idea from the realm of public discourse because contrary to such a transcendent value. This is true even of the fundamental

[217] See T. Emerson, above n. 156, at 159–60.

norms expressed in the constitution itself, for all provisions of the *Charter*—including the equality and the multiculturalism provisions—are subject to change through public discourse leading to constitutional amendment.[218]

It is of course possible to imagine a constitutional scheme that expressly declares certain provisions to be exempt from the amendment process, and hence arguably from the testing grounds of public discourse. It would be interesting to consider the status of a hate speech law under a constitution that had a free speech provision but also had an equality provision that could not be altered or eliminated by amendment. But even then there would be strong arguments that speech that denounces the vision of equality entrenched in this hypothetical constitution should none the less be protected by the free speech provision. If the constitution in question does not purport to limit the right of the people to institute an entirely new constitution, then the equality provision is not in fact immutable even within the framework of the present constitution, but remains open to modification. But more significantly, even if a constitution purports to make a provision forever immutable (a questionable proposition both from a practical and a theoretical standpoint) it does not follow that a free speech principle would not protect the denunciation of this provision. Although from within the framework of such a constitution criticism is powerless to alter the equality provision legally, the autonomy protecting function, and perhaps even the truth finding function, of a free speech principle would remain applicable, and hence justify protection of speech contrary to this politically immutable norm.

But whatever might be said about a constitutional scheme that expressly attempts to exempt society's commitment to equality from the potential change inherent in a democracy, and thus arguably has removed criticism of this value from the rigors of public discourse, this is neither the Canadian nor the US scheme. Accordingly, the majority in the hate speech cases had no principled way to exempt the commitment to equality expressed in the, *Charter* from the dialectics of public discourse to which all other values are subject. But perhaps there are Canadian legal traditions that make such a move, if not exactly principled, at least legitimate. From my limited exposure to Canadian jurisprudence, it seems to me that Canadian legal culture

---

[218] The procedure for amending the Constitution of Canada is set forth in s. 38–49 of the *Charter*.

is more natural-law oriented than is the highly positivistic, post-Realist US legal system. Such a belief in immutable transcendent values would seem to explain why, even before there was a *Charter* expressly providing a constitutional right of free expression, the Canadian courts discovered a free speech principle that trumped positive law.[219] Ironically, this same belief in transcendent values might explain the Court's now exalting equality and multiculturalism above all other values in the *Charter*, including free speech.

Finally, I want to raise the possibility that in criticizing the Canadian Court's failure to articulate a cabinable rationale for the punishment of hate speech I have taken the Court's opinions too literally. Perhaps a deeper message of the Canadian hate speech opinions is that just as in every culture there are certain things that people do not eat, there are also certain things that just must not be said. And just as there is no principled explanation of why Canadians do not eat dogs, there is no principled explanation of why hate speech is beyond the bounds of public discourse in Canada. Perhaps every society has its speech taboos that are better explained by sociology than by legal principle. Consider, for example, the longstanding American prohibition against explicit descriptions of sexual conduct. Although there have been recent attempts to justify this prohibition based on the harm that it causes to women, it is significant that the Supreme Court has never adopted a harm-based rationale for the exclusion of obscenity from first amendment protection.[220] Moreover, I am certain that if tomorrow the empirical data showed beyond cavil that obscenity did not lead to violence or discrimination against women, few proponents of antiobscenity laws would change their minds. Similarly, the harm that the Canadian Court says may flow from hate speech seems to me to be window dressing for a deep-seated but as yet unexplained objection to such expression.

Just as individuals repress unconscious thoughts that prove too threatening to their self image, perhaps the Canadian hate speech and the American obscenity taboos are society's attempt to repress troubling thoughts bubbling up from society's collective identity. And perhaps these images are troubling not because they threaten to change anyone's mind about racial or gender equality but because they reveal some dark truth about all of us, or at least what we fear may be the truth—that our sexual lust is to some uncomfortable

---

[219] *Keegstra*, at 726–7.   [220] See text accompanying n. 127–8, above.

extent indistinguishable from that of beasts, and that on some level we are all racists. Just as different individuals repress different types of unconscious thoughts, so too different societies will have different speech taboos. And just as it is sometimes desirable or even necessary for an individual to repress unconscious thoughts, societal speech taboos may arguably serve a legitimate purpose. But often it is healthier, both for individuals and societies, to listen to and deal openly with their darker thoughts.

8. Hate Propaganda in Canada

JOSEPH MAGNET

1

The relationship between ideas and acts is striking in the history of anti-Semitism. 'Jew-hating' is a core idea with a long history. In the new nation-states of the early enlightenment the idea of Jew hating became 'The Jewish Question'. The 'Jewish Question' referred to the peculiar persistence of the Jewish people in the midst of rising nationalisms. Posing the 'Jewish Question' challenged the new nations to find 'solutions'.

Throughout the nineteenth century the European countries produced more ideas—'solutions'. Nineteenth-century Europe flirted with 'solutions' such as these: converting the Jews, segregating the Jews, deporting the Jews. Pobyedonostsev, chief advisor to Alexander III, provided his Czar with this modest proposal in 1881: one-third of the Jews were to emigrate, one-third were to convert and one-third were to die of hunger. The European nations turned these nineteenth century ideas into action by manifold legal measures. In the twentieth century Germany produced a totally new idea, a 'solution'. unique in history; a conclusive idea—the Final Solution. That idea was carried into action by the modern German state, which transformed Germany's sickening ideology into bureaucratic action by the systematic mass murder of the Jewish people.[1]

The relationship between ideas and acts is indelibly emblazoned on the modern mind. Some ideas are so terrible, so hellish, that they should not be thought about. They should not be expressed. Their expression should be prohibited and punished.

This is the thinking of the community of nations in the post war period. Since 1945 many states in the international community ratified four treaties obligating their countries to eliminate ideas promoting hatred. States party to the treaties enacted new laws to control hate propaganda pursuant to their treaty obligations. The treaties are

[1] Lucy Dawidowich, *The War Against the Jews,* Bantam, New York, (1975), P. I.

the International Convention on the Elimination of All Forms of Racial Discrimination,[2] International Covenant on Civil and Political Rights,[3] Convention on the Prevention and Punishment of the Crime of Genocide,[4] and Convention for the Protection of Human Rights and Fundamental Freedoms.[5] The language of the treaties is interesting. Article 4 of the Racial Discrimination Convention requires states party to the treaty to condemn all propaganda based on ideas of racial or ethnic superiority, and to adopt positive measures to eliminate discrimination. Article 20 of the Civil and Political Rights Covenant requires that 'any advocacy of ... hatred that constitutes incitement to discrimination ... shall be prohibited by law'.

The Racial Discrimination Convention and the Civil and Political Rights Covenant are monitored by two elected committees of eighteen members. Countries must report to the committees about measures they have taken to implement their Convention obligations within one year of ratification. Every two years thereafter, each country must report on the current status of Convention guarantees. Under optional protocols, individuals may complain to the committees against a state party for violation of a treaty right. The Committees will mediate, and, if necessary, adjudicate the complaint, advising the country complained against of the committee's views as to whether a violation has occurred. States have the obligation to bring their laws and practices into line with the committee's views. The Crime of Genocide Convention is supervised by the International Court of Justice. This mechanism can only be triggered by states party to the treaty which are involved in a dispute. It cannot be activated by individuals.

2

It is fascinating to examine the variety of measures states party to the treaties have taken to implement their obligations to eliminate dis-

[2] (1969) 660 UNTS 212 (hereafter Racial Discrimination Convention).

[3] (1976) 999 UNTS 172 (hereafter Civil and Political Rights Covenant).

[4] (1948) 78 UNTS 278 (hereafter Crime of Genocide Convention).

[5] (1950) 213 UNTS 222. Canada has ratified all of the Conventions except the Convention for the Protection of Human Rights and Fundamental Freedoms. This Convention is specific to the countries of the European Community. In ratifying the other three Conventions Canada has made no express reservations to the contents of the Conventions.

criminatory ideas. A survey of states party to the treaties reveals four types of national response.

A first group of countries legislates against hate propaganda through the criminal law. The criminal sanctions of each country vary, but all explicitly outlaw and punish hate propaganda. The prohibitions identify specific types of statements and communication modes which are prohibited, and enumerate groups to be protected.[6]

A second group of countries utilizes weaker criminal measures. These states outlaw hate propaganda, but do not identify illegal modes of communication or catalogue groups to be protected. The

---

[6] Cyprus: The government of Cyprus responded to its Convention obligations by s. 47 of the Criminal Code which states: 'Any person who (a) conspires with any other person or persons to do any act in furtherance of any seditious intention common to both or all of them; or (b) publishes any words or documents or mails any visible representations whatsoever with a seditious intention, is guilty of a felony and liable to imprisonment for five years.' See *International Convention on the Elimination of All Forms of Racial Discrimination; Seventh Periodic Report by Cyprus (1982)*, UN Doc No. CERD/C/91/Add.16; Czechoslovakia: The government of Czechoslovakia, although noting that hate propaganda is rare, have enacted s. 260 of the Penal Code which makes it an offence, punishable by one to five years imprisonment to '(1) support or propagate fascism or another similar movement which aims at suppressing the rights and freedom of the working people or which preaches national, racial or religious hatred'. See *International Convention on the Elimination of All Forms of Racial Discrimination; Ninth Periodic Report by Czechoslovakia (1986)*, UN Doc. No. CERD/C/149/Add.2; Federal Republic of Germany: s. 131 of the Penal Code makes illegal any writings which incite to racial hatred and criminalizes the production, sale import, export, and advertisements of such writings. In 1986, 31 people were prosecuted under this section. See *International Convention on the Elimination of All Forms of Racial Discrimination; Eighth Periodic Report by Federal Republic of Germany (1984)*, UN Doc. No. CERD/C/118/Add.19; German Democratic Republic: The German Democratic Republic has extensive sanctions on persecution and have included in the Criminal Code s. 92 which states: 'A person who engaged in fascist propaganda or in such manifestations of hatred against peoples or races as are apt to incite others to the preparation or commission of a crime against humanity shall be liable to between two and ten years imprisonment.' See *International Convention on the Elimination of All Forms of Racial Discrimination; Fourth Periodic Report by German Democratic Republic (1980)*,. UN Doc. No. CERD/C/64/Add.1; Greece: The government of Greece enacted Act No. 927 of 28 June 1979. The Act provides for: 'the punishment of international incitement to acts that may endanger discrimination, hatred or violence against persons or groups of persons solely on account of their racial or national origin.' The acts in question must have taken place publicly, orally or in written form. The Act also punishes any person who publicly, orally or in written texts expresses ideas which are offensive to other persons or groups of persons because of their racial or national origin. See *International Convention on the Elimination of All their racial or national origin. See International Convention on the Elimination of All Forms of Racial Discrimination; Sixth Periodic Report by Greece (1981)*, UN Doc. No. CERD/C/76/Add.1; Italy: Italy ratified CERD by an Act which implements Art. 4 by the following provision: 'any person who, in any way whatsoever, disseminates ideas based on racial superiority or racial hatred; any person who, in any way whatsoever,

instigates or inspires the commission of acts of violence or provocation against persons because they belong to a national ethnic or racial group shall be imprisoned for a period of one to four years.' See *International Convention on the Elimination of All Forms of Racial Discrimination; Third Periodic Report by Italy (1983)*, UN Doc. No. CERD/C/104/Add.2; Netherlands: The Netherlands combats hate propaganda by its Criminal Code. S. 137(c) states: 'any person by means of the spoken or written word or pictorially gives deliberate public expression to views insulting to other persons or groups on account of their race, religion, or conviction shall be liable to up to one year imprisonment or a fine of up to 10,000 guilders.' Between 1 Jan. and 31 Dec. 1988 a total of 101 cases involving the section were recorded. Fifty-four resulted in prosecution, 30 were dismissed and in 17 cases a decision is still pending on whether to prosecute. See *International Convention on the Elimination of All Forms of Racial Discrimination; Ninth Periodic Report by Netherlands (1990)*, UN Doc. No. CERD/C/184/Add.4; Norway: The Norwegian Penal Code deals with dissemination of hate propaganda under s. 135(a) which states: 'Anyone who threatens insults or exposes any person or group of persons to hatred presentation or contempt on account of their religion, race, colour or national or ethnic origin by means of public utterance or by other means of communication brought before, or in any other way disseminated among the general public will be punished.' See *International Convention on the Elimination of All Forms of Racial Discrimination; Ninth Periodic Report by Norway (1986)*, UN Doc. No. CERD/C/132/Add.5; Poland: Poland's Penal Code s. 274(1) 'Makes liable to imprisonment anyone who insults, scoffs or degrades a group or an individual because of national, ethnic or racial origin. If this is done in print or by any other means of public information the sentence can be up to ten years. Also penalized are persons who make, hold, transport, carry, dispatch with a view of dissemination ... periodicals, printed matter or any other object which constitutes strife, insult, public abuse or humiliation or a group of persons or person'. See *International Convention on the Elimination of All Forms of Racial Discrimination; Seventh Periodic Report by Poland (1982)*, UN Doc. No. CERD/C/91/Add.19; Portugal: Portugal's Criminal Code s. 189(2) states: 'Anyone who at a public meeting, in writing intended for circulation or by any other means of social communication: (a) slanders or libels any person or group of persons or holds them up to public scorn on the ground of race, colour or ethnic origin, (b) incites acts of violence against a person or group of persons of a given race, colour or ethnic origin is guilty of an offence.' See *International Convention on the Elimination of All Forms of Racial Discrimination; Initial Report by Portugal (1984)*, UN Doc. No. CERD/C/101/Add.8; Romania: The Romanian Criminal Code in Art. 166(1) states: 'Fascist propaganda disseminated by any public means shall be punishable by five to fifteen years imprisonment and disqualification from the exercise of certain rights.' See *International Convention on the Elimination of All Forms of Racial Discrimination; Sixth Periodic Report by Romania (1982)*, UN Doc NO. CERD/C/76/Add.3; Sweden: Sweden recently revised ch. 16, s. 8 of their Penal Code to read: 'If a person in a statement or in other communication which is disseminated, threatens or expresses contempt for, an ethnic group or other such group of persons with allusions to race, colour, national or ethnic origin or religious creed, he shall be sentenced for agitation against an ethnic group to imprisonment of no more than two years, or if the offence is minor, to a fine.' See *International Convention on the Elimination of All Forms of Racial Discrimination; Ninth Periodic Report by Sweden (1989)*, UN Doc. No. CERD/C/184/Add.1; United Kingdom: S. 70 of the Race Relations Act makes it an offence for 'Any person to publish or distribute written matter, or to use words in any public place or at any public meeting, where the matter or words are threatening, abusive or insulting and likely to stir up hatred against any racial group in Great Britain.' See *International Convention on the Elimination of All Forms of Racial Discrimination; Eighth Periodic Report by United Kingdom (1984)*, UN Doc. No. CERD/C/118/Add.7.

legislation is framed in broad language which attempts to capture all possibilities.[7]

A third approach combats hate propaganda through extensive education in the school system. Iceland has a compulsory social studies curriculum dealing with hate and discrimination which continues from first to ninth grades in school. The curriculum is very detailed. Iceland claims that its curriculum produces a person who, at the age of 10, is acquainted with various customs and habits of others and realizes how unfamiliarity with these customs leads to prejudice and conflict. In the fifth grade, the curriculum centres on the Second World War and its consequences for the European nations. In the sixth grade the focus is on racial problems. Iceland attempts to eliminate hate propaganda positively, through cultural measures, as opposed to negatively, through criminal prohibitions.[8]

A fourth group of states either refrains from legislating against hate propaganda or legislates conditionally. Some countries in this group claim they have no problem in this area.[9] Others believe direct

[7] Bulgaria: Bulgaria's legal system, pending advocacy of racial discrimination gives injured parties the right to compensation for material or non-material damage. See *International Convention on the Elimination of All Forms of Racial Discrimination; Eighth Periodic Report by Bulgaria (1984)*, UN Doc. No. CERD/C/118/Add.17; Fiji: The offence of sedition is defined in the Penal Code to include 'the issue or circulation of a seditious publication ... (appearing) to have the object of promoting feelings of hostility between classes or races of the community'. See *International Convention on the Elimination of All Forms of Racial Discrimination; Fifth Periodic Report by Fiji (1982)*, UN Doc. No. CERD/C/89/Add.3; Hungary: s. 148(1)(d) makes illegal 'All organizations or propaganda activity professing or inciting to racial discrimination'. See *International Convention on the Elimination of All Forms of Racial Discrimination; Seventh Periodic Report by Hungary (1982)*, UN Doc No. CERD/C/91/Add.5; Luxembourg: In Luxembourg it is an offence to engage in propaganda activities which promote discriminatory practices or demonstrations based on racism. A lesser penalty attaches to 'any person who orally, in words addressed to the public or pronounced in public or in writing, print, pictures or symbols published, posted distributed, sold, placed on sale or exhibited in public, incites any one to acts in the above offence'. See *International Convention on the Elimination of All Forms of Racial Discrimination; Second Periodic Report by Luxembourg (1981)*, UN Doc. No. CERD/C/72/Add.2.

[8] Iceland: Iceland's educational approach is described in its second Report to the Racial Discrimination Committee: See *International Convention on the Elimination of All Forms of Racial Discrimination; Second Periodic Report by Iceland (1980)*, UN. Doc. No. CERD/C/66/Add.7. Additionally, Iceland's Criminal Code prohibits 'attacking a group of persons, whether by ridicule, slander, insult, threat or other measures on the basis of their origin, colour, race or religion'.

[9] Malta: The government of Malta states they do not have a problem with hate propaganda, but if it existed the provisions of the countries constitution would suffice. See *International Convention on the Elimination of All Forms of Racial Discrimination; Sixth Periodic Report by Malta (1983)*,. UN Doc. No. CERD/C/90/Add.8; Tonga: The Kingdom has not carried out its obligations under Art. 4 because of multiple

adherence to Article 4 jeopardizes the fundamental freedoms of speech, association, and religion. This group has ratified the Racial Discrimination Convention and the Civil and Political Rights Covenant but expressly reserved a right of non-compliance with Article 4 of the Racial Discrimination Convention and Article 20 of the Civil and Political Rights Covenant.[10]

The USA fits most closely in this fourth category. Although the USA has signed and ratified the Crime of Genocide Convention, the American ratification was subject to a reservation that the USA was not required or authorized to enact any legislation or take any other action prohibited by the United States Constitution, as interpreted by the USA. In addition, although the USA has signed both the Civil and Political Rights Covenant and the Racial Discrimination Convention, neither has ever been ratified. This means that the USA is not bound by the terms of the treaties.[11]

---

reasons, including the claim that Tonga has no hate problem, according to their United Nations report. See *International Convention on the Elimination of All Forms of Racial Discrimination; Fourth Periodic Report by Tonga (1981)*, UN Doc. No. CERD/C/75/Add.3.

[10] Australia: The government has passed the Racial Discrimination Act and Crimes Act, 1914, but both are subject to freedom of speech and association. Australia complies with Art. 4 except where it requires the prohibition of the dissemination of ideas and the outlawing of organizations. See *International Convention on the Elimination of All Forms of Racial Discrimination; Third Periodic Report by Australia (1981)*, UN Doc. No. CERD/C/63/Add.3; Austria: Austria ratified CERD with a reservation to Art. 4. S. 283(1) of the Penal Code states: 'Whoever in a manner likely to endanger public order urges or incites to commit a hostile act against groups on account of its membership of parties, race, people tribe or State . . . shall be punished up to one year.' See *International Convention on the Elimination of All Forms of Racial Discrimination; Sixth periodic Report by Austria (1984)*, UN Doc. No. CERD/C/106/Add.12; Belgium: The Belgian Government refuses to legislate where freedom of thought, religion, assembly or association will be sacrificed. See *International Convention on the Elimination of All Forms of Racial Discrimination; Second Periodic Report by Belgium (1979)*, UN Doc. No. CERD/C/16/Add.2; New Zealand: New Zealand has enacted a Race Relations Act. It is, however, subject to their reservation to protect fundamental freedoms first and foremost. See *International Convention on the Elimination of All Forms of Racial Discrimination; Fifth Periodic Report by New Zealand (1984)*, UN Doc. No. CERD/C/106/Add.10; Papua New Guinea: The government ratified CERD with a reservation to Art. 4 in light of the fundamental freedoms. For this reason they state it is unnecessary to legislate in the area of hate propaganda. See *International Convention on the elimination of All Forms of Racial Discrimination; Initial Report by Papua New Guinea (1983)*, UN Doc. No. CERD/C/101/Add.1.

[11] M. J. Matsuda, 'Public Response to Racist Speech: Considering the Victims Story', *Mich. L. Rev.* 87 (1989), 2320 at 2345 suggests that signature without ratification means that the USA is bound to refrain from defeating the objective of the treaty. But see J. J. Paust, 'Rereading the First Amendment in Light of Treaties Proscribing Incitement to Racial Discrimination or Hostility', *Rutgers L. Rev.* 43 (1991), 565 for a different view.

3

Canada is the most enthusiastic consumer of hate propaganda norms in the international community. Canada has ratified everything—all three treaties and every optional protocol. Canada reserved nothing from its treaty obligations.

Canada is equally enthusiastic about implementing its treaty obligations. Canada has more hate propaganda legislation than any other country in the world. In general orientation, Canada is a 'first group' country, responding to its treaty obligations by enacting strong criminal prohibitions. The Criminal Code[12] outlaws advocacy of genocide on pain of five years imprisonment, and forbids communicating provocative statements in public places which incite hatred against identifiable groups on pain of two years imprisonment.[13] A separate Code section punishes by two years imprisonment everyone who knowingly publishes false news that is likely to injure a 'public interest'.[14]

Dissemination of hate propaganda is dealt with indirectly by other Canadian legislation. Defamation and sedition are classed as crimes.[15] People who use the mail system to distribute hate propaganda may lose their right to post mail or to have mail delivered to them.[16] Importation of hate propaganda to Canada is forbidden; importers are liable to payment of a fine, and to the seizure and destruction of their materials.[17] A unique Canadian invention is the use of conciliation, and, if necessary, coercive machinery in the Human Rights Codes to prohibit hate propaganda and provide remedies for its circulation.[18]

[12] R.S.C. 1985, c. C-46.   [13] Criminal Code, ss. 318, 319.
[14] Criminal Code, s. 181 (ruled unconstitutional in *R. v. Zundel* (1992), 140 N.R. 1 (S.C.C.)).
[15] Defamatory Libel: Criminal Code, s. 298. See generally, Canada, Law Reform Commission of Canada, *Defamatory Libel*, working paper n. 35 (1984). Seditious Libel: Criminal Code, ss. 59–61. See generally *Boucher* v. *The King*, [1951] SCR 265 (The intention to produce hatred, by itself, is insufficient to convict. There must be an additional intent to disturb the established order or to resist authority).
[16] Canada Post Corporation Act, R.S.C. 1985, chap. C-10, s. 43. Ernst Zundel and John Ross Taylor lost their mailing rights under this section.
[17] Customs Tariff Act, R.S.C. 1985, chap. 41 (3rd supp.), s. 14.
[18] Human Rights Act, R.S.C. 1985, chap. H-6. S. 13 makes it a discriminatory practice to use the telephone to communicate racial hatred. The communication must be repeated and it must be likely to expose a person or persons to hatred or contempt on the basis of race, nationality, ethnicity, religion, age, sex, family or marital status, disability, or pardoned conviction. The Human Rights Code, C.C.S.M. c. H175, s. 18 and the Human Rights Code, R.S.N.B. 1973, s. 6(1) contain similar provisions to the federal Act.

Notwithstanding Canada's extensive legislation about hate propaganda, the legislative provisions are seldom utilized. There have been only six prosecutions and almost no convictions in the twenty years since hate control laws first appeared in the Criminal Code.[19] There are also few complaints received by provincial and municipal pölice forces. In Toronto, for example, hate propaganda complaints are turned over to the Joint Forces Pornography/Hate Literature Section, a combined unit of the Ontario Provincial Police and the Metropolitan Toronto Police Department. Two officers investigate potential Criminal Code violations, largely on a complaints received basis, or by special request of the provincial Attorney General as to a specific occurrence. After investigation, the Branch submits its opinion to a Crown Attorney who specializes in hate literature. In 1989 the Branch investigated fifty possible hate literature violations. None were followed by prosecution. The section expected to complete fifty to sixty further investigations in 1990.

At the border, the Prohibited Importations Unit of Revenue Canada reviews four to five hundred items of suspected hate propaganda annually. Virtually all of this material is white supremacist literature which is sent to the unit by regional Customs officers at border stations. These officers follow Hate Propaganda guidelines released by Revenue Canada in 1985.[20] The average review process of 'detained' material takes seven to eight days. The four to five hundred items number is misleadingly large because much of the material seized consists of multiple issues of only a few white supremacist magazines.

---

[19] *R.* v. *Buzzanga and Durocher*, convicted at trial (unreported), reversed on appeal, (1979), 49 C.C.C. (2d) 369; *Nealy* v. *Johnston* (1989), 10 C.H.R.R. D/6450 (Human Rights Tribunal); *R.* v. *Zundel* (1987), 31 C.C.C. (3d) 97 (Ont. C.A.); *R.* v. *Andrews* (1990), 77 D.L.R. (4th) 128 (S.C.C); *R.* v. *Keegstra* (1990), 3 C.R.R. (3d) 193 (S.C.C.); *R.* v. *Taylor* (1990), 3 C.R.R. (2d) 116, 75 D.L.R. (4th) 577 (S.C.C.). A conviction was upheld in *Andrews*, and in the *Nealy* and *Taylor* cases decided under the Canadian Human Rights Act. Zundel and Keegstra have been sent back to trial. The charge against Zundel was dismissed in 1992 on constituitional grounds. On 10 July 1992 Keegstra was convicted at a second trial, but has expressed his intention to appeal.

[20] Authority to detain hate propaganda is provided by Schedule VII to the Customs Tariff Act and Tariff Code 9956. A recent controversy which prompted a change in procedure involved Salmon Rushdie's novel, *The Satanic Verses*. The book was detained at the border following complaints by sympathizers of Ayatollah Khomeni. In response to the outcry over censorship, headquarters officials were given authority to provide 'advance rulings' and field officers were stripped of authority to detain books until a review is taken to determine whether the book violates Canada's hate propaganda legislation. There is an appeal process: *Customs Act,* s. 71.

4

How was it that Canada decided to attack hatemongering through the criminal sanction? What thinking led to this approach? Is that thinking still sound?

In the early 1960s Canada experienced increased activity by neo-Nazi and white supremacist organizations based largely in the USA. The Minister of Justice established a Special Committee (the 'Cohen Committee') to survey and report on the problem. The Cohen Committee reported[21] that most of the hate materials circulating in Canada were anti-Semitic. The majority were produced by the American Nazi party in the USA. Two individuals, Adrien Arcand and John Ross Taylor, were the primary Canadian distributors.

Cohen concluded that the number of persons involved in hate propaganda was limited, involving about fourteen organizations, mostly splinter groups expelled from the Social Credit movement; a few Nazi-type parties; and a few indigenous fascist associations. Cohen believed that none of the organizations represented a really effective political or propaganda force.[22]

Even though Cohen concluded that the disseminators of hate propaganda were small in number and inefficient in method, the 'deeply offensive' nature of the materials to many Canadians led his Committee to infer that 'it would be a mistake to ignore the potential of prejudice developed by these groups and their continuing "hate" activities'.[23] Cohen feared that the activities of such groups, if left unchecked, could fester into 'a climate of malice, destructive to the central values of Judaeo-Christian society, the values of our civilization' as in Europe of the 1930s. The Committee concluded that 'the "hate" situation in Canada, although not alarming, clearly is serious enough to require action', however small the number of groups and individuals actively promoting hate.[24]

Even though Cohen's principal empirical observation was that the hate phenomenon in Canada was small and ineffective, he concluded that the problem of hate propaganda 'nevertheless ... is a serious one'.[25] This conclusion was based entirely on speculation—the hypothesis, altogether untested in the Committee's research, that if left alone hate propaganda might become effective and lead to social breakdown. Cohen phrased his conclusion this way:

[21] Canada, *Report of the Special Committee On Hate Propaganda in Canada* (Queen's Printer, Ottawa, 1966) (hereafter *Cohen Report*).
[22] Ibid. 14.   [23] Ibid.   [24] Ibid. 24–5.   [25] Ibid. 59.

We believe that, given a certain set of socio-economic circumstances, such as a deepening of the emotional tensions or the setting in of a severe business recession, public susceptibility might well increase significantly. Moreover, the potential psychological and social damage of hate propaganda, both to a desensitized majority and to sensitive minority target groups, is incalculable.[26]

This speculation led to Cohen's central recommendation— that hate propaganda should be suppressed by a criminal prohibition. Parliament agreed with that recommendation, and enacted Criminal Code amendments outlawing hate propaganda in 1970.

The limited evidence Cohen brought forward tends to suggest the opposite of the conclusion he reached, i.e. that a small, inefficient phenomenon was serious enough to require a massive criminal law response. One could go further and ask to what extent the evidence unearthed by the Committee justified its three central hypotheses. These were that hate propaganda might fester into something seriously destructive, that the effect on victims was severe, and that criminal prohibition would be an effective prophylactic means to address the problem. As evidence for these hypotheses, the Committee relied on existing governmental files, interviews with various federal and provincial politicians and police officers, and two studies done at the request of the Committee.[27] The Committee held no public hearings because:

Remembering the Minister's invitation to embark on a study which would not take too long to complete, but nevertheless a study which was to be as thorough as possible, the Committee decided that, in the interests of effective operation, no public hearings would be held, or briefs solicited, over and above the variety of submissions already on file.[28]

Moreover, the survey study, although favouring legislative action against hate, saw the law 'as an aspect of education or as a means of improving the social climate rather than as a final solution'.[29] One must observe that criminal prosecution and imprisonment is a harsh

---

[26] Ibid.

[27] These studies were a review of the offence of sedition in England, the United States and Canada, and a survey of the literature on hate propaganda: ibid., Appendices 1 and 2.

[28] Ibid. 3.

[29] Ibid. 32. The Cohen Committee itself found a 'need for a serious general study of efforts through education to deal with the problems of hate propaganda' (33), although it was felt this was beyond the scope of their enquiry.

means of education. As a prime objective education is at least a controversial use of the criminal sanction.

It would appear that the Cohen Committee's primary concern was to complete an analysis of the existing legal position with a view to law reform, and only tangentially did the Committee see its mandate as the gathering of evidence about the phenomenon of hate propaganda in Canada. Nor did the Cohen Committee undertake any serious study of the effect of hate propaganda on its victims or on the general public. When considering the social-psychological effects of hate propaganda, the Committee felt that this was an area 'in which all conclusions are tentative and few things can be scientifically measured'.[30] Thus, the Committee lacked any evidentiary foundation from which to support one of its central conclusions: that the impact of hate propaganda on its victims as well as on society generally was sufficiently severe as to justify criminal prosecution. The Committee simply assumed that 'in view of the increasing public concern about such propaganda, it seemed unnecessary to belabour the notoriously offensive character of "hate materials"'.[31] Again, one must observe that the use of criminal measures to address an assumed problem, an assumption based on no evidence, is a dangerous precedent.

All justifications for the present criminal prohibitions on hate propaganda stem from the *Cohen Report*. There are three reports subsequent to Cohen's which agree with continued use of the criminal sanction.[32] None of the subsequent reports test or add to Cohen's empirical research, sketchy though that research was. These reports continue to rely on the conjectures and untested hypotheses of the *Cohen Report*.

The Supreme Court of Canada considered the constitutional validity of the hate propaganda provisions in three recent decisions, *Keegstra*, *Andrews*, and *Taylor*.[33] The opinions of the Court in these cases find the provisions to be free expression violations, but violations which are justifiable under section 1 of the Charter as reasonable limits in a free and democratic society. The justifications for the

---

[30] Ibid. 28.   [31] Ibid. 4.

[32] J. D. McAlpine, *Report Arising Out of the Activities of the Ku Klux Klan in British Columbia*, (1981); *Hate Propaganda*, Law Reform Commission, Working Paper 50 (The Commission, Ottawa, 1986); *Equality Now*, Canada, House of Commons, Special Committee on Participation of Visible Minorities in Canadian Society (Supply and Services, Ottawa, 1984); *Report of the Special Committee on Racial and Religious Hatred*, Canadian Bar Association (1984).

[33] Above, n. 19.

limits are based on the conclusions of the *Cohen Report* and its progeny, without questioning the premises on which those reports were based. In *Keegstra*, Dickson CJC refers to the *Cohen Report*, cites the subsequent reports mentioned above, and uses these sources to support his conclusion that the legislative objective was sufficiently powerful to justify a limit on freedom of expression.[34] The unsound evidentiary foundation of the *Cohen Report* thus finds its ways into the Supreme Court's opinion without ever being independently tested as required by the evidentiary dimensions of section 1 of the *Charter*.[35] Canada's constitutional guarantee of freedom of expression is being limited by the Supreme Court's acceptance of the self-contradictory conclusions of the *Cohen Report*. There is nothing in the Court's opinion or its sources which add independent evidence about Canadian hate propaganda to the *Cohen Report*.

Canada's constitutional jurisprudence establishes that violation of Charter rights by use of the criminal sanction demands a stringent standard of justification on the evidence.[36] The use of the criminal sanction to address hate propaganda is contrary to the stringent evidentiary burden required by the jurisprudence, as fortified by common sense, when the State appears as 'singular antagonist' to a criminal accused. The hate phenomenon the Cohen Committee described was small, inefficient and ineffective. This poses a difficulty for Canadian hate propaganda doctrine, despite the prestige of the hate propaganda sources, because the evidence in the hate propaganda reports contradicts the Cohen Committee's recommendations and Parliament's legislative response. There was no evidence, beyond conjecture, which justified use of the criminal sanction, which all agree should be used sparingly. The *Cohen Report*'s central conjecture is counter-intuitive because it requires the assumption that Canadian hate propaganda might become something it is not.

[34] Dickson CJC's conclusion was that 'the nature of Parliament's objective is supported not only by the work of numerous study groups, but also by our collective historical knowledge of the potentially catastrophic effects of the promotion of hatred'. See *Keegstra*, above, n. 19 at 236.

[35] Below, n. 36.

[36] 'It is important in considering the issues raised by a case like the present to note that judicial evaluation of the state's interest will differ depending on whether the state is the "singular antagonist" of the person whose rights have been violated, as it usually will be where the violation occurs in the context of the criminal law.' The difference is that in the criminal context, 'the courts will be able to determine whether the impugned law or other government conduct is the "least drastic means" for the achievement of the state interest with a considerable measure of certainty'. *Vancouver General Hospital* v. *Stoffman*, [1990] 3 S.C.R. 483, 521.

Why should the Cohen Committee's counter-intuitive conjecture, unsupported by evidence, be accepted as an elementary building block of Canadian constitutional law?

Cohen's first answer—that the materials are offensive— raises obvious difficulties with Canada's constitutional commitment to freedom of expression, a problem which Professor Weinstein has exhaustively considered elsewhere in this volume. Cohen's second reason for recommending use of the criminal law to suppress hate propaganda—the spectre of the holocaust—is more troubling. The holocaust marks a savage appearance of hate in modern times, requiring stern vigilance against such fiendishness. If Cohen was right in hypothesising that the Canadian hate situation might grow into something significant if left unchecked by the criminal sanction, then Parliament's enactment of criminal hate prohibitions would certainly seem less paradoxical.

At twenty-five years remove from enactment of Canada's hate laws, it would be useful to re-examine Cohen's speculation about the potential of Canada's small hate propaganda phenomenon to mushroom into something serious. With the benefit of Canada's twenty-five-year experience in administering comprehensive prohibitions on hate propaganda, we may inquire again whether Canadian hate laws effectively combat Canadian racism and anti-Semitism. We may also attempt to document the change in Canada's hate profile in the past twenty-five years in order to assist a re-evaluation of Cohen's conjecture that without the intervention of the criminal law, Canada's hate problem 'might well increase significantly'.

5

There is some difficulty for present day researchers, as it was difficult for the Cohen committee, to track Canadian hate propaganda, as it is largely an underground literature. Nevertheless, police, prosecutors, human rights commissions, customs officials, and private enforcers monitor distribution of hate material; newspapers report on it; organized groups distribute it. These sources were surveyed in the period 1989–90. The results offer a portrait of Canada's modern day hate profile at least as accurate as the depiction provided by the Cohen committee twenty-five years ago.

Hate activity increased in the mid-1970s with the revival of the Ku Klux Klan in Ontario and British Columbia, new activity by the

Edmund Burke Society, later the Western Guard Party, and the Nationalist Party of Canada. In substance, Canadian hate propaganda changed little from what the Cohen Committee described. It is the same racist, white supremacist invective, except that today, hate speech goes beyond anti-Semitism and attacks on people of colour. Hate propaganda in present-day Canada includes hate missives directed also at East Indians, Orientals, Catholics, Aboriginal Peoples, and Francophones.

What is the filthy speech of the hatemongers in Canada? At its core is the taunting insult, spiked with hate: 'kike, nigger, cunt.' It secretes substance around its foul pith, urging others on to loathing. The hatemonger embellishes a malicious missive of hate with content, sneering at his targets, blaming them for humanity's woes—jeering, belittling, hurting. This is the hate monger's squalid sermon:

'Hitler was right', 'Nigger go home';[37] 'the allegation that six million Jews died during the second world war is utterly unfounded . . . a brazen fantasy . . . marking with eternal shame a great European nation, as well as wringing fraudulent monetary compensation from them';[38] 'A nation which allows a small alien community to dominate its financial life and its resources cannot expect to remain in good health';[39] 'America is being swamped by coloureds who do not believe in democracy and harbour a hatred for white people!';[40] 'Wake up Canadians Your Future is at stake! . . . The French minority who support the building of the French language high school are in fact a subversive group and most French Canadians are opposed to the building of the school'.[41]

Methods of dissemination have evolved. Hatemongers now distribute their messages by telephone, video and audio cassette, and computer link-up, in addition to leaflets. There is also a mock academic literature characterized by 'revisionist' histories, typically Holocaust denial.

[37] This is the language of Messrs Andrews and Smith, members of the Nationalist Party of Canada, who were prosecuted under s. 319.2 of the *Criminal Code* for *inter alia* these published statements: *R.* v. *Andrews*, above, n. 19, 132.

[38] This is the language of Ernst Zundel who was prosecuted for, *inter alia*, this statement under s. 181 of the Criminal Code: see *R.* v. *Zundel* (1987), 58 O.R. (2d) 129, 142.

[39] *R.* v. *Andrews*, above, n. 19, 132.

[40] *R.* v. *Andrews*, above, n. 19, 132.

[41] These are the words, satirically published, of Robert Buzzanga and Jean Durocher, prosecuted under s. 319.2 of the Criminal Code: *R.* v. *Buzzanga and Durocher* (1979), 25 O.R. (2d) 705, 711.

Materials from the USA still make up a substantial amount of the hate propaganda circulating in Canada. Racist organizations such as the US Ku Klux Klan overlap with Canadian counterparts and exchange materials across the border. The *List of Material Reviewed by the Prohibited Importations Unit at Revenue Canada*[42] suggests pseudo religious, white supremacist literature as the most prevalent hate propaganda coming to Canada from the USA.

The usual audience for hate literature incubates in Canada's ultra right wing. The ultra right furnishes a potential following which 'is substantial, but not out of proportion with that in other countries... [It has] a significant religious basis... but probably not more so than elsewhere'.[43] It is difficult to know how many Canadians belong to or support radical right organizations. Professor Barrett's statistics suggest that most groups have few active members.[44] Active members, however, are vocal, and this contributes to enhanced visibility. In addition, a very small percentage of Canadians lend support, both financially and in spirit, from a discreet distance.[45] Whatever the potential audience lurking in the far right, paid subscriptions to hate publications contribute the largest source of hate funding. Paying subscribers appear to be few.

It is more difficult to know what appeal hate publications have to the much greater number of Canadians who pay lip service to the

---

[42] The material is itemized in the *List of Material Reviewed by the Prohibited Importations Unit at Revenue Canada* for a three year period, as follows: 16 advertisements; 225 audio cassettes, 171 by Dr W. A. Swift; 2 films; 164 booklets; 129 books; 33 brochures; 5 catalogues; 8 comic books; 20 issues of '*National Vanguard*' magazine; 2 other magazines; 29 newsletters; 7 leaflets; Newspapers: 31 issues of *Attack*, 4 issues of *CDL Report*, 18 issues of *Christian Vanguard*, 17 issues of *National Vanguard*, 53 issues of *The Thunderbolt*, and 18 others, 141 total; 105 pamphlets, 19 by *Sons of Liberty*; 38 video cassettes; 5 miscellaneous items; 929 individual items total. Information on this programme is available from Manager, Prohibited Importations Tariff Programs, Revenue Canada, Customs and Excise, Ottawa.

[43] S. Barrett, *Is God A Racist? The Right Wing in Canada*, 355. Prof. Barrett claims that there 'is a virtual explosion of right wing activity' in Canada. He counts 161 organizations, 79 on the 'radical right' and 82 on the 'fringe right'.

[44] Ibid. The groups are not forthcoming about such matters during personal interviews. Our impression is that they inflate paid subscribers.

[45] e.g. Ian MacDonald, who lately has become less discreet. See Generally, W. Kinsella, 'The Somewhat Right of Centre Views of Ian MacDonald', *Ottawa Magazine*, Sept. 1989, 24. MacDonald is an ex-diplomat, who, as senior trade counsellor at Canada's embassy in Beirut in 1966, was the second most powerful Canadian in the Middle East. Kinsella describes MacDonald's blatantly racist and anti-Semitic views (mental and social inferiority of the negro; Canada should have co-operated with Hitler) and associations (Ku Klux Klan).

Canadian paradigm of multiculturalism and 'mosaic', but who really espouse xenophobic 'melting pot' sentiments more commonly associated with the USA. While Canada holds itself out as a racially tolerant country, Canadian traditions reveal a different agenda. In recent history the virtual exclusion of European Jewry from Canada during the Second World War[46] and the internment of Japanese Canadians are painful reminders of racial intolerance pushed to the surface by crisis. Professor Frances Henry has described convincingly how in the past few decades, overt racism has been replaced by a systemic, semi-conscious discrimination.[47] A recent Angus Reid–Southam News survey found that 60 per cent of Canadians want ethnic minorities to abandon their customs and language to become 'more like Canadians'. Reid suggests that 'it may well be that up to one third of Canadians are bigots'.[48] While this seems an assertion difficult to verify, it does suggest a continuing tradition of intolerance to minorities in Canada. In at least some cases one would expect these attitudes to be susceptible to hate propaganda.

The number of groups and individuals circulating hate propaganda in today's Canada and the quantity of hate literature distributed remains relatively limited. A striking point revealed by the survey is that the hate literature situation in Canada has not changed very much from what Cohen described twenty-five years ago. Although cause and effect is always difficult to establish in the legislative field, the hate control laws do not appear to have altered the hate literature condition Cohen portrayed in the Canada of the mid-1960s. The hate laws induce some small scale customs seizures relating to a few authors and magazines at the border and less than one prosecution every three years.

The hate laws prompt only a small number of complainants to come forward. This is significant because it indicates that the general public does not view the hate laws as an effective remedy against racism and prejudice. Nor have the hate laws apparently provided the police with incentives or instruments to eradicate hate literature. Few police resources are devoted to hate literature enforcement. The hate

---

[46] See generally, I. Abella and H. Troper, *None is Too Many: Canada and the Jews of Europe* (1984).

[47] See generally, The *Toronto Star*, 6 May 1985, p. C4.

[48] Julian Beltrame, 'Bigotry increasing in Canada' *The Ottawa Citizen*, 23 Feb. 1990.

laws occasion few investigations, almost no prosecutions, and virtually zero convictions.

It is worth inquiring into the phenomenon of hate in the USA for comparative study of a democracy that approaches hate propaganda differently from Canada. US jurisdictions generally refrain from strong prohibition of hate speech. On the contrary, US constitutional law protects hate speech from legislative incursion.[49] The comparative example may help us speculate about the relative effectiveness of Canada's hate prohibitions.

From the heyday of the Ku Klux Klan in the first half of the twentieth century, where the membership of the KKK were numbered in the millions and enjoyed the solid backing of preachers, business people, and politicians in the South,[50] memberships have drastically declined to their lowest levels this century. In 1925 KKK membership was estimated at four to five million. Today, membership stands at ten to twelve thousand.[51] This decline extends beyond the KKK; all of the traditional racist groups are experiencing dwindling numbers.[52] In 1990 the Anti-Defamation League of the B'nai B'rith estimated that there are fewer than twenty thousand members in all American hate groups, and no more than 5,500 members in the KKK. Based on the criteria of membership, influence, and potential for violence, the League reported that most hate groups have declined.[53]

Despite the decline of hate groups, racist crimes and incidents are reported to be on the rise. In 1988 B'nai B'rith inventoried the highest

---

[49] *R.A.V.* v. *St. Paul Minn.*, Us Sup. Ct. No. 90–7675, 60 *U.S.L. Week* 4667 (6–23–92).

[50] *The Economist*, 24 Feb. 1990, 26.

[51] Thomas Young, 'Violent Hate Groups in Rural America', *International Journal of Offender Therapy and Comparative Criminology* 34 (1990), 15 at 16. Young claims that the KKK membership has increased from the mid-1970s, when the Southern Poverty Law Center estimated KKK membership at 1,500.

[52] 'Hate Crimes Increase and Become more Violent', *Wall Street Journal*, 14 July 1989, A12.

[53] The exception is the skinheads. From a membership of less than 100 in 1985, B'nai B'rith estimates that there were more than 5,000 members in 1990. In 1991 the FBI estimated that there are more than 3,000 skinheads in the United States, a threefold increase since 1987. Although there is no strong national organization of skinheads, B'nai B'rith believes that traditional hate organizations are recruiting skinheads to shore up their dwindling ranks. In 1989 B'nai B'rith reported that there were 3,000 skinheads belonging to outwardly racist organizations in 31 states, an increase from 2,000 in 21 states from 1988. See Floyd I. Clarke, 'Hate Violence in the United States' *FBI Law Enforcement Bulletin* 60 (1991), 14 at 16.

number of anti-Semitic incidents reported in more than five years.[54] Additionally, the increase in the incidents of violence is accompanied with an increase in the degree of violence used.[55] In response to the increase in reporting of hate-motivated crimes, the US Attorney General vowed to prosecute members of hate groups to address 'the shocking re-emergence of hate-group violence', and make the prosecution of hate crimes a top priority.[56] In addition, the FBI has two criminal investigative programmes which are designed specifically to address hate violence.[57]

On 23 April 1990, Congress enacted the Hate Crime Statistics Act after almost five years of debate and hearings. The Act requires the Attorney General to collect data about crimes motivated by hate until 1995.[58] The Act is intended to bring the picture of hate crimes into sharper focus by providing detail on who commits these crimes, who are the victims, what geographic locations show a concentration of hate violence and so on. Perhaps this clearer statistical portrait will

[54] There were 823 acts of vandalism and desecration, and 458 threats and physical attacks against Jews. For 1989 a total of 1,432 acts of anti-Semitic vandalism, desecration and harassment were reported, the highest level since 1979 when such incidents were first tracked. See Joseph M. Fernandez, 'Bringing Hate Crimes into Focus', *Harv. C.R.-C.L.L.* 26 (1991) 261.

[55] The National Gay and Lesbian Task Force also monitors hate-motivated violence. In 1989, there were 7,031 anti-gay incidents reported. A Task Force on Education Bigotry formed in 1991 in Illinois cited a 200% increase in racial incidents on campuses across the USA within the past few years. The Puerto Rican Legal Defense & Education Fund reported a marked increase in racial violence in 1990. Various states and local governments that collect data on hate violence also report increases in hate crimes. The Arab-American Anti-Discrimination Society counted incidents of violence during 1990; from Jan. to August, there were 5 incidents of violence reported, whereas in the period from August—the start of the Iraq invasion of Kuwait—to Dec., 37 acts of violence were reported. Cited in Jeff Peters, 'When Fear Turns to Hate and Hate to Violence', *Human Rights* 18 (1991), 22; Tanya Kateri Hernandez, 'Bias Crimes: Unconscious Racism in the Prosecution of "Racially Motivated Violence"', *Yale L.J.* 99 (1990), 845, 846. Also see 'Decade Ended in Blaze of Hate', *Los Angeles Times*, 23 Feb. 1990, B3; 'Hate Crimes Rise Sharply', *Los Angeles Times*, 7 Sept. 1990, B1, which report a dramatic increase in hate violence. In Los Angeles County in 1989, there were 378 hate crimes (crimes motivated by race, religion, or sexual orientation); in the first 6 months of 1990, there had already been 272 hate crimes reported.

[56] He appears to be making good on his word: from Jan. to May inclusive, 17 prosecutions for racial violence by organized hate groups were initiated by federal prosecutors, more than the total brought during any previous full year. See above, n. 52.

[57] Above, n. 53, 15.

[58] S. (b)(1) of the *Hate Crime Statistics Act* directs the Attorney General to collect data for 'crimes that manifest evidence of prejudice based on race, religion, sexual orientation, or ethnicity'. S. (b)(2) authorizes the Attorney General to establish guidelines for the collection of the data.

aid policy makers to fashion a better targeted response to US experience with hate.

Since most hate groups have declining memberships, why are the reported incidents of hate-motivated violence on the rise? Various explanations have been advanced by prosecutors and advocacy groups, although both groups admit that these explanations are tentative and not firmly supported by empirical evidence. First, the expansion of youth 'white power' groups, such as the skinheads, has been blamed for the increase. Second, affirmative action programmes may be seen to give an unfair advantage to blacks and other minorities, and thus to provoke a backlash. Third, the greater visibility of gays may provoke more homophobic attacks. Finally, a study commissioned by the Justice Department and done by Abt Associates Inc. in Massachusetts suggested that hate crimes may be growing in part 'because of a perceived decrease in government efforts to prevent discrimination in education, housing and development'.[59]

Although these explanations may partially account for the rise in reported hate violence, none appear broad enough to account for the consistent reports of an increase in hate crimes in the United States. It is possible the rise in *reporting* of hate crimes is simply that: an increase in *reported* incidents, not an increase in *actual* incidents. This could be accounted for by heightened public awareness.[60]

Although the hate phenomena in Canada and the USA are obviously different, there are certain broad similarities. Organized hate is not growing appreciably in Canada and is in fact declining in the USA. Organized hate is small in both countries. There is heightened public awareness of and sensitivity to hate propaganda. Given these similarities in broad long-term trends in both countries, one with strong hate control laws and one without such laws, it is difficult to see that Canada's hate laws have made a difference in Canada's hate profile. The comparative example appears to throw doubt on Cohen's

[59] Above, n. 52.

[60] This is similar to the phenomenon of sexual harassment. Although reports of sexual harassment in the work-place 10 years ago were significantly lower than today, it is unlikely that the work-place was freer of such incidents in the past. More likely, increased public awareness and support for those coming forward have played a substantial role in the increased reports of sexual harassment. It is probable that a similar pattern can be drawn for hate crimes. The significant increase in the number of federal prosecutions for racial violence by organized hate groups may simply reflect the increase in public awareness and support for victims that exists today. See 'Sharp Rise in Hate Crimes', *Washington Post*, 15 Sept. 1990, B4.

conjecture that without strong hate control laws hate propaganda in Canada could mushroom into a serious problem.

No one has ever suggested that Canada's hate laws have ameliorated racism in Canada, and this would seem an extravagant claim on the evidence. Professor Barrett's study suggests that the Canadian hate phenomenon is unaffected by criminal hate propaganda prohibitions. One can see in Barrett's study that there is little difference in the rise of hate activity in Canada and the USA in recent history. Canada has strong hate laws; the USA does not.[61] Canada's hate laws have had no observable effect on Canada's hate perpetrators in the sense of curtailing their organizations or activities. In the twenty years since Canada enacted the hate laws, hate groups have augmented slightly. Given that the police and general public do not rely substantially on the hate laws to combat racism, it seems extravagant to suggest that hate would have spread more widely or rapidly but for the hate laws. Is it any less extravagant to conjecture that the spectacular decline in US hate group membership would have been any more dramatic if there had been hate propaganda prohibitions in place in the USA during this period?

Professors Winn and Weimann studied the effect of media exploitation of Ernst Zundel's trial for spreading hateful Holocaust-denial lies.[62] They concluded that sensational media coverage of Zundel's case did not weaken support for Zundel among his constituency. Zundel's support strengthened in this group because the trial imbued him with a martyr's aura. Nor can one confidently say that the Zundel trial weakened support for racist sentiment in the larger group of Canadians with weak sentiments of prejudice. Following reversal of Keegstra's conviction for hate propaganda by the Alberta Court of Appeal[63] on technical constitutional grounds, the *Edmonton Journal* proclaimed in its headline: 'Keegstra Vindicated.' Is it likely that such media coverage by a major paper would diminish support for either Keegstra, or the anti-Semitism which he represents?

In light of the present survey it is difficult to resist the conclusion that in the twenty years of their operation, Canada's hate propaganda controls have had little or no real effect on Canada's hate literature

---

[61] Nor would a system of strong hate propaganda prohibitions be possible in light of court interpretation of the first amendment. The Supreme Court has rules such laws constitutionally infirm: *R.A.V.* v. *St. Paul, Minn.*, US Sup. Ct., No 90–7675, 22 June 1992 (60 *U.S.L. Week*, no. 50, p. 4667).

[62] C. Winn and G. Weimann, *Hate on Trial* (1986).

[63] *R.* v. *Keegstra* (1989), 43 C.C.C. (3d) 150 (Alta. C.A.).

predicament or the underlying causes of racism and intolerance which motivate it.

Since 1965 Great Britain has had hate laws similar to those of Canada, but tougher in their administration. Britain has more prosecutions than Canada, and quite a few British hate propagandists actually go to jail.[64] The British experience has been studied. The researchers found no empirical evidence that suggests that censoring racist speech counters British racism at all, or that British hate laws have had any impact on neo-Nazi and other hate groups operating in Britain.[65] 'To the contrary, psychological research shows that censored speech, merely by virtue of the censorship, becomes more appealing and persuasive to many listeners.'[66]

The Canadian, US, and British experience would appear to confirm what we already know from the example of Nazi Germany. There were strong hate propaganda prohibitions on the statute books during the period of Hitler's rise to power.[67] These laws were actively enforced by energetic prosecution of anti-Semitic speech during the Weimar Republic. Yet,

> all too often, the defendants were allowed to use the court room as a forum for the dissemination of their ideas ... [show trials] were turned by skilful Nazi attorneys ... into trials of Jewish rituals, Jewish religious texts, Jewish

[64] The chart below indicates the activity and results of prosecutions in United Kingdom, 1965–89:

Accused	Verdict	Sentence
Cole	Not guilty	Nil
Jones	Not guilty	Nil
Weston	Guilty	£50
Relf	Guilty	9 months
Cole	Guilty	6 months suspended + £250
Knight	Guilty	£1,000
Heron	Guilty	£1,000
Pearce	Guilty	2 years conditional discharge
Hume	Guilty	3 months detention
McLaughlin	Guilty	4 months
Webster	Guilty	6 months suspended + £150

[65] A. Neier, *Defending My Enemy: American Nazis, The Skokie Case, and the Risks of Freedom* (1979), 154–5.

[66] N. Strossen, 'Regulating Racist Speech on Campus: A Modest Proposal?' *Duke L.J.* (1990), 484, 559.

[67] 'pre-Hitler Germany had law very much like our anti-hate law, and it was used quite vigorously.' A. Borovoy, 'Language as Violence v. Freedom of Expression', *Buffalo L. Rev.* 37 (1988–9) 337, 344.

leaders ... [slT]he Nazis not only welcomed show trials but actually tried to provoke them'.[68]

Obviously, vigorous use of hate propaganda laws were ineffective at stemming the spread of anti-Semitism at this critical juncture of history.

In light of how the hate laws really work, it is difficult to have confidence that Cohen's second rationale for invoking the criminal sanction against hate speech is sound. The hate laws do not seem to combat anti-Semitism and racism effectively, if at all. They do not seem to stop or slow society's slide into Nazism if other powerful socio-economic forces impel a particular culture on that path. The evidence would appear to suggest that criminalization of hate propaganda does not alter racism or anti-Semitism as social phenomena.

6

Since Canada's criminal law approach to hate propaganda has no discernible benefits, it is appropriate to ask: what are the costs?

All serious commentators[69] recognize that Canada's hate propaganda laws have an uneasy relationship with the free speech principle. Although the Supreme Court of Canada has rejected the counsel of Professor Weinstein[70] and others to invalidate the hate control laws, the Court is clear that constitutional validity depends on keeping such

[68] Cyril Levitt, 'Racial Incitement and the Law: The Case of the Weimar Republic', in D. Scheiderman, ed. *Freedom of Expression and the Charter* (1991), 211 at 212, 239. Levitt's careful study merits close attention. At 231 he details how Julius Streicher, editor of *Der Stuermer*, turned his libel trials into trials of the Talmud, a phenomenon not unlike the Zundel trial where the Court took weeks to determine whether it was proven, beyond a reasonable doubt, that the Holocaust happened.

[69] Here is a sample of the more interesting articles. D. Riesman, 'Democracy and Defamation: Control of Group Libel', *Columbia Law Review* 42 (1942) 727; A. Borovoy, *When Freedoms Collide: The Case for our Civil Liberties* (1988); A. Borovoy, K. Mahoney, B. Brown, J. Cameron, D. Goldberger, M. Matsuda, 'Language as Violence v. Freedom of Expression: Canadian and American Perspectives on Group Defamation', *Buffalo Law Rev.* 37, (1988–9), 337; W. Tarnopolsky, 'Freedom of Expression v. Right to Equal Treatment: The Problem of Hate Propaganda and Racial Discrimination' *U.B.C. Law Review* (1967) 43; H. W. Arthurs, 'Hate Propaganda: An Argument Against Attempts to Stop it by Legislation', *Chitty's Law Journal*, 18 (1970), 1; M. Cohen, 'The Hate Propaganda Amendments: Reflections on a Controversy' *Can. Com. Law Review* 4 (1972), 243.

[70] See his essay in this volume.

statutes narrow.[71] Sections 318 and 319 of Canada's Criminal Code are narrowed by defences. One of the most important of these is the defence of truth. By s. 319(3)(a) no person may be convicted of hate propaganda 'if he establishes that the statements communicated were true'.

Consider the cases of a racist accused arraigned for stating that people of colour commit more crimes, and produce more single mothers living on welfare than whites; or a sexist defendant charged with stating that women do less well at mathematics than men, or other accused persons charged with communicating similar stereotyped ideas. These accused may defend by proving that the statements are true. The problem is that these statements operate in many contexts. Defence counsel will call expert testimony to support the truth of these statements in some contexts. The prosecution must prove the falsity of these statements in all contexts beyond a reasonable doubt. As a sometime prosecutor, I am certain that there will be many acquittals on this ground. Are we willing to have trials on these propositions with the certain result that some courts will dignify them by adjudicating that they are true or that reasonable doubt exists as to the facts? Do we want our courts to be in the business of ruling that a reasonable doubt exists that people of colour are less intelligent or that women learn more slowly?[72]

In this light it is surprising to read the view of Chief Justice Dickson [as he then was] that '[t]here is very little chance that statements intended to promote hatred against an identifiable group are

---

[71] In *Keegstra*, above n. 19 at 251, Dickson CJC addresses the argument of overbreadth and vagueness, and concluded that the defences significantly reduce the danger that s. 319(2) is overbroad or unduly vague. In McLachlin J's analysis, 308, she refers to the chilling effect due to vagueness and subjectivity in s. 319. In *Taylor*, above, n. 19 at 165, McLachlin J (dissenting) expands on overbreadth in the context of s. 13 of the Canadian Human Rights Act. She concludes that s. 13 is overly broad for several reasons. The terms 'hatred' and 'contempt' are vague and subjective, there is no clear and precise indiction to members of society as to what the limits of impugned speech are, there is no requirement for intent or foreseeability, there are no defences, and there is wide administrative discretion granted. Dickson CJC does not agree: 'The terms of the section, in particular the phrase "hatred or contempt", are sufficiently precise and narrow', 148.

[72] See *Doe* v. *University of Michigan*, 721 F. Supp. 852 (E. D. Mich, 1989). In this case a student was disciplined under a campus anti-harassment code for making the comment in class that 'homosexuality was a disease that could be psychologically treated'. The policy gave as an example of sanctionable conduct a remark in like: 'Women just aren't as good in this field as men, thus creating a hostile learning atmosphere for female classmates.'

true'...[73] Consider the statement that 'Jews are overrepresented in universities'. This statement is true. Certain speakers express this statement to promote hatred of Jews.[74] Most Courts would acquit a person charged with making this statement under s. 319 of the Criminal Code, on the finding that the statement is true.

It is complicated to explain how this statement can be true, and still be used to promote hatred, something that would probably not be relevant to a court considering the defence of truth. In the late 1930s Canada was a country rife with anti-Semitism. Whole areas of the economy were closed to Jews.

Banks, insurance companies, department stores and large industrial and commercial interests did not hire Jews. Jewish doctors could not get hospital appointments. There was not one Jewish judge in the entire country. Law firms rarely hired Jews. ... There was not one Jewish professor at any Canadian University. There were no Jewish school principals, very few teachers, and almost no Jewish engineers, architects or nurses. [When the first Jewish intern was hired at a hospital in Montreal] every intern on staff walked out, refusing, as they explained to the press, to work with a Jew ... [Bora Laskin], a brilliant legal scholar with two Masters degrees could not get a job in a Toronto law firm [and was hired at the University of Toronto only after the Dean assured the University President that although] Laskin was Jewish ... he will not disgrace the University.[75]

The reasons why Jews are over-represented in the universities is that universities relaxed exclusion of Jews before the professions, finance, banking, and government. Universities were one of the few places professionally minded Jews could work.

Is there any alternative to narrowing Canada's hate propaganda statutes by the defence of truth? The only alternative appears to be creation of official dogmas. We could establish that in Canadian society, as official dogma, Jews are not over-represented in universities. As official dogma, we could proclaim that men and women are equal. These propositions cannot be questioned in any context on pain of jail, whether or not true. The problem with this alternative is that official dogma is the antithesis of a free society. In any event, it is hard to see why we would want to go in this direction. This is where

[73] *R.* v. *Keegstra*, above, n. 19, 239.

[74] Like most Jewish professors, I have heard my share of this statement. Like most Jewish professors, I got the message the speaker was intending to convey.

[75] I. Abella, 'The Making of a Chief Justice: Bora Laskin, The Early Years' *The Cambridge Lectures* (1989), 159.

the Eastern Bloc countries have been, and what the Eastern Bloc now reject, in light of their unhappy ordeal.[76]

The experience of countries around the world that criminalize hate propaganda is that hate control laws are used in bizarre ways. Members of minority groups which the laws intend to protect are the usual targets of punishment under these laws. The first prosecutions under the British statutes were against black power leaders. Since 1965 the British law has been used regularly to curb the speech of black leaders, trade unionists, and anti- nuclear activists.[77] In nineteenth-century France, none of the anti-Semites responsible for inflaming opinion against Captain Alfred Dreyfus was prosecuted for group libel. Zola, however, had to flee to England to escape punishment after he was prosecuted for libelling the French clergy and military in his *J'Accuse*. So too in the USA. Speech-limiting ordinances aimed at Skokie Nazis never were applied to the Nazis. But they were enforced against the Jewish war veterans. Canadian experience is the same. The hate laws attract bizarre prosecutions, against French Canadian nationalists, against opponents of full financing for Catholic schools, against trade unionists, against Salman Rushdie's spectacular novel, *The Satanic Verses*. So too with the pornography laws which the Supreme Court upheld as measures to protect women. The first targets of the police after these laws were upheld were lesbian and gay groups.[78]

The international experience suggests that it is difficult, if not impossible, to target hate propaganda laws with precision. The determinations which are required are very fact intensive. The discretion

[76] The creation of official dogma would steer us towards the constitutions of the former Soviet Union and other Eastern Bloc countries. The system of free expression operating under these constitutions was particularly unsuccessful. The now defunct *Constitution of the Soviet Union* created an 'all people's state' in which the will of the people, as expressed by the Communist Party of the Soviet Union, and that of the State, as expressed by the party, are inseparable (Art. 2, Art. 6, Soviet Constitution). If we opt for official dogma, we are accepting this type of thinking. All socialist constitutions subordinate individual free expression to the 'general interest', 'socialist order', 'objectives of the State', or 'interests of the whole community'. Recent developments in the Eastern Bloc suggest that the will of the individual should prevail. The proposition that there should be limits on the exercise of free speech inspired by official dogma would seem to have been disproved by the recent history of Communist constitutions.

[77] [I]n Great Britain a substantial percentage of "hate speech" prosecutions have been against members of minorities.' Kent Greenawalt, 'Free Speech in the United States and Canada', *Law and Contemporary Problems*, 55 (1992), 1, 24.

[78] On 30 Apr. 1992, a gay and lesbian bookstore, Glad Day Book Store was raided for the first time in 11 years: see 'Police Raid Gay Bookstore', *Globe and Mail*, 1 May 1992, A10.

to make these factual findings are widely decentralized in police forces, prosecutors, customs and other administrative officials, and the judiciary. Many authorities therefore have great latitude to determine which speakers and what words will actually be prosecuted and punished. The experience of all countries is that hate propaganda laws are used against the very disempowered people they are designed to protect, while many vicious racial epithets continue to go unpunished. No country has been successful in solving this structural problem.

Hate propaganda laws chill free speech. This is important, because our democratic societies need more speech, not less, to nourish the self-government premise of our political systems. The chilling effect is also important to our attempts to combat racism. Hate propaganda laws diminish opportunity for intergroup discussion because they inhibit free discussion and airing of misunderstandings.[79] These interchanges are more likely to promote positive intergroup relations than legal battles. It is undesirable that intercommunity exchanges be forced to pass through the filter of criminal sanctions on speech.

The most weighty objection of all to using the criminal sanction against hate propaganda is that the criminal approach exacerbates the problem of racism. It is important for us to know who the racists are and what they are saying. The presence of racist speech is a challenge to public morality about and public complicity in the underlying societal problem of racism. Hate speech is a dramatic reminder of the need for constant vigilance against our baser human tendencies. If racist speech is suppressed, there is less opportunity for societal mobilization to attack the real racism problem.

Banning racist speech perpetuates a paternalistic view of people of colour and other minorities, suggesting that they are incapable of defending themselves. As a Jew, I resent this paternalism. I want to know who the anti-Semites are. I want to hear their speech so I can decide what to do about it. It is not good for me that they be driven underground. I prefer my enemies to be visible.

Finally, the censorship approach makes it easier for communities to avoid coming to grips with the harder, expensive, but more meaningful methods for dealing with the underlying problem of racism and its effects. Persecuted communities need a greater weight in the balance of power. They need jobs, education, training, and in some cases affirmative preference. Our polity may feel it has addressed the

[79] See *Doe* v. *University of Michigan*, above, n. 72.

needs of victimized minorities by enacting questionable hate statutes. As I have tried to show, the statutes do little or nothing for the persecuted. They are a cheap, smug way of flattering ourselves that we have done the righteous thing. To take the obvious example: the international treaties on hate propaganda do nothing to remedy the mass murder of European Jews. Nor will these pitiful laws prevent another Holocaust. They were on the German statute books during Hitler's administration. The real way to prevent another mass murder of Jews is to create the State of Israel and the Israeli army. This is real devolution of power to a persecuted community that solves a real problem of powerlessness. The post-war treaties agreeing that hate propaganda should be banned provoked an interesting academic debate in the countries, like Canada, that closed their doors to Jews fleeing Hitler. When faced with the next Hitler, I would rather have Israel and the Israeli army than Canada's *Criminal Code*.

In any event, Canada's criminal prohibitions are not the obvious response to the international morality that requires measures to combat hate propaganda. As indicated above by my survey of the international community, there are a multitude of legal measures which act positively to combat racism and anti-Semitism. Among these are the use of State-sponsored initiatives in education and culture which promote equality and condemn discrimination, the use of government speech with all its prestige to condemn racist ideas expressed by private speakers, government funding of anti-racist, equality-seeking groups, and of course the use of affirmative promotion of historically excluded groups by means of government largesse. Some of these measures actually seem to work in the fight against hate and its causes.[80] This is more than can be said for Canada's hate propaganda laws.

However, Canada's hate propaganda laws do have an enthusiastic constituency. Disempowered groups want government to do *something*, and those attracted to a simple law-and-order political response can be satisfied that government is doing something when it enacts or toughens hate control measures. Such a response

---

[80] See R. Seltzer and G. M. Lopes, 'The Ku Klux Klan: Reasons for Support or Opposition Among White Respondents' *J. Black Studies* 17 (1986), 91, 105. The researchers found that the level of education was clearly the most important variable influencing support for the KKK, with higher education correlating to lower levels of support. In R. J. Bryon and R. L. Lenton, 'The Distribution of Anti-Semitism in Canada in 1984', *Canadian Journal of Sociology* 16 (1991), 411 at 416, it was found that higher levels of education correlated with lower levels of anti-Semitism.

makes resort to the criminal law tempting to government because policy-makers know that such prohibitions are extremely cheap to administer. It is easy to see why policy makers prefer the cheap criminal sanction that has high political visibility when they contrast the criminal approach with the vaguer, expensive, long term measures that over time, sometimes imperceptibly, with little political visibility, really work.

If the proponents of Canada's hate propaganda laws could demonstrate that these statutes really did combat racism, anti-Semitism and other forms of hatred, many civil libertarians would be all for them. If it could be proved that these laws are effective, many civil libertarians, including myself, would be seriously tempted to put civil liberties scruples aside, and support these prohibitions. Most defenders of free speech are for equality. However, our instinct and experience is that these laws are counter productive. Like the death penalty and the war on drugs, the hate laws are a quick fix that makes people feel better because they perceive, falsely, that something is being done about a visible, irritating problem. If, however, that perception proves to be a cruel illusion, as I have tried to demonstrate, the hate propaganda statutes will only cripple our political capacity to take serious action against intolerance.

Index

hate propaganda 57, 153–250;
balancing of interests 156–63; British
restrictions and prosecutions 243;
and campus codes 201, 206–7; and
conciliation 229; definition of 176;
description of 236; and emotional
distress 205–7; and falsehood 183–4,
186, 202; importation of materials
229; and individual liberty vs. social
equality 153–4, 158; ineffectiveness
of criminal prohibitions against 232,
238; laws against counterproductive
242; legal defenses for 160, 178, 183,
245; methods 236; most restricted in
Canada 229; and parody 206–7;
produces harms 232; and public
policy 160; and remedies 229;
restriction justified by Canadian
Charter values 206, 213–18;
restriction justified since harmful to
individuals 206–10; restriction
justified since harmful to society 206,
210; severely affects victims 232;
small number of Canadian charges
230; and speculative consequentialist
calculations 173; and truth 245–7;
see also anti-Semitic speech, 'clear
and present danger' test, group libel,
racist speech, speech vs. action
hate speech, *see* hate propaganda
hearer-based interests 65, 108, 114, 138,
144–5
Heidegger, Martin 50 n 51
Henry, Frances 238
Henry, J 115, 121
Hernandez, Tanya Kateri 240 n 55
Hess, see *Hess* v. *Indiana*
Higginbotham, Cir. J 99 n 14
Hilberg, Raul 55 n 64
Hitler, Adolf 90, 243, 249
Hobbesian state of nature 61
Holocaust 88, 170, 177, 183, 201,
235–6, 249
Hohfeld, Wesley 96 and n 9, 97 n 12,
111, 133
Holmes, Oliver Wendell, Jr. 33 and n 6,
42 and n 37, 70–1, 190 and n 80, 203
and n 145, 216 n 209
Hugessen, ACJ 140
human rights 53, 55; inalienable 50–1;
in Canadian Charter 137; in US
Constitution 187
Hutcheon, JA 107

Hutchinson, Allan ix, 118 n 35, 122–3
and n 43, 129, 133

ideas and acts, *see* speech vs. action
identification, with society 14–15, 146;
with social group 150
immigration 54
importation of materials 229
individual autonomy 46–7, 99–100, 121,
139, 153, 168, 179, 182, 186, 202, 205,
219, 248
individual identity 138
individual vs. social 27, 138–40, 151,
153–4, 158, 232
information, as commodity 111–12
informed economic choices, right
to 111–13
instrumental reason, and Canadian
Charter 118
internal vs. external limits: of Canadian
free speech rights 165–8; significance
of 166–7; of US free speech
rights 165
interpretation of Canadian Charter:
incorporating pre-existing rights 165;
s. 2(b) rights as absolute or
limited 164–5
intuitionism 7
Iwanicki, Jack 130 n 52

Jackson, Thomas H. 95 n 7, 133
Janis, Mark W. 31 n 1, 32 n 2, 45
n 43
Jefferson, Thomas 37–41, 39 nn 21–3,
40 n 27, 51, 200 n 129
Jeffries, John Calvin, Jr. 95 n 7, 133
Jehovah's Witness 179

Kadue, D. 196 n 112, 208 n 176
Kalven, Harry, Jr. 44 n 42, 57, 57 nn
68–9
Karst 179 n 21
Katz, Jacob 56 n 65
Kay, Richard S. 31 n 1, 32 n 2, 45 n 43
Kaye, David 175 n
Keegstra, James 155; see *R.* v. *Keegstra*
Kelman, Mark 5 n 7
Kennedy 8
Kennedy, J 195 n 103
King, Martin Luther 180
Kinsella, W. 237 n 45